Scott, Foresman Mathematics

L. Carey Bolster
Supervisor of Mathematics
Baltimore County Public Schools
Towson, Maryland

E. Glenadine Gibb
Professor of Mathematics Education
The University of Texas at Austin
Austin, Texas

Viggo P. Hansen
Professor, Mathematics Education
California State University
Northridge, California

Joan E. Kirkpatrick
Professor, Elementary Education
University of Alberta
Edmonton, Alberta, Canada

Charles R. McNerney
Professor of Mathematics
University of Northern Colorado
Greeley, Colorado

David F. Robitaille
Associate Professor
of Mathematics Education
University of British Columbia
Vancouver, British Columbia, Canada

Harold C. Trimble
Professor of Education
The Ohio State University
Columbus, Ohio

Irvin E. Vance
Associate Professor of Mathematics
New Mexico State University
Las Cruces, New Mexico

Ray Walch
Teacher of Mathematics
Florida Institute of Technology
Jensen Beach, Florida

Robert J. Wisner
Professor of Mathematics
New Mexico State University
Las Cruces, New Mexico

Scott, Foresman and Company
Editorial Offices: Glenview, Illinois

Regional Sales Offices: Palo Alto, California •
Tucker, Georgia • Glenview, Illinois •
Oakland, New Jersey • Dallas, Texas

Consultants, Grades 1-8

Linda Cox
Associate Professor of Education
Pacific Lutheran University
Tacoma, Washington

Jane Gawronski
Coordinator—Mathematics
Department of Education
San Diego County
San Diego, California

Alejandro Gonzalez
Mathematics Teacher
Gay Junior High School
Harlingen, Texas

Harriet Haynes
Junior High School Mathematics Teacher
Intermediate School 88
Brooklyn, New York

William Nibbelink
Associate Professor of Early Childhood
and Elementary Education
University of Iowa
Iowa City, Iowa

Thomas Pagan
Mathematics Consultant
William E. Wilson Education Center
Jeffersonville, Indiana

Glenn Prigge
Associate Professor of Mathematics
University of North Dakota
Grand Forks, North Dakota

Sidney Sharron
Supervisor in the Educational
Communications and Media Branch
Los Angeles Unified School District
Los Angeles, California

Advisors, Grade 4

Mary Sing
Teacher
Phoenix, Arizona

Marjorie Chamberlayne
Parent
New York, New York

Acknowledgments

For permission to reproduce indicated information on the following pages, acknowledgment is made to:

Riddles on 24–25 from MORE RIDDLES, RIDDLES, RIDDLES by Helen Hoke, copyright 1976 by Helen Hoke. Used by permission of the Publisher. Data on 46–47 on birds, reptiles, and amphibians from "Length of Life of Animals," cited in THE WORLD BOOK ENCYCLOPEDIA, Volume 12, 1978, p. 244. Life span data on 47 from Flower, S.S. (1925), "The Duration of Life in Animals," PROCEEDINGS OF THE LONDON ZOOLOGICAL SOCIETY, 1925: 911–918. Riddles on 58 and in Exercises 28–30 on 108 from A POCKETFUL OF RIDDLES by William Wiesner. Copyright, ©, 1966 by William Wiesner. By permission of the publisher, E. P. Dutton. Data in Exercise 16 on 63 from "National League Home Run Champions," INFORMATION PLEASE ALMANAC, 1977, Thirty-First Edition, edited by Ann Golenpaul. Copyright © November 1976 by Dan Golenpaul Associates. Reprinted by permission of Dan Golenpaul Associates. Data in Exercises 13–18 on 89 from THE WORLD ALMANAC® & Book of Facts 1978, p. 880. Copyright © Newspaper Enterprise Association, Inc. Reprinted by permission. Riddle on 96 from THE SIX-MILLION DOLLAR CUCUMBER by E. Richard Churchill. Copyright 1976 by E. Richard Churchill. Used by permission of the publisher. Riddle in Exercises 25–27 on 108 from HEY RIDDLE RIDDLE! by Ann Bishop. Copyright © 1968 by Albert Whitman & Company. Riddle in Exercises 31–33 on 108 from BIGGEST RIDDLE BOOK IN THE WORLD by Joseph Rosenbloom, p. 249. Copyright © 1976 by Joseph Rosenbloom. Reprinted by permission of Sterling Publishing Co., Inc. Riddle in Exercises 34–37 on 109 from RIDDLE RADDLE, FIDDLE FADDLE by Ann Bishop. Copyright © 1966 by Albert Whitman & Company. Riddle in Exercises 38–43 on 109 from BENNETT CERF'S BOOK OF RIDDLES. Copyright © 1960 by Bennett Cerf. Reprinted by permission of Random House, Inc. Riddle in Exercises 44–48 on 109 from SOUP WITH QUACKERS by Mike Thaler. Copyright © 1976 by Michael C. Thaler. Used by permission of Franklin Watts, Inc.
Continued on page 369.

Acknowledgments for photographs appear on page 369.

ISBN: 0-673-11814-2

Unit 1

Unit 2

Unit 3

Unit 4

Unit 5

Unit 6

Unit 1

Chapter 1 Numeration

Digits and Numbers

0, 1, 2, 3, 4, 5, 6, 7, 8, and 9
are called **digits.**

A. Joan and Carl counted license
plates when they went on a
trip.

Carl wrote tally marks as they
counted. Joan used digits to
show each number.

	Tally	Digit
New York	ℳℋ /	6
California	////	4
Texas	///	3
Ontario	//	2
Illinois	ℳℋ	5
Colorado	ℳℋ ///	8

B. Joan wrote this two-digit
number to show how many
license plates they counted.

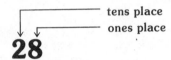

28

twenty-eight

•**Discuss**   Use the digits 3 and 5
to make as many two-digit numbers
as you can. Do not repeat a
digit in a number.

Use digits to give each number.

1. ///
2. ////
3. 𝍷𝍷𝍷𝍷𝍷 ///
4. 𝍷𝍷𝍷𝍷𝍷 //
5. 𝍷𝍷𝍷𝍷𝍷 𝍷𝍷𝍷𝍷𝍷 /
6. 𝍷𝍷𝍷𝍷𝍷 𝍷𝍷𝍷𝍷𝍷 ///

What digit is in the ones place?

7. 13   8. 27   9. 60

10. 45   11. 92   12. 98

What digit is in the tens place?

13. 63   14. 27   15. 45

16. 91   17. 18   18. 50

Use digits to give each number.

19. eleven   20. fourteen

21. twenty-five   22. fifty-seven

23. seventy-one   24. ninety-six

For each exercise, give as many two-digit numbers as you can. Do not repeat a digit in a number.

25. 4 and 2   26. 7 and 4

27. 6 and 3   28. 5 and 1

29. 8 and 9   30. 8 and 4

*31. Use the digits 1, 7, 5, and 9 to give as many four-digit numbers as you can. Do not repeat a digit in a number.

Place Value: Numbers Through 999

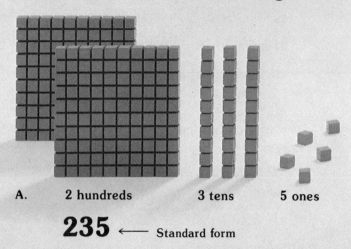

A.　　2 hundreds　　　3 tens　　　5 ones

235 ← Standard form

You can also show this number on a counter.

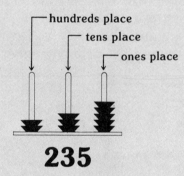

hundreds place
tens place
ones place

235

two hundred thirty-five

B.

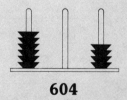

604

six hundred four

Give each number.

Here's how

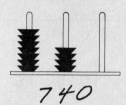

740

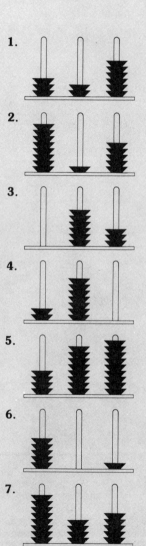

1.

2.

3.

4.

5.

6.

7.

Tell what each 3 means.

Here's how

635   *3 tens*

8. 273   9. 381   10. 553

11. 938   12. 236   13. 301

Tell what each 7 means.

14. 672   15. 357   16. 786

17. 788   18. 179   19. 597

Give each number.

Here's how

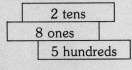

528

20.
| 7 tens |
| 6 hundreds |
| 5 ones |

21.
| 3 hundreds |
| 4 tens |
| 1 one |

22.
| 1 hundred |
| 8 tens |
| 2 ones |

23.
| 9 ones |
| 5 hundreds |
| 4 tens |

24.
| 7 tens |
| 8 hundreds |
| 5 ones |

25.
| 7 hundreds |
| 3 ones |
| 1 ten |

26.
| 4 hundreds |
| 2 tens |

27.
| 5 ones |
| 9 hundreds |

Give the standard form.

28. nineteen
29. thirty-five
30. eighty-seven
31. six hundred forty-three
32. two hundred sixteen
33. fifty-eight
34. nine hundred ninety-one
35. one hundred two

Give each number in words.

Here's how

45   *forty-five*

36. 28   37. 61   38. 899

39. 580   40. 732   41. 407

Use the digits 3, 9, and 5 to make a three-digit number with

42. 9 in the ones place.
43. 3 in the tens place.
44. 5 in the hundreds place.

Use the digits 8, 2, and 6 to make a three-digit number with

45. 6 in the ones place.
46. 2 in the tens place.
47. 8 in the hundreds place.

Place Value: Numbers Through 9999

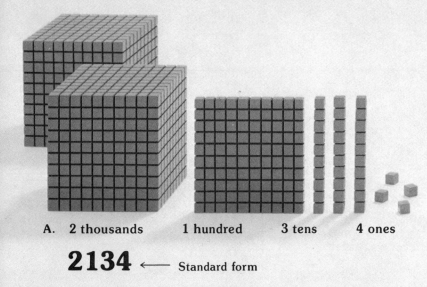

A. 2 thousands   1 hundred   3 tens   4 ones

2134 ⟵ Standard form

You can also show this number on a counter.

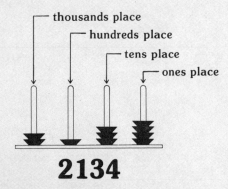

thousands place
hundreds place
tens place
ones place

2134

two thousand one hundred thirty-four

B.

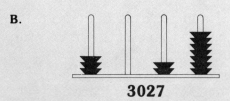

3027

three thousand twenty-seven

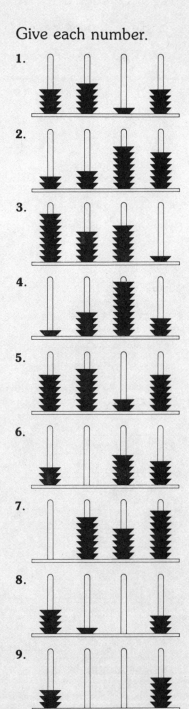

Give each number.

1.

2.

3.

4.

5.

6.

7.

8.

9.

Tell what each 6 means.

10. 4316 **11.** 9631 **12.** 5268

13. 6882 **14.** 5060 **15.** 6119

Tell what each 2 means.

16. 5126 **17.** 2004 **18.** 1602

19. 2347 **20.** 9235 **21.** 1728

Give each number.

22.
| 4 hundreds |
| 3 ones |
| 6 thousands |
| 1 ten |

23.
| 6 ones |
| 8 tens |
| 5 hundreds |
| 2 thousands |

24.
| 5 thousands |
| 4 ones |
| 2 tens |
| 3 hundreds |

25.
| 7 ones |
| 9 thousands |
| 4 tens |
| 6 hundreds |

26.
| 2 hundreds |
| 1 one |
| 8 tens |
| 4 thousands |

27.
| 3 thousands |
| 6 tens |
| 5 hundreds |
| 7 ones |

28.
| 6 ones |
| 8 thousands |
| 9 hundreds |
| 3 tens |

29.
| 1 thousand |
| 4 hundreds |
| 2 tens |

30.
| 5 thousands |
| 9 hundreds |
| 7 ones |

31.
| 3 thousands |
| 2 tens |
| 8 ones |

Give the standard form.

32. six thousand three hundred eighty-one

33. two thousand six hundred seventeen

34. five thousand nine hundred forty-three

35. six thousand four hundred sixty-two

36. two thousand five hundred ninety-seven

37. five thousand three hundred twelve

38. eight thousand two hundred

39. three thousand fifty-seven

40. one thousand twenty-eight

41. nine thousand six

Give each number in words.

42. 3267 **43.** 2191

44. 4853 **45.** 5041

46. 8230 **47.** 6009

★48. Use the digits 3, 4, 9, and 1 to make the least four-digit number possible. Do not repeat digits.

★49. Use the digits 6, 2, 8, and 4 to make the greatest four- digit number possible. Do not repeat digits.

Comparing Numbers

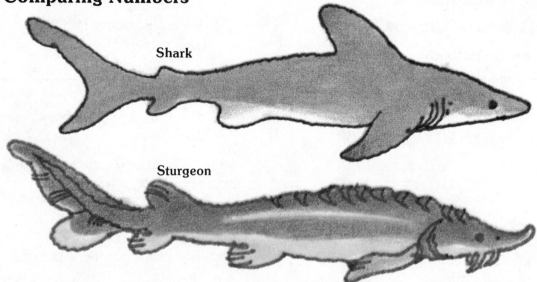

Shark

Sturgeon

A. A white shark weighs 1243 kilograms and a sturgeon weighs 1211 kilograms. Which weighs more?

Which is greater, 1243 or 1211?

1243 ● 1211 The thousands digits are the same.
The hundreds digits are the same.

1243 ● 1211 Compare the tens digits.
4 is greater than 1.

1243 > 1211 1243 is greater than 1211.

The white shark weighs more because 1243 > 1211.

B. Compare the numbers. Use < or >.

5448 ● 5943 The thousands digits are the same.

5448 ● 5943 Compare the hundreds digits.
4 is less than 9.

5448 < 5943 5448 is less than 5943.

Which number is greater?

1. 58 or 53   **2.** 72 or 74

3. 462 or 468   **4.** 659 or 653

5. 1342 or 1821   **6.** 4368 or 4349

Which number is less?

7. 87 or 83   **8.** 91 or 98

9. 731 or 736   **10.** 831 or 830

11. 1097 or 1473   **12.** 5627 or 5283

Compare the numbers.
Use < or >.

13. 41 ● 51   **14.** 67 ● 48

15. 688 ● 382   **16.** 234 ● 439

17. 5552 ● 6558   **18.** 7654 ● 7650

Use the table for each exercise.
Which fish weighs more?

Fish	Weight in kilograms
Cod	34
Opah	227
Sailfish	54
Swordfish	538
Tarpon	242
Tuna	545

19. Cod or Sailfish

20. Tarpon or Opah

21. Sailfish or Opah

22. Cod or Tarpon

23. Swordfish or Cod

24. Tuna or Tarpon

25. Tuna or Opah

26. Swordfish or Tuna

**More practice
Set 1, page 370**

Time Out

Arrange six pennies as shown. Think of this as one row of four pennies and one row of three pennies.

By moving just one penny, make two rows of the same length, with four pennies in each row.

Ordering Numbers

A. Give 465, 431, 526, and 418 in order
from least to greatest.

Write the hundreds digits in order.	When the hundreds digits are the same, write the tens digits in order.	Complete each number. Now the numbers are in order.
4	**41**	**418**
4	**43**	**431**
4	**46**	**465**
5	**5**	**526**

B. Give 4732, 4952, and 4161 in order
from least to greatest.

4161   4732   4952

Study these patterns.

C. 560	D. 862	E. 642
570	962	1642
580	1062	2642
590	1162	3642
600	1262	4642
610	1362	5642

Each number is 10 greater than the number before it.	Each number is 100 greater than the number before it.	Each number is 1000 greater than the number before it.

Give the numbers in order from least to greatest.

1. 66   84   20   44
2. 96   73   16   41
3. 371   659   721   124
4. 98   768   22   385
5. 576   595   721   724
6. 383   347   421   405
7. 1234   2568   1432
8. 2267   2177   2361

What number is 10 greater?

9. 32   10. 49   11. 361
12. 472   13. 313   14. 4675
15. 5600   16. 6390   17. 2898

What number is 100 greater?

18. 683   19. 327   20. 452
21. 2764   22. 3800   23. 9065
24. 5814   25. 18   26. 37

What number is 1000 greater?

27. 5124   28. 1260   29. 3457
30. 4389   31. 7621   32. 2999
33. 345   34. 862   35. 790

**More practice
Set 2, page 370**

Expanded Form

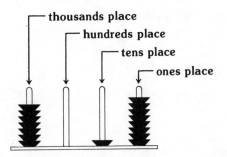

— thousands place
— hundreds place
— tens place
— ones place

7018 ← Standard form

7000 + 10 + 8 ← Expanded form

Give the expanded form.

1. 27   2. 49   3. 691
4. 385   5. 539   6. 8156
7. 7238   8. 3040   9. 9001

Give the standard form.

10. 60 + 3
11. 800 + 70 + 6
12. 9000 + 500 + 40 + 3
13. 7000 + 300 + 80 + 1
14. 500 + 2
15. 6000 + 10 + 7
16. 4000 + 3

11

Rounding Numbers

There were 8679 people at a hockey game between Boston and Chicago. A magazine reported the attendance as 9000. The attendance was given as a **rounded number.**

A. Round 78 to the nearest ten.

80

78

50   60   70   80   90

78 is closer to 80.
Round to 80.

B. Round 326 to the nearest hundred.

300

326

100   200   300   400   500

326 is closer to 300.
Round to 300.

c. Round 6500 to the
nearest thousand.

7000

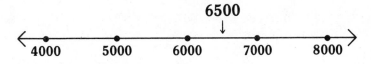

6500 is halfway between 6000
and 7000. Round to 7000.

● **Discuss**   When are rounded numbers used?

Round to the nearest ten.

1. 33   **2.** 47   **3.** 56   **4.** 63   **5.** 19   **6.** 85

7. 408   **8.** 794   **9.** 412   **10.** 375   **11.** 121   **12.** 643

Round to the nearest hundred.

13. 144   **14.** 286   **15.** 525   **16.** 853   **17.** 372   **18.** 419

19. 1358   **20.** 4845   **21.** 2498   **22.** 7682   **23.** 1736   **24.** 8206

Round to the nearest thousand.

25. 7134   **26.** 6280   **27.** 3784   **28.** 1625   **29.** 2318   **30.** 5900

31. 4500   **32.** 8195   **33.** 2500   **34.** 5005   **35.** 3246   **36.** 8872

Complete the table. Round each number.

Hockey game	Attendance	Nearest 10	Nearest 100	Nearest 1000
Pittsburgh and Colorado	7331	**37.**	**38.**	**39.**
Vancouver and Detroit	9435	**40.**	**41.**	**42.**
Montreal and Atlanta	7821	**43.**	**44.**	**45.**
New York and Washington	3764	**46.**	**47.**	**48.**
Los Angeles and Minnesota	9083	**49.**	**50.**	**51.**

Ten-Thousands and Hundred-Thousands

A. 1000 marbles
one thousand

hundred-thousands	ten-thousands	thousands	hundreds	tens	ones
		1	0	0	0

B. 10,000 marbles
ten thousand

hundred-thousands	ten-thousands	thousands	hundreds	tens	ones
	1	0	0	0	0

C. 100,000 marbles
one hundred thousand

hundred-thousands	ten-thousands	thousands	hundreds	tens	ones
1	0	0	0	0	0

D. Tell what each 8 means.

	hundred-thousands	ten-thousands	thousands	hundreds	tens	ones	
34,872 →		3	4	8	7	2	→ 8 hundreds
148,536 →	1	4	8	5	3	6	→ 8 thousands
894,210 →	8	9	4	2	1	0	→ 8 hundred-thousands
86,453 →		8	6	4	5	3	→ 8 ten-thousands

Tell what each 5 means.

1. 58,346
2. 517,613
3. 49,153
4. 95,381
5. 571,601
6. 156,112
7. 652,191
8. 580,003

Tell what each 9 means.

9. 92,613
10. 34,957
11. 71,890
12. 96,241
13. 982,561
14. 579,306
15. 891,742
16. 920,500

Tell what each 6 means.

17. 615,742
18. 23,631
19. 39,486
20. 61,275
21. 650,743
22. 946,735
23. 467,029
24. 642,001

Give each number.

25. 5 ten-thousands
9 hundreds
4 tens
8 ones

26. 3 hundred-thousands
8 ten-thousands
2 hundreds
9 ones

27. 1 hundred-thousand
7 ten-thousands
4 thousands
5 tens

28. 5 hundred-thousands
3 tens
6 ones

29. 8 ten-thousands
2 ones

30. 7 hundred-thousands
4 tens

Millions

A. The length of the earth's orbit around the sun is about 934,000,000 kilometers.

hundred-millions	ten-millions	millions	hundred-thousands	ten-thousands	thousands	hundreds	tens	ones
9	3	4	0	0	0	0	0	0

934,000,000

nine hundred thirty-four million

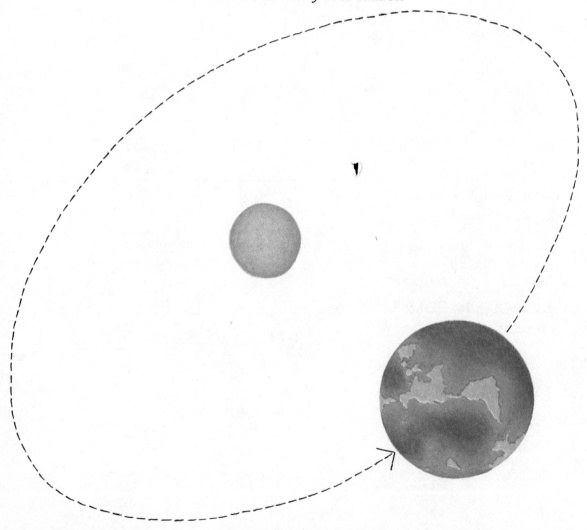

Read each number.

B. **4,341,032**   four million, three hundred forty-one thousand, thirty-two

C. **81,675,000**   eighty-one million, six hundred seventy-five thousand

D. **505,002,500**   five hundred five million, two thousand, five hundred

E. **70,006,310**   seventy million, six thousand, three hundred ten

Tell what each 2 means.

1. 6,235,864
2. 2,803,413
3. 25,600,000
4. 52,813,000
5. 123,800,000
6. 283,641,000
7. 192,530,000
8. 629,100,000

Give the standard form.

9. forty-three thousand, five hundred sixteen

10. eight hundred seventy-one thousand, forty-nine

11. six million, fifteen thousand, two hundred nineteen

12. nine hundred eighty-seven million, three hundred twelve thousand, one hundred sixteen

13. two hundred sixty-six million, eight hundred thirty-five

14. nine hundred million, four

Give each number in words.

15. 109,300,000
16. 207,800,000
17. 23,550,420
18. 38,730,690
19. 5,367,200
20. 6,123,400

Give the standard form.

21. The planet Mercury orbits around the sun at a distance of about fifty-eight million kilometers.

22. The planet Jupiter's outer satellite is about twenty-three million, five hundred thirty thousand kilometers away.

23. The planet Venus orbits around the sun at a distance of about one hundred eight million, two hundred thirty thousand kilometers.

Giving Sensible Answers

Chin and Sue Ling live in New York City.

Choose the best answer.

1. Sue Ling is (8   80   800) years old.

2. Chin is (6   60   600) years old.

3. There are (4   400   4000) members in their family.

4. Their father is (4   40   400) years old.

5. Chin and Sue Ling walk (1   100   1000) kilometers to school each day.

6. There are (3   30   300) students in Sue Ling's room at school.

7. There are (8   800   8,000,000) students in the whole school.

8. Chin and Sue Ling's family went to Los Angeles. They traveled about (4   40   4000) kilometers.

9. They visited an amusement park and went on (10   1000   10,000) rides.

10. Sue Ling spent ($5.00 $150.00 $1500.00) to buy a small stuffed bear.

Keeping Skillful

Which number is greater?

1. 43 or 39

2. 78 or 88

3. 524 or 693

4. 459 or 456

5. 2581 or 2384

6. 4675 or 4863

Which number is less?

7. 56 or 25

8. 31 or 41

9. 302 or 305

10. 7458 or 7589

11. 9247 or 9329

Compare the numbers. Use < or >.

12. 32 ● 25

13. 74 ● 86

14. 187 ● 190

15. 652 ● 573

16. 8568 ● 8540

17. 4289 ● 4391

18. 6832 ● 6731

Census Taker

A census taker gathers information about a group of people. In the United States, a census is taken every ten years. The information below was gathered by some census takers in 1970.

The population of Fort Stockton, Texas, is 8283. Round this number

1. to the nearest ten.

2. to the nearest hundred.

3. to the nearest thousand.

4. The population of Illinois is about 11,114,000. Give this number in words.

5. The population of Pennsylvania is about 11,794,000. Give this number in words.

6. The population of Alaska is about three hundred thousand, three hundred eighty. Give the standard form of this number.

7. The population of Idaho is about 713,000. The population of New Hampshire is about 738,000. Which state has fewer people?

8. The population of Nevada is about 489,000. The population of Wyoming is about 332,000. Which state has more people?

Large Numbers

A beam of light travels about 298,000 kilometers per second.
This distance is about 7 times around the earth.
The chart below shows how far light travels.

Time	Distance traveled in kilometers	
1 second	298,000	two hundred ninety-eight thousand
1 minute	17,900,000	seventeen million, nine hundred thousand
1 hour	1,070,000,000	one billion, seventy million
1 day	25,700,000,000	twenty-five billion, seven hundred million
1 year	9,380,000,000,000	nine trillion, three hundred eighty billion

Give the standard form.

1. four billion, three million, seven hundred thousand

2. sixty-three billion, five hundred million

3. one hundred five billion, thirty-two million, four hundred

4. five hundred eighty billion, six million, twenty thousand, nineteen

5. nine hundred trillion, two billion, sixty-one million, four thousand

Chapter 1 Test
Numeration, pages 2–20

Tell what each 6 means.

1. 68   2. 346

3. 5627   4. 16,245

5. 62,480   6. 671,053

Give the standard form.

7. sixty-two

8. three hundred ninety-eight

9. one thousand five hundred forty-seven

10. thirty-two thousand, fifty-one

11. five million, six thousand

Give the number.

12.
| 4 hundreds |
| 5 ones |
| 9 tens |

13.
| 7 thousands |
| 8 tens |
| 2 ones |
| 6 hundreds |

14.
| 3 ten-thousands |
| 5 thousands |
| 1 hundred |
| 6 tens |
| 4 ones |

Complete each sentence.
Use < or >.

15. 46 ● 93   16. 53 ● 57

17. 348 ● 251   18. 821 ● 824

19. 6147 ● 9264   20. 2871 ● 2763

Give the numbers in order from least to greatest.

21. 13   81   31   27

22. 279   300   211   356

Round to the nearest 10.

23. 37   24. 82

25. 534   26. 956

Round to the nearest 100.

27. 643   28. 288

29. 209   30. 473

Round to the nearest 1000.

31. 7891   32. 9221

33. 3610   34. 5173

Terry's father is 35 years old.
Choose the best answer.

35. Terry is (7, 70, 700) years old.

Chapter 2 Addition

Addition Basic Facts

There are 7 dinosaurs and 5 flying reptiles.
How many animals are there in all?

$$7 + 5 = 12$$

↑ Addend ↑ Addend ↑ Sum

$$5 + 7 = 12$$

The sum is 12.

$$
\begin{array}{c}
7 \\
+5 \\
\hline
12
\end{array}
\quad
\begin{array}{c}
\leftarrow \text{Addend} \rightarrow \\
\leftarrow \text{Addend} \rightarrow \\
\leftarrow \text{Sum} \rightarrow
\end{array}
\quad
\begin{array}{c}
5 \\
+7 \\
\hline
12
\end{array}
$$

The sum is 12.

Add.

1. 2
   +2

2. 4
   +4

3. 0
   +5

4. 6
   +1

5. 3
   +4

6. 1
   +1

7. 1
   +8

8. 5
   +5

9. 3
   +3

10. 2
    +4

11. 1
    +7

12. 3
    +2

13. 3
    +6

14. 8
    +2

15. 5
    +4

16. 2
    +7

17. 9
    +3

18. 3
    +9

19. 6
    +5

20. 5
    +6

21. 7
    +3

22. 3
    +7

23. 9
    +8

24. 8
    +9

25. 9 + 6
26. 5 + 3
27. 7 + 4
28. 6 + 2
29. 5 + 7
30. 3 + 8

31. 7 + 2
32. 4 + 9
33. 8 + 6
34. 7 + 8
35. 9 + 5
36. 8 + 4

37. 8 + 5
38. 7 + 6
39. 9 + 7
40. 5 + 9
41. 6 + 8
42. 9 + 4

43. 4 + 0
44. 6 + 0
45. 0 + 7
46. 9 + 0
47. 0 + 3
48. 8 + 0

For each exercise, tell
how many in all.

49. There were 8 turtles in a
    pond and 7 on the bank.

50. A bear had 4 fish. It
    caught 5 more.

51. There were 6 bears and
    9 reptiles in a cave.

• **Discuss**   What is the answer when
you add 0 and another number?

• **Discuss**   Does the order in which
you add two numbers change the
answer?

**More practice
Set 3, page 370**

23

Using Addition Facts

Find each sum. Use the code to find the riddle and the answer.

Code			
3	B	11	N
4	R	12	D
5	E	13	H
6	U	14	W
7	I	15	T
8	O	16	G
9	A	17	C
10	S		

Here's how

8 + 8   16 G

Riddle

Word 1

1. 9 + 5
2. 6 + 7
3. 1 + 8
4. 6 + 9

Word 2

5. 4 + 3
6. 9 + 1

Word 3

7. 5 + 4
8. 2 + 8

Word 4

9. 0 + 3
10. 2 + 5
11. 7 + 9

Word 5

12. 6 + 3
13. 5 + 5

Word 6

14. 0 + 9

Word 7

15. 6 + 6
16. 5 + 2
17. 4 + 7
18. 3 + 5
19. 6 + 4
20. 2 + 7
21. 3 + 3
22. 4 + 0

Word 8

23. 8 + 1
24. 5 + 6
25. 9 + 3

Word 9

26. 4 + 8
27. 2 + 6
28. 3 + 2
29. 1 + 9

Word 10

30. 8 + 3
31. 4 + 4
32. 7 + 8

Word 11

33. 8 + 6
34. 4 + 1
35. 0 + 7
36. 8 + 8
37. 9 + 4

Word 12

38. 3 + 6
39. 7 + 4

Word 13

40. 5 + 3
41. 4 + 2
42. 2 + 9
43. 9 + 8
44. 2 + 3

Complete the tables.

	+6
3	9
0	6

		+6
61.	7	
62.	4	
63.	8	
64.	5	
65.	9	

	+9
6	15

		+9
66.	5	
67.	8	
68.	3	
69.	7	
70.	1	
71.	4	
72.	9	

Answer

Word 1

45. 7 + 2

Word 2

46. 9 + 3

47. 1 + 6

48. 6 + 5

49. 1 + 7

50. 8 + 2

51. 4 + 5

52. 2 + 4

53. 1 + 3

54. 3 + 7

Word 3

55. 4 + 6

56. 5 + 8

57. 9 + 0

58. 5 + 7

59. 6 + 2

60. 7 + 7

Keeping Skillful

Round to the nearest ten.

1. 13 **2.** 34

3. 87 **4.** 66

5. 18 **6.** 91

7. 82 **8.** 62

9. 29 **10.** 45

Round to the nearest hundred.

11. 182 **12.** 427

13. 396 **14.** 689

15. 138 **16.** 241

17. 753 **18.** 324

19. 914 **20.** 550

Round to the nearest thousand.

21. 1386 **22.** 4526

23. 6872 **24.** 5943

25. 9407 **26.** 8178

27. 8614 **28.** 7241

29. 2758 **30.** 3500

25

Estimating Sums

A. 317 books were checked out in the morning and 452 were checked out in the afternoon. About how many books were checked out in all?

Estimate 317 + 452.

317 + 452
↓   ↓
300 + 500 = 800

Round 317 and 452 to the nearest hundred. Add.

Actual sum

317
+452
‾‾‾‾
769

About 800 books were checked out.

B. Estimate 56 + 71.

56 + 71
↓   ↓
60 + 70 = 130

Round 56 and 71 to the nearest ten. Add.

Actual sum

56
+ 71
‾‾‾‾
127

C. Estimate 2642 + 3206.

2642 + 3206
↓   ↓
3000 + 3000 = 6000

Round 2642 and 3206 to the nearest thousand. Add.

Actual sum

2642
+3206
‾‾‾‾‾
5848

D. Estimate 431 + 52.

431 + 52
↓   ↓
430 + 50 = 480

Round 431 and 52 to the nearest ten. Add.

Actual sum

431
+ 52
‾‾‾‾
483

Estimate by rounding to the nearest ten.
Then find the actual sum.

1. 15 + 11   2. 62 + 16   3. 41 + 52   4. 23 + 21   5. 35 + 52

6. 63 + 86   7. 51 + 82   8. 71 + 46   9. 308 + 89   10. 50 + 638

Estimate by rounding to the nearest hundred.
Then find the actual sum.

11. 421 + 128   12. 543 + 254   13. 263 + 415   14. 201 + 526

15. 613 + 931   16. 714 + 525   17. 205 + 2733   18. 1424 + 562

Estimate by rounding to the nearest thousand.
Then find the actual sum.

19. 4231 + 2643   20. 3259 + 1420   21. 5462 + 1327   22. 2056 + 3713

23. 6578 + 3211   24. 8305 + 2671   25. 7145 + 6812   26. 8723 + 7254

Estimate each answer. Tell about how many in all.

Month	Books checked out
April	8340
May	7231
June	8403
July	6012

27. Books checked out in April and May

28. Books checked out in May and June

29. Books checked out in June and July

30. There were 37 monthly magazines and 12 weekly magazines in the library.

31. Sandy read a book with 343 pages. She read another book with 254 pages.

32. The book review was attended by 42 people in the morning and 54 in the afternoon.

33. There were 16 volumes in one set and 24 volumes in another set.

34. There were 115 books returned on Monday and 62 on Tuesday.

Renaming

A. Rename 3 tens 16 ones. Give the standard form.

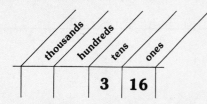

Put 10 ones together to make another ten. 6 ones are left.

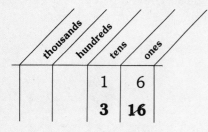

Put the tens together.

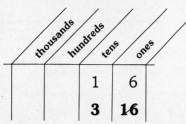

46 ← Standard form

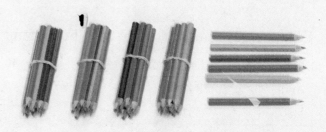

Tell what was done in each example.

B.

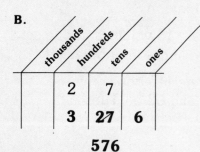

576

C.

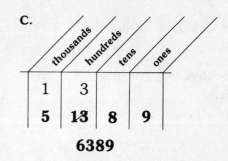

6389

28

Rename. Give the standard form.

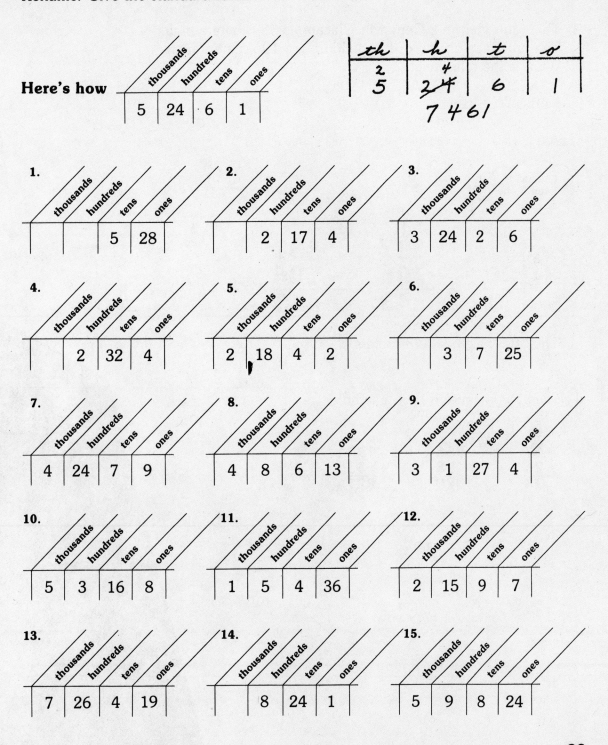

Here's how

	thousands	hundreds	tens	ones
	5	24	6	1

th	h	t	o
2	4		
5	24	6	1

7461

1.

thousands	hundreds	tens	ones
		5	28

2.

thousands	hundreds	tens	ones
	2	17	4

3.

thousands	hundreds	tens	ones
	3	24	2	6

4.

thousands	hundreds	tens	ones
	2	32	4

5.

thousands	hundreds	tens	ones
2	18	4	2

6.

thousands	hundreds	tens	ones
	3	7	25

7.

thousands	hundreds	tens	ones
4	24	7	9

8.

thousands	hundreds	tens	ones
4	8	6	13

9.

thousands	hundreds	tens	ones
3	1	27	4

10.

thousands	hundreds	tens	ones
5	3	16	8

11.

thousands	hundreds	tens	ones
1	5	4	36

12.

thousands	hundreds	tens	ones
2	15	9	7

13.

thousands	hundreds	tens	ones
7	26	4	19

14.

thousands	hundreds	tens	ones
	8	24	1

15.

thousands	hundreds	tens	ones
5	9	8	24

29

Addition: One Renaming

A. The John Hancock Center in Chicago is 337 meters high. The antennas on top of the building are 106 meters high. What is the total height?

Find 337 + 106.

Add the ones. Add the tens. Add the hundreds.

13 ones =
1 ten 3 ones

$$
\begin{array}{r}
\overset{1}{3}37 \\
+106 \\
\hline
3
\end{array}
\qquad
\begin{array}{r}
\overset{1}{3}37 \\
+106 \\
\hline
43
\end{array}
\qquad
\begin{array}{r}
\overset{1}{3}37 \\
+106 \\
\hline
443
\end{array}
$$

The total height is 443 meters.

Tell what was done in each example.

B.
$$
\begin{array}{r}
\overset{1}{4}7 \\
+26 \\
\hline
73
\end{array}
$$
C.
$$
\begin{array}{r}
\overset{1}{9}56 \\
+\ 73 \\
\hline
1029
\end{array}
$$
D.
$$
\begin{array}{r}
\overset{1}{1}924 \\
+6352 \\
\hline
8276
\end{array}
$$

Add.

1. 63 +19	**2.** 37 +17	**3.** 28 +45	**4.** 59 +92
5. 329 +247	**6.** 538 +445	**7.** 161 +362	**8.** 827 +453
9. 2157 +1433	**10.** 6513 +8249	**11.** 9881 +4073	**12.** 4263 +8801
13. 268 + 80	**14.** 982 + 43	**15.** 2362 + 574	**16.** 7540 + 632
17. 641 +795	**18.** 361 + 75	**19.** 3942 +2301	**20.** 4825 +7026

21. 537 + 15   **22.** 49 + 127

23. 673 + 184   **24.** 581 + 295

25. 6832 + 651   **26.** 7320 + 492

27. 9302 + 9851   **28.** 2045 + 8271

★29. 91,783 + 702   **★30.** 10,552 + 8645

31. In the Hancock Center, apartments begin
on the 45th story. Some apartments are
47 stories higher. What story are they on?

32. The Sky Lobby swimming pool is 165 meters
above the ground. The observatory is
150 meters higher. How high is it?

**More practice
Set 4, page 371**

Addition: More Than One Renaming

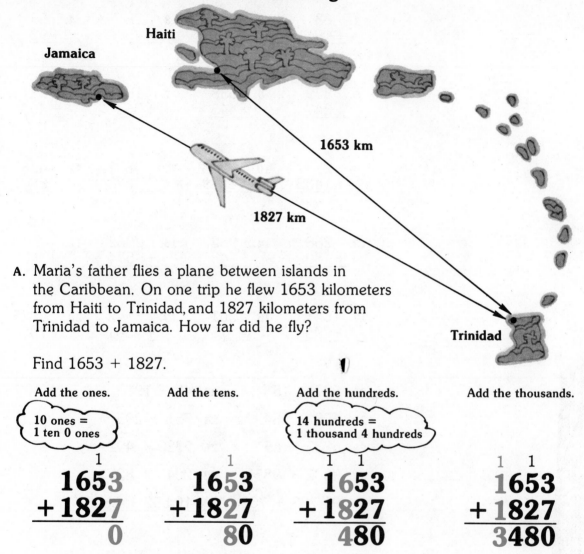

Jamaica

Haiti

1653 km

1827 km

Trinidad

A. Maria's father flies a plane between islands in the Caribbean. On one trip he flew 1653 kilometers from Haiti to Trinidad, and 1827 kilometers from Trinidad to Jamaica. How far did he fly?

Find 1653 + 1827.

Add the ones.	Add the tens.	Add the hundreds.	Add the thousands.
10 ones = 1 ten 0 ones		14 hundreds = 1 thousand 4 hundreds	

$$
\begin{array}{r}
\overset{1}{1653} \\
+1827 \\
\hline
0
\end{array}
\qquad
\begin{array}{r}
1 \\
1653 \\
+1827 \\
\hline
80
\end{array}
\qquad
\begin{array}{r}
1\ 1 \\
1653 \\
+1827 \\
\hline
480
\end{array}
\qquad
\begin{array}{r}
1\ 1 \\
1653 \\
+1827 \\
\hline
3480
\end{array}
$$

He flew 3480 kilometers.

Tell what was done in each example.

B.
$$
\begin{array}{r}
^{1\ 1}367 \\
+458 \\
\hline
825
\end{array}
$$

C.
$$
\begin{array}{r}
^{1\ 1}993 \\
+\ \ 47 \\
\hline
1040
\end{array}
$$

Add.

1. 583
  +249

2. 368
  +593

3. 262
  +178

4. 348
  +396

5. 385
  +595

6. 876
  +145

7. 1739
  +4541

8. 4507
  +7636

9. 9378
  +2139

10. 3476
   +4194

11. 2687
   +2951

12. 9953
   +3352

13. 635
   + 89

14. 19
   +582

15. 6409
   + 629

16. 918
   +8534

17. 5378
   +1054

18. 7348
   +8075

19. 5162
   +3983

20. 2638
   +5427

21. 7219
   + 386

22. 6423
   +9947

23. 8956
   +1782

24. 5783
   +4766

25. 954 + 476

26. 499 + 128

27. 4792 + 3761

28. 7980 + 485

29. 3906 + 8506

30. 2535 + 2748

31. 4860 + 853

32. 4684 + 5670

This table shows the air distance between some islands.

Islands	Distance in kilometers
Haiti to Aruba	653
Aruba to St. Thomas	768
Puerto Rico to Aruba	787
Aruba to Martinique	915
Martinique to Haiti	1057
St. Thomas to Haiti	686
Puerto Rico to Jamaica	1073
Jamaica to Trinidad	1827
Haiti to Trinidad	1653

Find the total distance flown on each trip.

33. From Haiti to Aruba
    From Aruba to St. Thomas

34. From Puerto Rico to Aruba
    From Aruba to Martinique

35. From Martinique to Haiti
    From Haiti to Aruba

36. From Puerto Rico to Jamaica
    From Jamaica to Trinidad

37. From St. Thomas to Haiti
    From Haiti to Trinidad

38. From Martinique to Haiti
    From Haiti to Trinidad

**More practice
Set 5, page 371**

Using Addition

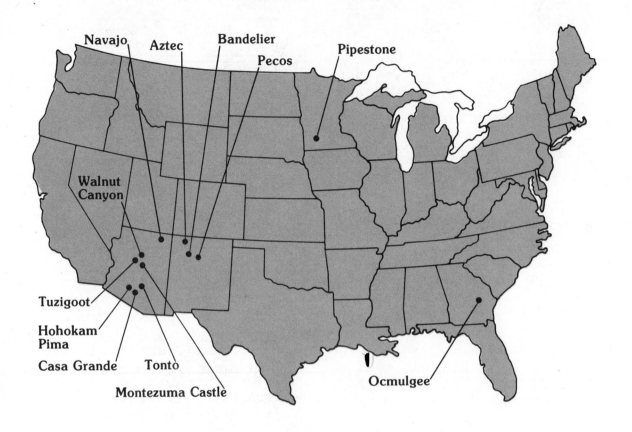

The tables show the number of acres in twelve outdoor national monuments. These are monuments to different Native American cultures.

Monument	Acres
Aztec	27
Bandelier	36,970
Casa Grande	473
Hohokam Pima	1,690
Montezuma Castle	842
Navajo	360

Monument	Acres
Ocmulgee	683
Pecos	365
Pipestone	282
Tonto	1,120
Tuzigoot	58
Walnut Canyon	2,249

How many acres are in the two parks?

1. Aztec and Casa Grande
2. Casa Grande and Pecos
3. Pecos and Ocmulgee
4. Ocmulgee and Hohokam Pima
5. Hohokam Pima and Tonto
6. Tonto and Walnut Canyon
7. Walnut Canyon and Navajo
8. Navajo and Montezuma Castle
9. Montezuma Castle and Tuzigoot
10. Tuzigoot and Pipestone
11. Pipestone and Walnut Canyon
*12. Walnut Canyon and Bandelier

Add.

13. $\begin{array}{r} 97 \\ + 65 \\ \hline \end{array}$
14. $\begin{array}{r} 76 \\ + 41 \\ \hline \end{array}$
15. $\begin{array}{r} 58 \\ + 33 \\ \hline \end{array}$
16. $\begin{array}{r} 748 \\ + 615 \\ \hline \end{array}$
17. $\begin{array}{r} 378 \\ + 193 \\ \hline \end{array}$
18. $\begin{array}{r} 327 \\ + 67 \\ \hline \end{array}$

19. $\begin{array}{r} 168 \\ + 63 \\ \hline \end{array}$
20. $\begin{array}{r} 6405 \\ + 7023 \\ \hline \end{array}$
21. $\begin{array}{r} 4295 \\ + 3912 \\ \hline \end{array}$
22. $\begin{array}{r} 2985 \\ + 806 \\ \hline \end{array}$
23. $\begin{array}{r} 2138 \\ + 456 \\ \hline \end{array}$
24. $\begin{array}{r} 219 \\ + 846 \\ \hline \end{array}$

25. $\begin{array}{r} 566 \\ + 347 \\ \hline \end{array}$
26. $\begin{array}{r} 3189 \\ + 2047 \\ \hline \end{array}$
27. $\begin{array}{r} 2837 \\ + 4316 \\ \hline \end{array}$
28. $\begin{array}{r} 6120 \\ + 2952 \\ \hline \end{array}$
29. $\begin{array}{r} 4238 \\ + 9622 \\ \hline \end{array}$
30. $\begin{array}{r} 853 \\ + 784 \\ \hline \end{array}$

31. 86 + 42
32. 476 + 284
33. 3180 + 4530
34. 4126 + 319
35. 413 + 572
36. 8071 + 1276
37. 5314 + 6657
38. 153 + 82
39. 290 + 291
40. 135 + 182
41. 37 + 35
42. 5856 + 427
43. 9706 + 8534
44. 1752 + 2387
45. 9943 + 865
46. 3745 + 6529

Estimate each sum.

47. The Navajo National Monument had 56 visitors in the morning and 43 in the afternoon. About how many visitors were there in all?

48. The Aztec National Monument had 3406 visitors one month and 4572 the next month. There were about how many visitors in the two months?

Three or More Addends

A. The team's scores were 7, 5, and 3. What was the total score for the first round?

Jean added down.

$$
\begin{array}{r}
7 \\
5 \\
+3 \\
\hline
15
\end{array}
$$

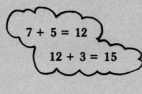

7 + 5 = 12
12 + 3 = 15

Steve looked for sums of 10.

$$
\begin{array}{r}
7 \\
5 \\
+3 \\
\hline
15
\end{array}
$$

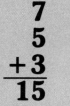

7 + 3 = 10
10 + 5 = 15

The team's total score was 15.

Tell what was done in each example.

$$
\text{B.} \quad
\begin{array}{r}
61 \\
52 \\
+76 \\
\hline
189
\end{array}
\qquad
\text{C.} \quad
\overset{1\ 2}{
\begin{array}{r}
245 \\
438 \\
+359 \\
\hline
1042
\end{array}}
\qquad
\text{D.} \quad
\overset{1\ 2}{
\begin{array}{r}
7961 \\
583 \\
74 \\
+\quad 40 \\
\hline
8658
\end{array}}
$$

36

Add.

1.   4
   7
+6
	2. 6
	   7
	+5
		3. 7
		   8
		+6
			4. 9
			   7
			+8

5.   27
  35
+63
	6. 55
	  69
	+42
		7. 38
		  26
		+17
			8. 76
			  59
			+45

9.   67
  18
+89
	10. 39
	  24
	+10
		11. 71
		  64
		+23
			12. 16
			  29
			+34

13. 634 218 +735	14. 374 163 +217	15. 268 485 +173	16. 527 812 +134
17. 3423 8562 +9850	18. 4861 3674 +1233	19. 7410 6392 +4747	20. 5025 4311 +3162

21. 393
  21
  87
+456
	22. 892
	  55
	  73
	+146
		23. 1580
		  754
		 3062
		+ 91
			24. 2384
			 4682
			  590
			+1971

25. 825 + 6309 + 747   26. 3245 + 1496 + 87

27. 6703 + 432 + 57   28. 2593 + 482 + 60

*29. 18,756 + 947 + 23   *30. 37,645 + 2872 + 89

More practice
Set 6, page 371

Clifton drew a clock face. He drew a line across it to separate the numbers into two groups. He added the numbers in each group. Did he get the same sum?

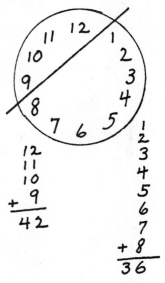

Copy the clock face. Draw a line across so that the sum of the numbers in each group is the same.

37

Using Addition

Add.

1. 243
  +119

2. 336
  +257

3. 195
  + 62

4. 61
  +974

5. 362
  +484

6. 619
  +509

7. 798
  + 27

8. 94
  +386

9. 385
  +576

10. 149
  +273

11. 786
  +616

12. 267
  +873

13. 3784
  +2042

14. 2930
  +1965

15. 5924
  +2749

16. 4065
  +2397

17. 2089
  +3117

18. 4395
  +2488

19. 361
  42
  +853

20. 638
  927
  + 15

21. 658
  215
  + 20

22. 493
  71
  +260

23. 305
  237
  +414

24. 342
  592
  +233

25. 248
  95
  +578

26. 159
  43
  +436

27. 226
  538
  +157

28. 894
  242
  +331

29. 437
  264
  +125

30. 169
  640
  +379

31. 426 + 137 + 3008

32. 1437 + 604 + 1718

33. 7621 + 502 + 433

34. 9234 + 325 + 2048

35. 4610 + 1311 + 2724

36. 8973 + 2512 + 134

This table shows the distance
a plane flew each day.

Day	Distance
Monday	2183 kilometers
Tuesday	975 kilometers
Wednesday	1641 kilometers

Give the number of kilometers
traveled on

37. Monday and Tuesday.

38. Tuesday and Wednesday.

39. Wednesday and Monday.

40. Monday, Tuesday, and Wednesday.

Palindromes

Numbers like 232, 7447, and 51615 are called palindromes.
A palindrome does not change when you reverse the digits.
You can make a palindrome by adding. A calculator can
help with the addition.

Carlos started with 529. He used a calculator and
showed the addition on his paper.

$$
\begin{array}{r}
529 \\
+925 \\
\hline
1454 \\
+4541 \\
\hline
5995
\end{array}
$$

Write a number.

Reverse the digits and add.

Is this number a palindrome? No.

Reverse the digits and add.

Is this number a palindrome? Yes.

Carlos reversed the digits two times to make this palindrome.

Add to make a palindrome from each of these numbers.

1. 48
2. 63
3. 79
4. 86
5. 648
6. 235
7. 287
8. 7413
9. 7543
10. 5716

Prime Numbers

You can use blocks to represent numbers.

A. Use two blocks. You can make only one rectangle.

Rectangle

B. Use three blocks. You can make only one rectangle.

Rectangle

Not a rectangle.

C. Use four blocks. You can make more than one rectangle.

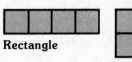

Rectangle

Rectangle

Not a rectangle.

You can make only one rectangle with two blocks.

The number 2 is a **prime number.**

You can make only one rectangle with three blocks.

The number 3 is a prime number.

You can make more than one rectangle with four blocks.

The number 4 is not a prime number.

1. Copy and complete the table.

Number of blocks used		2	3	4	5	6	7	8	9	10	11	12	13	14	15	16
Number of rectangles	One	√	√													
	More than one			√												

2. How many rectangles can you make with five blocks?

3. Is 5 a prime number?

4. List all the prime numbers between 2 and 16.

5. Which numbers between 16 and 25 are prime numbers?

Add.

1. 4
  +5

2. 6
  +7

3. 7
  +3

4. 8
  +9

5. 9
  +5

6. 8
  +6

Give the standard form.

7.
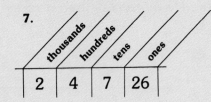

8.
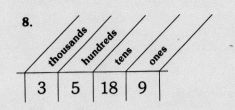

9.
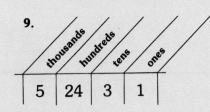

Add.

10. 59
   +17

11. 148
   + 36

12. 234
   +681

13. 763
   +442

14. 385
   + 98

15. 475
   +267

16. 1406
   +7534

17. 5683
   +5148

18. 3566
   + 891

19. 6097
   +7435

20. 16
    23
   +48

21. 252
    465
   + 77

22. 1325
    3284
   + 276

23. 4621
    7835
   +5392

Estimate each answer.

24. Juan had 57 shells and Chan had 41 shells. About how many shells did they have in all?

25. Gina had 126 baseball cards and Barbara had 163 baseball cards. They had about how many cards in all?

Chapter 3 Subtraction

Subtraction Basic Facts

A. There were 15 cars in a parking lot. After 7 were driven away, how many were still there?

$$15 - 7 = 8$$

↑
Difference

8 cars were still there.

B. Gail parked 13 cars and 4 trucks. She parked how many more cars than trucks?

$$\begin{array}{r} 13 \\ -\ 4 \\ \hline 9 \end{array}$$ ← **Difference**

She parked 9 more cars than trucks.

Subtract.

1. 7
   − 3

2. 9
   − 5

3. 5
   − 3

4. 7
   − 4

5. 6
   − 4

6. 5
   − 2

7. 6
   − 5

8. 4
   − 4

9. 7
   − 2

10. 5
    − 4

11. 6
    − 3

12. 4
    − 2

13. 7
    − 5

14. 5
    − 0

15. 10
    − 6

16. 14
    − 5

17. 11
    − 4

18. 12
    − 8

19. 15
    − 6

20. 10
    − 2

21. 18
    − 9

22. 7 − 0
23. 3 − 3
24. 9 − 0
25. 5 − 5
26. 2 − 0

27. 14 − 6
28. 12 − 7
29. 6 − 2
30. 15 − 9
31. 13 − 4

32. 10 − 7
33. 16 − 9
34. 12 − 6
35. 11 − 2
36. 14 − 8

37. 11 − 7
38. 13 − 5
39. 11 − 3
40. 12 − 3
41. 13 − 6

42. 10 − 8
43. 11 − 9
44. 16 − 7
45. 15 − 8
46. 17 − 9

47. Jack parked 12 vans and 9 cars. He parked how many more vans than cars?

48. There were 16 cars in the lot. 8 were driven away. How many were left?

49. There were 13 empty parking places. After 7 were filled, how many were still empty?

50. Last weekend, Gail worked 15 hours and Jack worked 9 hours. Gail worked how many more hours than Jack?

In one day, Gail parked 14 trucks, 9 station wagons, and 7 sports cars. She parked how many more

51. trucks than sports cars?

52. station wagons than sports cars?

53. trucks than station wagons?

• **Discuss** What is the answer when you subtract zero from a number?

• **Discuss** What is the answer when you subtract a number from itself?

More practice
Set 7, page 372

Using Subtraction Facts

Subtract to find each answer.

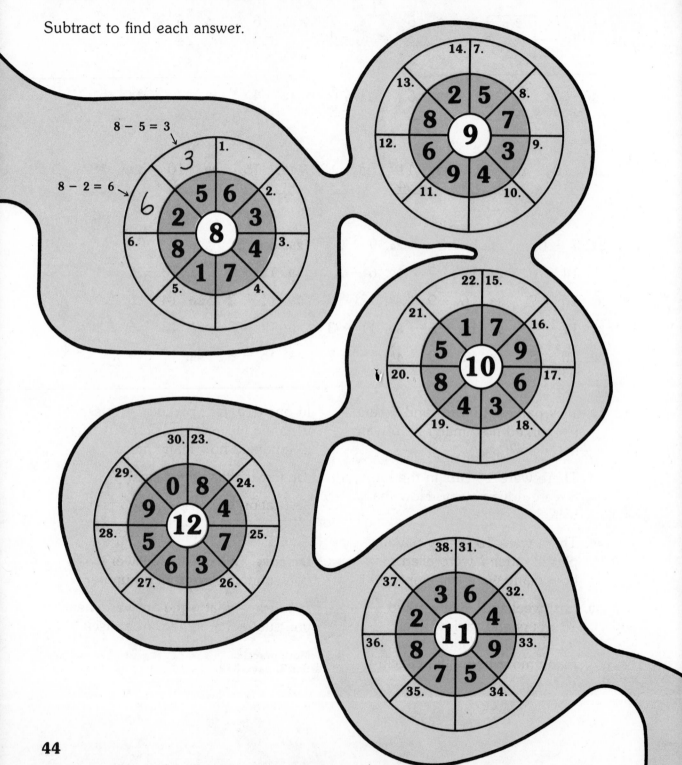

8 − 5 = 3

8 − 2 = 6

Complete each table.

	− 8
13	5
39. 16	
40. 14	
41. 17	
42. 15	

	− 6
9	3
43. 6	
44. 8	
45. 14	
46. 7	

	− 7
47. 7	
48. 14	
49. 16	
50. 13	
51. 15	

	− 9
52. 17	
53. 14	
54. 18	
55. 16	
56. 13	

Find each answer.

57. Tracy had 13 tennis balls. She gave away 6. How many tennis balls did she have left?

58. A team has 14 baseballs and 5 bats. They have how many more baseballs than bats?

59. Mrs. Peters sold 8 footballs and 17 helmets. She sold how many more helmets than footballs?

Keeping Skillful

Round to the nearest ten.

1. 24 **2.** 91

3. 38 **4.** 79

5. 45 **6.** 63

7. 432 **8.** 329

9. 176 **10.** 457

Round to the nearest hundred.

11. 123 **12.** 435

13. 493 **14.** 780

15. 347 **16.** 815

17. 2572 **18.** 4354

19. 1209 **20.** 3916

Round to the nearest thousand.

21. 3416 **22.** 4827

23. 1273 **24.** 9046

25. 2528 **26.** 5634

27. 8123 **28.** 1945

29. 6540 **30.** 7381

Estimating Differences

An owl can live
about 294 months.

A starling can live
about 180 months.

A. An owl can live about how many
months longer than a starling?

Estimate 294 − 180.

294 − 180
   ↓   ↓
300 − 200 = 100

Round 294 and 180
to the nearest hundred.
Subtract.

Actual difference

$$\begin{array}{r} 294 \\ -180 \\ \hline 114 \end{array}$$

An owl can live about 100 months
longer than a starling.

B. Estimate 3498 − 1263.

3498 − 1263
   ↓   ↓
3000 − 1000 = 2000

Round 3498 and 1263
to the nearest thousand.
Subtract.

Actual difference

$$\begin{array}{r} 3498 \\ -1263 \\ \hline 2235 \end{array}$$

C. Estimate 116 − 32

116 − 32
  ↓   ↓
120 − 30 = 90

Round 116 and 32
to the nearest ten.
Subtract.

Actual difference

$$\begin{array}{r} 116 \\ -32 \\ \hline 84 \end{array}$$

Estimate by rounding to the nearest ten.
Then find the actual difference.

1. 48 − 21   **2.** 88 − 13   **3.** 19 − 11   **4.** 53 − 32   **5.** 28 − 12

6. 77 − 42   **7.** 82 − 51   **8.** 124 − 32   **9.** 149 − 87   **10.** 184 − 92

Estimate by rounding to the nearest hundred.
Then find the actual difference.

11. 847 − 115   **12.** 386 − 153   **13.** 254 − 103   **14.** 618 − 406

15. 189 − 121   **16.** 1226 − 915   **17.** 1632 − 801   **18.** 1196 − 521

Estimate by rounding to the nearest thousand.
Then find the actual difference.

19. 6245 − 3112   **20.** 5627 − 3025   **21.** 1943 − 1021   **22.** 2838 − 1217

23. 8485 − 5350   **24.** 3918 − 2804   **25.** 9065 − 1024   **26.** 4568 − 2035

This table shows the average number of months certain animals can live.

Animal	Months
Giant tortoise	1788
Box turtle	1476
Alligator	672
Snapping turtle	540
Crocodile	162
Water snake	84
Garter snake	72

Estimate each answer.

A giant tortoise can live about how many months longer than

27. a box turtle?

28. a snapping turtle?

An alligator can live about how many months longer than

29. a snapping turtle?

30. a crocodile?

31. a garter snake?

32. A water snake can live about how many months longer than a garter snake?

Renaming

A. Rename 183 to show 10 more ones.

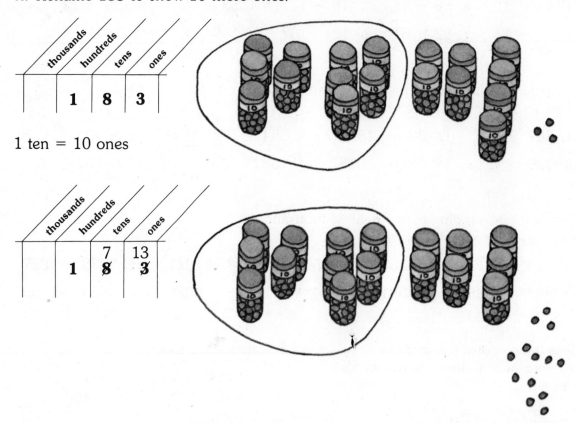

thousands	hundreds	tens	ones
	1	8	3

1 ten = 10 ones

thousands	hundreds	tens	ones
1	~~8~~ 7	~~3~~ 13	~~3~~

B. Rename to show 10 more tens.

thousands	hundreds	tens	ones
2	~~3~~ 18	~~8~~	5

C. Rename to show 10 more hundreds.

thousands	hundreds	tens	ones
4	~~5~~ 13	~~3~~	6	2

D. Rename to show 10 more tens.

thousands	hundreds	tens	ones
6	~~7~~	9 10 ~~0~~	16 ~~6~~	3

48

Rename to show 10 more ones.

Here's how

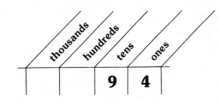

th	h	t	o
		8̶9	¹⁴4̶

1.
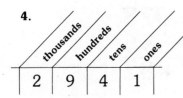
thousands | hundreds | tens | ones
| | 8 | 3 |

2.
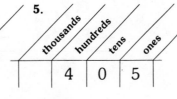
thousands | hundreds | tens | ones
| 1 | 5 | 2 |

3.
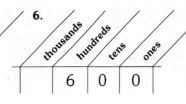
thousands | hundreds | tens | ones
| 3 | 7 | 0 |

4.
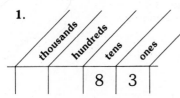
thousands | hundreds | tens | ones
2 | 9 | 4 | 1

5.
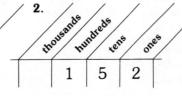
thousands | hundreds | tens | ones
| 4 | 0 | 5 |

6.
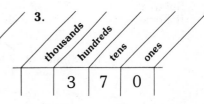
thousands | hundreds | tens | ones
| 6 | 0 | 0 |

Rename to show 10 more tens.

7.
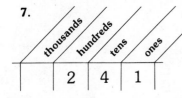
thousands | hundreds | tens | ones
| 2 | 4 | 1 |

8.
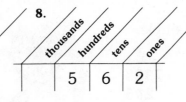
thousands | hundreds | tens | ones
| 5 | 6 | 2 |

9.
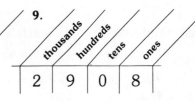
thousands | hundreds | tens | ones
2 | 9 | 0 | 8

10.
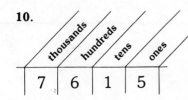
thousands | hundreds | tens | ones
7 | 6 | 1 | 5

11.
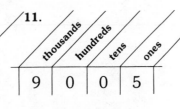
thousands | hundreds | tens | ones
9 | 0 | 0 | 5

12.
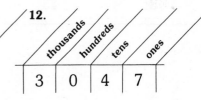
thousands | hundreds | tens | ones
3 | 0 | 4 | 7

Rename to show 10 more hundreds.

13.
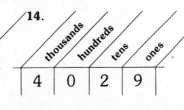
thousands | hundreds | tens | ones
7 | 6 | 3 | 4

14.
thousands | hundreds | tens | ones
4 | 0 | 2 | 9

15.
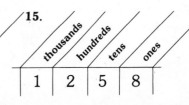
thousands | hundreds | tens | ones
1 | 2 | 5 | 8

49

Subtraction: One Renaming

A. There were 978 tickets for a play.
After 596 were sold, how many tickets
were left?

Find 978 − 596.

Subtract the ones.	You need more tens. Rename to show 10 more tens.	Subtract the tens.	Subtract the hundreds.

9 hundreds 7 tens =
8 hundreds 17 tens

```
        8 17        8 17        8 17
  978   9̸78̸       9̸78̸        9̸78̸
 −596  −596       −596       −596
 ─────  ─────      ─────      ─────
    2       2        82        382
```

There were 382 tickets left.

Tell what was done in each example.

```
        7 12              2 14               8 13
B.   98̸2̸     C.   3̸4̸56       D.   79̸3̸8
   − 146        − 1813           −  295
   ─────        ──────          ──────
     836          1643            7643
```

50

Subtract.

1. 37
   −18

2. 43
   −26

3. 64
   −37

4. 70
   −25

5. 85
   −47

6. 25
   −19

7. 826
   −340

8. 453
   −124

9. 581
   −416

10. 739
    −590

11. 450
    −137

12. 327
    −167

13. 4589
    −2816

14. 8745
    −1492

15. 4638
    −1352

16. 3621
    −1811

17. 8247
    −3128

18. 1924
    −1617

19. 687
    − 19

20. 326
    − 34

21. 245
    − 26

22. 537
    − 75

23. 5384
    − 192

24. 4259
    − 172

25. 618 − 345
26. 3678 − 293
27. 786 − 48
28. 228 − 193

29. 995 − 88
30. 421 − 105
31. 2349 − 1725
32. 8246 − 153

33. 591 − 263
34. 2850 − 634
35. 4516 − 2602
36. 3968 − 791

37. Ann sold 543 adult tickets and 372 student tickets. She sold how many more adult tickets than student tickets?

38. There are 35 dancers and 18 actors in the play. How many more dancers are there?

39. Ray had 1025 programs to sell. He has sold 618. How many does he have left to sell?

**More practice
Set 8, page 372**

Subtraction: More Than One Renaming

A. Mark and Julie went to the museum.
They saw a display of 715 gold coins and
348 silver coins. How many more gold
coins did they see?

Find 715 − 348.

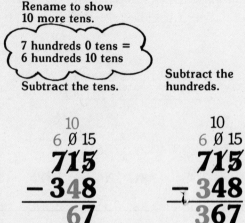

You need more ones.
Rename to show
10 more ones.

1 ten 5 ones =
0 tens 15 ones

Subtract the ones.

You need more tens.
Rename to show
10 more tens.

7 hundreds 0 tens =
6 hundreds 10 tens

Subtract the tens.

Subtract the
hundreds.

```
  0 15          10              10
              6 Ø 15          6 Ø 15
  715           715            715
− 348         − 348          − 348
─────         ─────          ─────
    7            67            367
```

They saw 367 more gold coins.

Tell what was done in each example.

```
      14
    2 4 11           3 12 7 10          1 4 13
B.  3514       C.   4280       D.   253
  − 1872           −  365           −  57
  ──────           ──────          ─────
    1642             3915            196
```

Subtract.

1. 321 − 65	**2.** 817 − 49	**3.** 634 − 86	**4.** 548 − 59	**5.** 260 − 75	**6.** 452 − 93
7. 245 −179	**8.** 456 −258	**9.** 384 −188	**10.** 736 −349	**11.** 913 −565	**12.** 543 −446
13. 2036 − 829	**14.** 7158 − 993	**15.** 5297 − 468	**16.** 5975 − 878	**17.** 8127 − 675	**18.** 3072 − 256
19. 4735 −1287	**20.** 8143 −1681	**21.** 6180 −4673	**22.** 6783 −5295	**23.** 7194 −1856	**24.** 8309 −6594

25. 783 − 94   **26.** 832 − 496   **27.** 5244 − 2718   **28.** 4516 − 925

29. 2455 − 1827   **30.** 340 − 93   **31.** 3129 − 275   **32.** 611 − 124

33. 1920 − 653   **34.** 950 − 378   **35.** 714 − 67   **36.** 8273 − 3490

37. Mrs. Lee had 247 wood carvings. She gave 59 to the museum. How many carvings did she have left?

38. On Friday, 1257 people came to the museum. 1915 people came on Saturday. How many more came on Saturday?

39. Mark and Julie saw a brass plate that was 416 years old. They saw a silver plate that was 267 years old. How much older was the brass plate?

More practice
Set 9, page 372

Using Subtraction

Name	Born	Died	Became President
George Washington	1732	1799	1789
Thomas Jefferson	1743	1826	1801
Abraham Lincoln	1809	1865	1861
Theodore Roosevelt	1858	1919	1901

How long did each man live?

1. Washington   2. Jefferson

3. Lincoln   4. Roosevelt

5. How old was Washington when he became President?

6. How old was Lincoln when he became President?

7. Jefferson died how many years after Washington died?

8. Lincoln became President how many years after Washington became President?

9. Roosevelt became President how many years after Lincoln died?

10. How old was Roosevelt when Lincoln became President?

54

Subtract across.
Subtract down.

		11.
516	32	
178	19	12.
13.	14.	15.

		16.
5234	317	
1618	228	17.
18.	19.	20.

Subtract.

21. 845 − 286   **22.** 6345 − 713

23. 4675 − 1250   **24.** 916 − 87

25. 340 − 215   **26.** 4121 − 740

27. 3863 − 1785   **28.** 709 − 97

29. 865 − 621   **30.** 5463 − 872

31. 3884 − 1267   **32.** 257 − 186

33. 284 − 57   **34.** 9017 − 1815

35. 8124 − 315   **36.** 726 − 37

37. 427 − 213   **38.** 2493 − 1507

39. 5637 − 246   **40.** 463 − 292

41. 9565 − 816   **42.** 3186 − 1994

Time Out

Who was the 34th President of the United States?
Use these clues to help you.

The fifth letter is N.

The ninth letter is E.

The seventh letter is O.

The second letter is I.

The tenth letter is R.

The first letter is E.

The sixth letter is H.

The third letter is S.

The eighth letter is W.

The fourth letter is E.

Zeros in Subtraction

A. Paul Bunyan cut 900 trees. His helper cut 132 trees.
Paul cut how many more trees than his helper?

Find 900 − 132.

You need to rename before you subtract. Rename to show 10 more tens.

9 hundreds 0 tens = 8 hundreds 10 tens

Rename to show 10 more ones.

10 tens 0 ones = 9 tens 10 ones

Subtract the ones. Subtract the tens. Subtract the hundreds.

```
  8 10
  900
 -132
```

```
    9
  8 10 10
  900
 -132
```

```
    9
  8 10 10
  900
 -132
  768
```

Paul cut 768 more trees.

Tell what was done in each example.

B.
```
      9
  4 10 12
  5028
 -2196
  2832
```

C.
```
      9
  7 10 17
   807
  - 89
   718
```

D.
```
      9
  2 10 10
  3004
 - 153
  2851
```

56

Subtract.

1. 706 −238	**2.** 900 −586	**3.** 200 −175	**4.** 503 −347
5. 100 − 58	**6.** 608 − 99	**7.** 300 − 43	**8.** 405 − 26
9. 8006 −4243	**10.** 2030 −1560	**11.** 5600 −2355	**12.** 7008 −3862
13. 4501 − 216	**14.** 8009 − 543	**15.** 2304 − 158	**16.** 5073 − 982
17. 3600 −1439	**18.** 1007 − 983	**19.** 2402 − 157	**20.** 3600 −1247

21. 3200 − 2143   **22.** 1038 − 746

★23. 9000 − 3528   **★24.** 5001 − 3999

25. Hot Biscuit Slim made 2500 biscuits. Paul ate 1356 of them. How many biscuits were left?

26. Babe, the blue ox, weighed 3506 kilograms. Paul weighed 398 kilograms. How much more did Babe weigh?

27. Paul cut 8007 trees. He used 342 for toothpicks. How many trees were left?

More practice
Set 10, page 373

Using Subtraction

Find each difference. Use the code to find the answer to the riddle.

At what time of his life did Paul Bunyan weigh the most?

Code			
228	N	1589	H
315	I	2158	A
387	S	2367	V
567	E	4257	T
851	W		

Word 1

1. 903 − 52
2. 1748 − 159
3. 1806 − 1239
4. 514 − 286

Word 2

5. 3049 − 1460
6. 700 − 133

Word 3

7. 1797 − 946
8. 5300 − 3142
9. 603 − 216

Word 4

10. 5601 − 1344
11. 8800 − 7211
12. 704 − 137

Word 5

13. 1706 − 117
14. 605 − 38
15. 4009 − 1851
16. 2513 − 146
17. 600 − 285
18. 1802 − 1235
19. 854 − 467
20. 4500 − 243

Subtract.

21. 302 − 187	**22.** 415 − 46	**23.** 6008 − 1352	**24.** 500 − 324
25. 9056 − 1238	**26.** 526 − 183	**27.** 5900 − 1562	**28.** 1850 − 478
29. 300 − 73	**30.** 4018 − 1246	**31.** 5706 − 2189	**32.** 9100 − 7015
33. 2308 − 1673	**34.** 183 − 96	**35.** 3490 − 1534	**36.** 601 − 375
37. 1100 − 150	**38.** 745 − 385	**★39.** 2000 − 199	**★40.** 4002 − 2005

Estimate each answer.

41. Paul moved 683 logs. Babe moved 897 logs. Babe moved about how many more logs than Paul?

42. Slim fried 896 eggs Monday and 813 eggs Tuesday. He fried about how many more on Monday?

43. Slim made 2826 flapjacks and 1635 biscuits. He made about how many more flapjacks?

44. There were 525 loggers in the camp. After 395 of them went to work, about how many were left in the camp?

45. Paul cut 5326 logs. He used 1845 to build a cabin. About how many logs were left?

Mental Computation: Addition and Subtraction

A. 66 + 28 = ▦
60 + 20 = 80
6 + 8 = 14
80 + 14 = 94
The answer is 94.

B. 99 + 34 = ▦
99 + 30 = 129
129 + 4 = 133
The answer is 133.

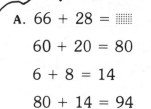

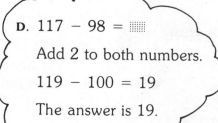

c. 91 − 52 = ▦
91 − 50 = 41
41 − 2 = 39
The answer is 39.

D. 117 − 98 = ▦
Add 2 to both numbers.
119 − 100 = 19
The answer is 19.

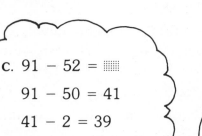

Find each sum or difference mentally.

1. $44 + 37$
2. $79 + 26$
3. $56 + 18$
4. $35 + 52$
5. $67 + 73$
6. $23 + 39$
7. $84 + 33$
8. $17 + 46$
9. $42 + 99$
10. $98 + 64$
11. $35 + 89$
12. $29 + 57$
13. $83 + 95$
14. $51 - 28$
15. $86 - 49$
16. $56 - 18$
17. $73 - 56$
18. $45 - 27$
19. $64 - 39$
20. $94 - 57$
21. $87 - 28$
22. $132 - 97$
23. $32 - 15$
24. $183 - 99$
25. $124 - 79$

Lab Activity

Add to 13

Tina and Betty used mental addition to play this game.

Rules:

1. The first player chooses 1, 2, or 3.

2. The second player adds 1, 2, or 3 to the first number and gives the sum.

3. At each turn, a player must add 1, 2, or 3 and give the sum.

4. The first player to reach the sum 13 is the winner.

Tina started. She chose 1.

Betty added 2.
$(1 + 2 = 3)$

Tina added 2.
$(3 + 2 = 5)$

Betty added 3.
$(5 + 3 = 8)$

Tina added 1.
$(8 + 1 = 9)$

Betty added 1.
$(9 + 1 = 10)$

Tina added 3.
$(10 + 3 = 13)$

Tina won the game.

Try the game with a friend.

Chapter 3 Test
Subtraction, pages 42–61

Subtract.

1. $\begin{array}{r} 12 \\ -\ 5 \\ \hline \end{array}$
2. $\begin{array}{r} 15 \\ -\ 6 \\ \hline \end{array}$
3. $\begin{array}{r} 11 \\ -\ 3 \\ \hline \end{array}$

4. $9 - 5$
5. $13 - 4$

Rename to show 10 more ones.

6.
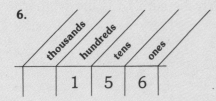

thousands	hundreds	tens	ones
	1	5	6

Rename to show 10 more tens.

7.
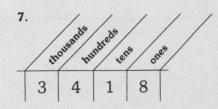

thousands	hundreds	tens	ones
3	4	1	8

Rename to show 10 more hundreds.

8.

thousands	hundreds	tens	ones
8	5	2	7

Subtract.

9. $\begin{array}{r} 528 \\ -\ 85 \\ \hline \end{array}$
10. $\begin{array}{r} 714 \\ -267 \\ \hline \end{array}$
11. $\begin{array}{r} 175 \\ -\ 98 \\ \hline \end{array}$

12. $\begin{array}{r} 9853 \\ -2016 \\ \hline \end{array}$
13. $\begin{array}{r} 381 \\ -157 \\ \hline \end{array}$
14. $\begin{array}{r} 638 \\ -389 \\ \hline \end{array}$

15. $\begin{array}{r} 406 \\ -138 \\ \hline \end{array}$
16. $\begin{array}{r} 902 \\ -556 \\ \hline \end{array}$
17. $\begin{array}{r} 8100 \\ -4260 \\ \hline \end{array}$

18. $\begin{array}{r} 1600 \\ -\ 429 \\ \hline \end{array}$
19. $\begin{array}{r} 4356 \\ -2932 \\ \hline \end{array}$
20. $\begin{array}{r} 5847 \\ -3918 \\ \hline \end{array}$

21. $\begin{array}{r} 3284 \\ -2758 \\ \hline \end{array}$
22. $\begin{array}{r} 6325 \\ -4035 \\ \hline \end{array}$
23. $\begin{array}{r} 2854 \\ -\ 196 \\ \hline \end{array}$

Estimate each answer.

24. On Monday 67 people came to the play. 32 people came on Tuesday. About how many more came on Monday?

25. Pam drove 345 kilometers in the morning and 232 kilometers in the afternoon. She drove about how many more kilometers in the morning?

Problems Around Us

**Six Longest Rivers
in the World**

River	Length (kilometers)
Nile	6632
Amazon	6400
Mississippi	5936
Ob-Irtysh	5536
Yangtze	5440
Huang Ho	4800

Which river is longer?

1. Amazon or Yangtze

2. Nile or Mississippi

3. Huang Ho or Ob-Irtysh

Which river is shorter?

4. Yangtze or Mississippi

5. Nile or Huang Ho

6. Amazon or Ob-Irtysh

Round the length of the

7. Nile (nearest ten).

8. Yangtze (nearest hundred).

9. Huang Ho (nearest thousand).

10. Mississippi (nearest ten).

Find each answer.

11. Hank Aaron hit 733 home runs in the National League and 22 more in the American League. He hit how many home runs in all?

12. A reindeer ran 48 kilometers the first hour, 35 kilometers the second hour, and 26 kilometers the third hour. How far did the reindeer run?

13. In 1926, Gertrude Ederle became the first woman to swim the English Channel. It took her 871 minutes. She broke the previous record of 993 minutes. How much less time did she take?

14. Edward Winslow brought the first cows to the American colonies in 1624. He became governor of Plymouth Colony 9 years later. In what year did he become governor?

15. A small Shetland sheepdog weighs 8 kilograms. A large Shetland sheepdog weighs 11 kilograms. How much heavier is the large sheepdog?

16. In 1968, Willie McCovey hit 36 home runs. The next year, he hit 45 home runs. How many home runs did he hit during this two-year period?

Individualized Skills Maintenance

Diagnose

A *pages 4–7*

Tell what each 3 means.

3,984,076

1376

9034

B *pages 22–25*

6 + 8

9 + 7

8 + 5

C *pages 42–45*

18 − 9

15 − 7

13 − 4

Practice

A Tell what each 5 means.

1. 4165 2. 50,722 3. 8,561,728 4. 115,740 5. 657

6. 5,786,241 7. 62,599 8. 9,500,001 9. 7795 10. 65,296

11. 6,968,759 12. 150,840 13. 5,910,068 14. 964,521 15. 10,005

B

16. 6 +9 17. 8 +6 18. 4 +9 19. 7 +3 20. 5 +9 21. 6 +5 22. 7 +8 23. 9 +2

24. 8 +9 25. 6 +7 26. 9 +9 27. 8 +5 28. 8 +4 29. 4 +7 30. 3 +8 31. 7 +9

C

32. 16 − 7 33. 13 − 8 34. 11 − 4 35. 17 − 8 36. 15 − 9 37. 12 − 5 38. 11 − 3

39. 11 − 2 40. 13 − 7 41. 12 − 9 42. 16 − 8 43. 14 − 9 44. 12 − 8 45. 14 − 7

Unit 1 Review

Chapter 1, pages 2–20
Tell what each 8 means.

1. 1824
2. 7628
3. 589
4. 8001
5. 819,450
6. 86,374

Give the standard form.

7. six hundred thousand, one hundred three
8. two thousand twenty-nine
9. nineteen million, six hundred eighty-seven thousand

Round to the nearest ten.

10. 35
11. 784

Round to the nearest hundred.

12. 349
13. 5680

Round to the nearest thousand.

14. 7320
15. 2560

Compare the numbers.
Use < or >.

16. 43 ● 57
17. 121 ● 212
18. 647 ● 638
19. 1762 ● 1627

Give the numbers in order from least to greatest.

20. 48 18 36 6
21. 376 307 367 360

Chapter 2, pages 22–40
Add.

22. 9
    +6

23. 7
    +4

24. 47
    +16

25. 325
    +295

26. 196
    +242

27. 5124
    +1638

28. 3298
    +2043

29. 67
     98
    +35

30. 682
     724
    +357

Chapter 3, pages 42–61
Subtract.

31. 16
    − 7

32. 14
    − 6

33. 27
    −19

34. 46
    −38

35. 756
    −397

36. 289
    −191

37. 503
    − 75

38. 2763
    −1825

39. 7048
    −1563

Unit 1 Test
Chapters 1–3, pages 2–62

Tell what each 7 means.

1. 3796   2. 7,301,458

Give the standard form.

3. six hundred forty-five

4. one million, two hundred thousand, four hundred eighteen

Round each number to

5. the nearest ten.   78

6. the nearest hundred.   216

7. the nearest thousand.   4621

Compare the numbers.
Use < or >.

8. 27 ● 72

9. 4138 ● 4813

Give the numbers in order
from least to greatest.

10. 48   45   31   47

11. 275   265   215   295

Add.

12.	8	13.	4	14.	6
	+7		+9		+8

15.	18	16.	61	17.	346
	+39		+59		+183

18.	526	19.	8833	20.	3728
	+295		+1079		+4863

21.	8	22.	48	23.	176
	9		31		353
	+6		+56		+213

Subtract.

24.	18	25.	13	26.	14
	− 9		− 7		− 9

27.	24	28.	81	29.	365
	− 6		−68		−172

30.	623	31.	9516	32.	8273
	− 89		−1624		−2354

33.	600	34.	7802	35.	2009
	−138		−3794		−1378

Unit 2

Checking Addition and Subtraction

Lake County School had a math contest. This is
how the winners checked their work.

Ronald used addition to check
subtraction.

Mio used subtraction to check
addition.

•*Discuss*   How can you use addition to check addition?

Check each answer. Tell if it is right or wrong.
If it is wrong, give the correct answer.

1. 582
   + 17
    609

2. 2639
   +5327
    7966

3. 64
   +59
   123

4. 7092
   + 653
    7645

5. 3741
   +2329
    5070

6. 478
   +972
   1450

7. 949
   +759
   1718

8. 8263
   + 435
    8698

9. 5649
   - 325
    5324

10. 297
   - 36
    251

11. 4683
   -3975
    1708

12. 974
   -489
    485

13. 2371
   -1290
    1081

14. 630
   -216
    424

15. 837
   - 84
    753

16. 7800
   - 325
    7485

Add or subtract. Watch the signs.
Check each answer.

17. 263
   +627

18. 395
   -174

19. 4506
   +1293

20. 8264
   -3017

21. 9767
   -8931

22. 1594
   + 762

23. 59
   +88

24. 275
   - 46

25. 5176
   + 316

26. 374
   + 23

27. 6218
   - 754

28. 672
   -583

29. 688
   +875

30. 6438
   +7821

31. 400
   - 26

32. 5008
   -2126

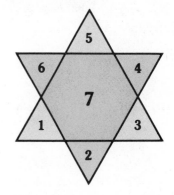
69

Problem Solving: Choosing the Operation

READ   Read the problem.
What facts are given?
What is the question?

A. The men who flew the balloon Double Eagle I traveled 4720 kilometers trying to cross the Atlantic Ocean. Later, the same men traveled 4992 kilometers in the Double Eagle II to cross the Atlantic. How far did they travel in all?

DECIDE   What must you do to solve the problem?

Add the distance traveled in Double Eagle I and the distance traveled in Double Eagle II.

Write an **equation**.

$$4720 + 4992 = n$$

SOLVE   Do the work.

$$\begin{array}{r} 4720 \\ +\ 4992 \\ \hline 9712 \end{array}$$

ANSWER   Read the question.
Give the answer.
Is the answer sensible?

$n = 9712$

9712 kilometers

READ   **B.** The trip on Double Eagle I took 64 hours. The trip on Double Eagle II took 137 hours. How many more hours did the second trip take?

DECIDE   Subtract the number of hours for the first trip from the number of hours for the second trip.

Write an equation.

$$137 - 64 = n$$

SOLVE

$$\begin{array}{r} 137 \\ -\ 64 \\ \hline 73 \end{array}$$

ANSWER $n = 73$

73 hours

For each problem, write an equation. Then give the answer.

1. Carmen traveled 827 kilometers in a balloon one year. Judy traveled 1250 kilometers. How many more kilometers did Judy travel? $(1250 - 827 = n)$

2. During one year, 83 passengers traveled in the Shooting Star balloon. The next year there were 254 passengers. How many passengers were there in all?

3. Lamar's balloon rose to a height of 165 meters. Carl's balloon rose to a height of 215 meters. How much higher did Carl's balloon rise?

4. The Sunshine balloon traveled 5296 kilometers one year and 3548 kilometers the next year. How many more kilometers did it travel the first year?

5. Kim traveled 742 kilometers in a balloon one year. The next year she traveled 1285 kilometers. How many kilometers did she travel in these two years?

6. A balloon school had 124 students one year and 97 students the next year. How many more students were there the first year?

7. The three passengers in a balloon weighed 52 kilograms, 85 kilograms, and 75 kilograms. What was the total weight of the passengers?

8. One year David flew 43 hours in a balloon. The next year he flew 97 hours. How many hours did he fly a balloon in these two years?

9. The club's balloon traveled 2429 kilometers one year and 2238 kilometers the next year. How many kilometers did it travel in all?

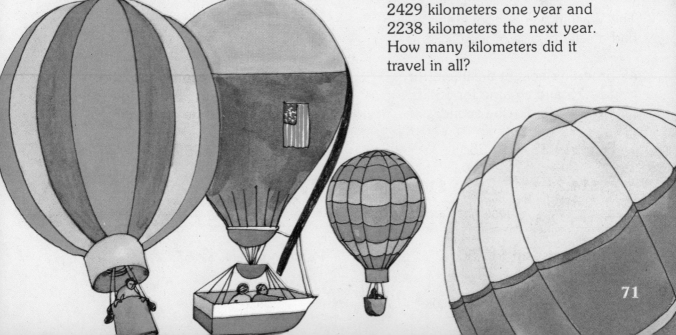

Addition and Subtraction of Money

The Washington School Hobby Club
had a sale to raise money.

A. Ernestine bought a camera for
$14.25 and a game for $3.25.
How much did she spend?

Find $14.25 + $3.25.

$$\begin{array}{r} \$14.25 \\ +\ \ 3.25 \\ \hline \end{array} \qquad \begin{array}{r} 1425 \\ +\ 325 \\ \hline 1750 \end{array} \qquad \begin{array}{r} \$14.25 \\ +\ \ 3.25 \\ \hline \$17.50 \end{array}$$

Ernestine spent $17.50.

B. Pablo bought a record for $2.35.
He paid for it with $5.00. How
much money did he get back?

Find $5.00 − $2.35.

$$\begin{array}{r} \$5.00 \\ -\ 2.35 \\ \hline \end{array} \qquad \begin{array}{r} 500 \\ -235 \\ \hline 265 \end{array} \qquad \begin{array}{r} \$5.00 \\ -\ 2.35 \\ \hline \$2.65 \end{array}$$

Pablo got back $2.65.

Add.

1. $24.35
  + 74.03

2. $5.24
  + 0.23

3. $3.42
  + 8.83

4. $1.89
  + 3.28

5. $68.28
  + 8.54

6. $23.74
  + 3.62

7. $9.77
  + 0.17

8. $56.18
  + 24.77

9. $0.99
  + 0.73

10. $43.49
   + 2.55

Subtract.

11. $9.87
  − 2.62

12. $67.88
  − 4.93

13. $79.54
  − 16.32

14. $5.41
  − 1.73

15. $9.60
  − 7.24

16. $96.83
  − 52.45

17. $1.22
  − 0.54

18. $29.94
  − 4.26

19. $5.26
  − 4.66

20. $94.91
  − 8.47

Find each answer.

21. Hiroko bought a paint brush for $0.94 and a football for $8.58. How much more did she pay for the football?

22. Mike bought a fish tank for $15.08 and a filter for $5.85. How much did he spend?

23. Jason bought a horn for $20.96 and a drum for $16.93. How much did he spend?

24. Elena had $16.50. She spent $3.79 at the sale. How much money did she have left?

25. Kenji spent $3.95 for a model airplane. He paid for it with $5.00. How much money did he get back?

26. Sally bought a mystery book for $3.19 and a dictionary for $5.96. How much did she spend?

27. Sharon bought a bicycle for $53.80 and a bicycle basket for $11.37. How much more did the bicycle cost?

28. Ricardo bought a record for $2.43 and a puzzle for $0.96. How much did he spend?

29. Donna bought a paint set for $6.50 and paid for it with $10.00. How much money did she get back?

**More practice
Set 11, page 373**

Using Addition and Subtraction

Endangered Species

Whooping crane
Estimated population 126

Sea otter
Estimated population 2196

Bighorn sheep
Estimated population 315

Bald eagle
Estimated population 3842

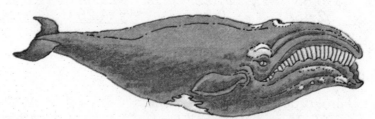

Right whale
Estimated population 956

Use the information in the picture.
Find each answer.

1. There are how many more bald eagles than whooping cranes?

2. If the number of right whales increases by 105, how many will there be?

3. What is the difference between the number of bald eagles and bighorn sheep?

4. What is the difference between the number of sea otters and right whales?

5. If the number of whooping cranes increases by 19, how many will there be?

6. There are how many more bald eagles than sea otters?

7. What is the difference between the number of bighorn sheep and whooping cranes?

8. If the number of bald eagles increases by 167, how many will there be?

Complete each table.

		− 93
	749	656
9.	898	
10.	507	
11.	352	
12.	471	

		+ 54
	405	459
13.	89	
14.	528	
15.	76	
16.	167	

		+ 273
17.	17	
18.	459	
19.	3963	
20.	861	
21.	6819	

		− 457
22.	3218	
23.	694	
24.	1897	
25.	6389	
26.	700	

		+ 5846
27.	725	
28.	2831	
29.	2143	
30.	116	
31.	8084	

		− 2386
32.	9437	
33.	7698	
34.	4297	
35.	5295	
36.	8500	

Keeping Skillful

Compare the numbers. Use < or >.

1. 27 ● 28
2. 31 ● 13
3. 18 ● 21
4. 401 ● 400
5. 389 ● 385
6. 256 ● 263
7. 7284 ● 7206
8. 5996 ● 6513
9. 3113 ● 3123

Give the numbers in order from least to greatest.

10. 28 22 26 25
11. 51 17 63 49
12. 81 79 80 78
13. 57 53 38 46
14. 326 521 384
15. 776 785 768
16. 214 207 212
17. 471 379 474
18. 5496 5964 5594
19. 1702 2701 1270
20. 3219 3116 3229

Missing Addends

A. Detective Dan and Detective Diane found 52 rubies in all. They found 34 rubies on Monday and the rest on Tuesday. How many rubies did they find on Tuesday?

Rubies found on Monday	Rubies found on Tuesday	Number of rubies in all

Write an equation.

$$34 + n = 52$$

Subtract to find the missing addend.

$$\begin{array}{r} 52 \\ -34 \\ \hline 18 \end{array}$$

$$n = 18$$

They found 18 rubies on Tuesday.

76

Tell what was done in each example.

B. $n + 347 = 596$

$$\begin{array}{r} 596 \\ -347 \\ \hline 249 \end{array}$$

$n = 249$

C. $n + \$3.76 = \$4.32$

$$\begin{array}{r} \$4.32 \\ -\ 3.76 \\ \hline \$0.56 \end{array}$$

$n = \$0.56$

Find the missing addend.

1. $286 + n = 674$
2. $n + 19 = 21$
3. $\$0.89 + n = \$7.64$
4. $n + 92 = 457$
5. $n + \$2.19 = \$5.26$
6. $n + 42 = 179$
7. $35 + n = 50$
8. $64 + n = 300$
9. $n + 435 = 849$
10. $n + \$0.30 = \$0.42$
11. $21 + n = 43$
12. $552 + n = 934$

13. Dan bought a secret-code book for $0.96. Then he bought a mystery-solving kit. He spent $5.95 in all. How much did he pay for the mystery-solving kit?

14. Diane found 524 of the missing gold coins and Dan found the rest. There were 906 gold coins in all. How many did Dan find?

15. Dan searched 35 cars for some missing money. He searched 19 cars on Thursday and the rest on Friday. How many cars did he search on Friday?

16. Diane bought a flashlight for $3.68. Then she bought a magnifying glass. She spent $9.45 in all. How much did she pay for the magnifying glass?

77

Problem Solving: Too Much Information

READ   The first year, 2735 runners entered the marathon. There were 4076 runners last year and 9135 runners this year.

How many more runners entered the marathon this year than last year?

DECIDE   There is too much information given. You only need to use the number of runners this year and the number of runners last year.

9135 ⟵ **Number of runners this year**
−4076 ⟵ **Number of runners last year**

SOLVE   **9135**
−4076
5059

ANSWER   5059 runners

Thousands Enter Marathon

For each problem, tell what information is used. Give the answer.

Here's how

Park Classes
Ballet lessons last 8 weeks and cost $7.35. Swimming classes last 10 weeks and cost $8.90.

How much does it cost to take the swimming class and the ballet class?

$ 7.35 ← *Ballet class*
+ 8.90 ← *Swimming class*
$16.25

78

1. Football Games

1356 people came to the first football game in November. There were 2974 people at the second game and 1496 people at the third game.

How many more people came to the second game than the first game?

2. School Attendance

Lincoln School has 956 students. King School has 901 students and Curie School has 844 students.

Lincoln School and Curie School have how many students in all?

3. Bottle Cap Contest

Ann Littlebird won the contest by collecting 97 bottle caps. Her brother, Jeff, came in second with 83 bottle caps. Virginia Jones came in third with 74 bottle caps.

How many bottle caps did Ann and Jeff have together?

4. Pool Passes

A family pool pass costs $12.75. An adult's pool pass costs $7.90 and a child's pool pass costs $4.95.

How much more does an adult's pool pass cost than a child's pool pass?

5. Stamp Collections

Mark Winn has 185 stamps in his collection. Linda Ruben has collected 125 stamps. Ken Wong has collected 98 stamps.

How many more stamps does Mark have than Ken?

6. Election Results

In the election, 9758 people voted for Rita Ortiz. 1350 people voted for John Brown. 839 people voted for Carl Hansen.

How many more people voted for Rita Ortiz than for Carl Hansen?

7. Art Fair

5496 people attended the first day of the fair. 4378 people attended the second day of the fair. 348 people attended the last day of the fair.

How many people attended the first and last days of the fair?

8. Recycling Center

The recycling center collected 2234 kilograms of newspaper in May, 2359 kilograms in June, and 2820 kilograms in July.

How many kilograms of newspaper were collected in June and July?

Addition and Subtraction of Large Numbers

How many beads are in the phone booth?

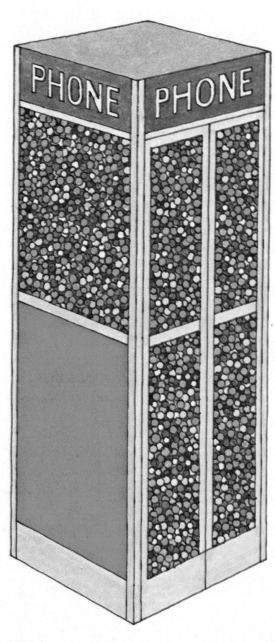

A. Carlos guessed that there were 1,342,976 beads in the booth. Karen guessed there were 3,150,276 beads in the booth. What is the difference between their guesses?

$$\begin{array}{r} 3,150,276 \\ -\,1,342,976 \\ \hline 1,807,300 \end{array}$$

The difference between their guesses is 1,807,300 beads.

B. This phone booth holds 2,456,973 beads. Another phone booth holds 5,279,342 beads. How many beads do you need to fill both phone booths?

$$\begin{array}{r} 2,456,973 \\ +\,5,279,342 \\ \hline 7,736,315 \end{array}$$

You need 7,736,315 beads to fill both phone booths.

Add.

1. 47,593
   + 65,219

2. 642,107
   + 954,638

3. 5,864,305
   + 9,428,016

4. 86,593,742
   + 2,639,561

5. 34,789
   + 45,629

6. 574,325
   + 826,357

7. 75,943,628
   + 6,321,754

8. 25,798,359
   + 61,375,946

Subtract.

9. 94,178
   − 53,459

10. 637,541
    − 594,786

11. 4,623,918
    − 2,157,632

12. 93,564,205
    − 1,479,824

13. 87,021
    − 59,346

14. 735,984
    − 239,895

15. 65,342,178
    − 2,956,019

16. 52,009,874
    − 27,945,392

	Peanuts	Beans	Grains of rice
Jar	95,216	283,516	4,965,420
Bucket	327,182	917,435	16,283,500
Barrel	1,053,276	2,810,783	59,463,218

Find each answer.

17. How many grains of rice are needed to fill the jar and the bucket?

18. The barrel holds how many more beans than peanuts?

19. How many peanuts are needed to fill a bucket and a barrel?

20. There are how many more beans in the bucket than in the jar?

21. How many beans are needed to fill the jar and the barrel?

22. How many more grains of rice are in the barrel than in the bucket?

Spin and Win

Randy, Mary, and Emily played this game. They made a spinner like this.

The players agreed that Randy would spin the pointer for the first round.

On the first spin, the pointer stopped on *You Lose*. Because this was the first spin, Randy spun again. This time, the pointer stopped on 19.

The players wrote 19 on their papers. Mary circled the 19 on her paper. This was her score for the round.

Randy spun again. The pointer stopped on 8. Randy and Emily wrote 8 on their papers. Then they added 19 + 8. Emily circled the sum 27 on her paper. This was her score for the round.

Randy spun the pointer again. It stopped on *You Lose*. The round was over. Since Randy had not circled a number on his paper, his score for this round was 0.

The players compared their scores. Emily had the highest score, so she won the first round.

Make a spinner. Find one or more partners and play 5 rounds. Find your total score at the end of 5 rounds. The player with the highest total wins the game.

Remember, once you circle a number during a round, you cannot change your mind.

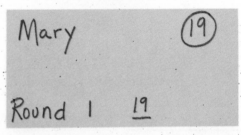

Mary   (19)

Round 1   19

Emily
$$19$$
$$+8$$
$$(27)$$

Round 1   27

Randy
$$19$$
$$+8$$
$$27$$

Round 1   0

Chapter 4 Test
Addition and Subtraction, pages 68–82

Add or subtract. Watch the signs.

1. $\begin{array}{r} 625 \\ -296 \\ \hline \end{array}$

2. $\begin{array}{r} 2739 \\ +5519 \\ \hline \end{array}$

3. $\begin{array}{r} 927 \\ +563 \\ \hline \end{array}$

4. $\begin{array}{r} 9600 \\ -4479 \\ \hline \end{array}$

5. $\begin{array}{r} 1873 \\ +\ 746 \\ \hline \end{array}$

6. $\begin{array}{r} 724 \\ -\ 83 \\ \hline \end{array}$

7. $\begin{array}{r} 8749 \\ -\ 582 \\ \hline \end{array}$

8. $\begin{array}{r} 845 \\ +\ 16 \\ \hline \end{array}$

9. $\begin{array}{r} 3846 \\ +\ 726 \\ \hline \end{array}$

10. $\begin{array}{r} 1496 \\ -\ 587 \\ \hline \end{array}$

11. $\begin{array}{r} \$75.36 \\ -\ 18.19 \\ \hline \end{array}$

12. $\begin{array}{r} \$21.93 \\ +\ 3.64 \\ \hline \end{array}$

13. $\begin{array}{r} \$4.88 \\ +\ 3.28 \\ \hline \end{array}$

14. $\begin{array}{r} \$8.35 \\ -\ 0.54 \\ \hline \end{array}$

Find the missing addend.

15. $n + 86 = 279$

16. $524 + n = 986$

Find each answer.

17. Pete's Pet Shop has 367 fish and 48 birds. The shop has how many more fish than birds?

18. The pet shop sold 2912 pets one year. 3254 pets were sold the next year. How many pets were sold in all?

19. 914 people went to the circus on Thursday. 1376 people went on Friday, and 1642 people went on Saturday. How many more people went on Saturday than on Thursday?

20. An art class costs $5.95. A dance class costs $5.75, and a guitar class costs $6.50. What is the total cost of an art class and a guitar class?

Chapter 5   Decimals

Tenths

A. Divide 1 one into ten equal parts. Each part is 1 tenth.

B. Six parts are shaded. This shows 6 tenths.

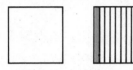

1 one   **1 tenth = 0.1**

6 tenths = 0.6

└── Decimal point ──┘

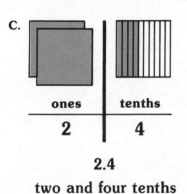

ones	tenths
2	4

2.4

two and four tenths

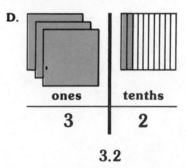

ones	tenths
3	2

3.2

three and two tenths

Numbers like 0.1, 0.6, 2.4, and 3.2 are **_decimals._**

Give a decimal to show how much is shaded.

1.

2.

3.

4.

5.

6.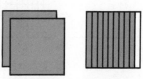

7.

8.

9.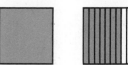

10.

Give each decimal.

11. two and eight tenths   12. nine and eight tenths

13. six and four tenths   14. three tenths

15. one and three tenths   16. five and two tenths

17. five tenths   18. three and seven tenths

19. four and five tenths   20. four tenths

Give the word name for each decimal.

Here's how   8.7   *eight and seven tenths*

21. 4.3   22. 7.8   23. 5.6   24. 1.2   25. 0.9   26. 9.2

Hundredths

A. Divide 1 one into one hundred equal parts. Each part is 1 hundredth.

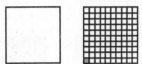

1 one   **1 hundredth = 0.01**

B. Twenty-four parts are shaded. This shows 24 hundredths.

24 hundredths = 0.24

C.

ones	tenths	hundredths
0	0	5

0.05

five hundredths

D.

ones	tenths	hundredths
1	0	7

1.07

one and seven hundredths

E.

ones	tenths	hundredths
1	5	8

1.58

one and fifty-eight hundredths

F.

ones	tenths	hundredths
2	2	0

2.20

two and twenty hundredths

Give a decimal to show how much is shaded.

1.

2.

3.

4.

5.

6.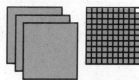

7.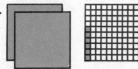

8.

9.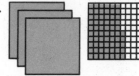

10.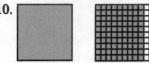

Give each decimal.

11. 26 hundredths

12. 47 hundredths

13. 5 and 61 hundredths

14. 7 and 19 hundredths

15. 2 and 33 hundredths

16. 4 and 1 hundredth

17. 9 hundredths

18. 60 hundredths

19. 3 and 36 hundredths

20. 8 and 12 hundredths

Give the word name for each decimal.

Here's how   9.82   *nine and eighty-two hundredths*

21. 5.62   22. 0.04   23. 9.19   24. 1.06   25. 7.25   26. 0.27

Place Value

A. Janet Guthrie first qualified for
the Indianapolis 500 auto race in 1977.
Her qualifying speed was 301.44 kilometers per hour.

hundreds	tens	ones	tenths	hundredths
3	0	1	4	4

B. Tell what each 4 means.

184.57   4 ones
263.94   4 hundredths
657.41   4 tenths
488.23   4 hundreds
345.06   4 tens

Tell what each 8 means.

1. 408.62 2. 829.74 3. 730.82 4. 265.78 5. 987.6 6. 64.28

7. 453.85 8. 358.2 9. 126.08 10. 732.82 11. 80.50 12. 803.06

Each of these drivers has been a winner of the Indianapolis 500.
Give each driver's winning speed as a decimal.

Here's how Hill

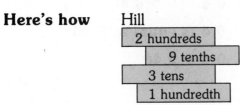

2 hundreds
9 tenths
3 tens
1 hundredth

230.91 kilometers per hour

13. Foyt
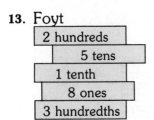

2 hundreds
5 tens
1 tenth
8 ones
3 hundredths

14. Unser
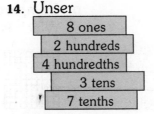

8 ones
2 hundreds
4 hundredths
3 tens
7 tenths

15. Donohue
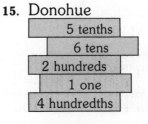

5 tenths
6 tens
2 hundreds
1 one
4 hundredths

16. Ward
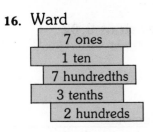

7 ones
1 ten
7 hundredths
3 tenths
2 hundreds

17. Rutherford
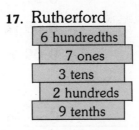

6 hundredths
7 ones
3 tens
2 hundreds
9 tenths

18. Andretti
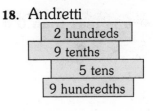

2 hundreds
9 tenths
5 tens
9 hundredths

Comparing Decimals

A. Compare the decimals.

0.1   **0.10**

0.1 is equal to 0.10

0.1 = 0.10

B. Compare the decimals.

0.4   **0.40**

0.4 is equal to 0.40

0.4 = 0.40

C. Compare the decimals.
Which is less?

0.6   **0.8**

0.6 is less than 0.8

0.6 < 0.8

D. Compare the decimals.
Which is greater?

0.09   **0.02**

0.09 is greater than 0.02

0.09 > 0.02

E. Compare the decimals.
Use <, >, or =.

54.62 ● 54.82

54.62 ● 54.82   **The tens are the same.**

54.62 ● 54.82   **The ones are the same.**

54.62 ● 54.82   **6 tenths is less than 8 tenths.**

54.62 is less than 54.82

54.62 < 54.82

F. Compare the decimals.
Use <, >, or =

4.39 ● 4.32

4.39 ● 4.32   **The ones are the same.**

4.39 ● 4.32   **The tenths are the same.**

4.39 ● 4.32   **9 hundredths is greater than 2 hundredths.**

4.39 is greater than 4.32

4.39 > 4.32

Compare the decimals. Which is less?

1.   2.   3.

4.   5.   6.

Compare the decimals. Which is greater?

7.   8. 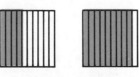   9.

10.   11.   12.

Compare the decimals.
Use <, >, or =.

13. 0.7 ● 0.8   14. 5.8 ● 5.3   15. 0.8 ● 0.80
16. 7.3 ● 7.5   17. 87.62 ● 87.62   18. 9.86 ● 9.90
19. 35.11 ● 35.01   20. 0.34 ● 0.47   21. 0.60 ● 0.6
22. 0.57 ● 0.59   23. 72.91 ● 72.82   24. 19.43 ● 19.23
25. 2.38 ● 2.08   26. 0.08 ● 0.18   27. 0.67 ● 0.63
28. 0.04 ● 0.05   29. 9.3 ● 9.30   30. 865.48 ● 865.49

**More practice
Set 12, page 373**

Money as Hundredths

A. 1 hundredth of a dollar $0.01   **1¢**

B. 5 hundredths of a dollar $0.05   **5¢**

C. 10 hundredths of a dollar $0.10   **10¢**

D. 25 hundredths of a dollar $0.25   **25¢**

E. 50 hundredths of a dollar $0.50   **50¢**

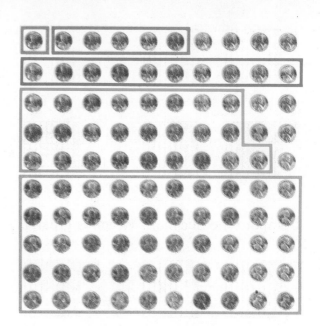

Give each amount with a dollar sign and a decimal point.

1.

2.

3.

4.

5.

6.

7.

8.

9.

10. 89¢   11. 145¢   12. 33¢   13. 150¢   14. 9¢   15. 5¢

Give each amount with a cent sign.

16.

17.

18.

19. $0.03	20. $0.51	21. $0.29
22. $0.60	23. $0.04	24. $0.62
25. $1.25	26. $0.08	27. $1.09

Give each amount with a dollar
sign and a decimal point.

Here's how

5 dollars and 19 cents   *$5.19*

28. 6 dollars and 20 cents

29. 37 dollars and 75 cents

30. 12 dollars and 95 cents

31. 14 dollars and 6 cents

32. 125 dollars and 8 cents

33. 399 dollars

34. 100 dollars and 1 cent

Keeping Skillful

Add.

| 1. 48 +27 | 2. 34 +96 | 3. 283 + 75 |

| 4. 159 +512 | 5. 678 +268 | 6. 4327 + 946 |

| 7. 1752 +6431 | 8. 3461 +2674 | 9. 9782 +2674 |

Subtract.

| 10. 93 −16 | 11. 45 −27 | 12. 526 − 98 |

| 13. 348 −167 | 14. 832 −256 | 15. 2803 − 572 |

| 16. 8121 −5608 | 17. 3245 −1773 | 18. 4600 −3415 |

Add or subtract.

19. 215 + 347	20. 97 − 58
21. 364 − 179	22. 873 + 67
23. 503 − 54	24. 15 + 9 + 385
25. 7563 + 854	26. 3527 − 2682
27. 3902 − 286	28. 43 + 29 + 94
29. 4783 + 2956	30. 700 − 428

Adding Tenths and Hundredths

A. Jamie and Tina ran in a 100-meter relay race.
Jamie's time for the first 50 meters was
8.7 seconds. Tina's time for the last
50 meters was 9.5 seconds. What was their
total time for 100 meters?

Find 8.7 + 9.5.

Line up the decimal points. Write the decimal point in the answer.	Add the tenths.	Add the ones.
	12 tenths = 1 one 2 tenths	
	1	1
8.7 +9.5	8.7 9.5 .2	8.7 9.5 18.2

Their total time was 18.2 seconds.

B. Find 0.81 + 4 + 1.29.

Write 4 as 4.00. Line up the decimal points. Write the decimal point in the answer.	Add the hundredths.	Add the tenths.	Add the ones.
	1	1 1	1
0.81 4.00 +1.29	0.81 4.00 +1.29 . 0	0.81 4.00 +1.29 .10	0.81 4.00 +1.29 6.10

Add.

1. 7.6
+1.2

2. 3.7
+4.8

3. 2.6
+5.5

4. 6.4
+0.9

5. 16.4
+ 8.6

6. 35.1
+16.3

7. 2.63
+9.16

8. 0.26
+1.74

9. 5.52
+3.68

10. 59.45
+ 0.61

11. 64.02
+42.79

12. 23.45
+67.46

13. 56.5 + 23.7

14. 73.2 +, 51.4

15. 7.81 + 3.23 + 24.72

16. 22.5 + 55.9

17. 72.4 + 21.6

18. 15.42 + 28 + 35.85

19. 62.7 + 86.3

20. 72.83 + 9.24

21. 0.57 + 3.16 + 0.09

22. 50 + 40.68

23. 34.5 + 8

24. 0.9 + 6.8 + 2.3

25. 19 + 46.7

26. 0.34 + 8.56

27. 2.9 + 3 + 14.5

28. 9 + 5.06

29. 12 + 6.7

30. 8 + 0.47 + 3.25

100-Meter Relay Race

Team	1	2	3
First 50 meters	7.52	7.47	7.36
Last 50 meters	8.53	7.42	7.75

Time shown in seconds.

Find each team's total time.

31. Team 1

32. Team 2

33. Team 3

Which team came in

★**34.** first?

★**35.** second?

★**36.** third?

More practice
Set 13, page 374

Using Addition of Decimals

Add. Use the code to help you find
the answer to the riddle.

Why is a barn so noisy?

Code					
6.38	B	52.51	S	73.24	V
16.2	C	59.34	O	90.95	N
23.86	E	66.53	W	91.02	H
47.4	A	70.16	U	98.72	R

Word 1

1. 3.76 + 2.62
2. 14.81 + 9.05
3. 8.4 + 7.8
4. 12.9 + 34.5
5. 47.16 + 23
6. 18.26 + 34.25
7. 16.24 + 7.62

Word 2

8. 3.4 + 12.8
9. 22.73 + 36.61
10. 19.62 + 46.91
11. 37.47 + 15.04

Word 3

12. 67.41 + 15 + 8.61
13. 5.02 + 26.37 + 16.01
14. 56.35 + 12.81 + 4.08
15. 7.30 + 5.62 + 10.94

Word 4

16. 45.31 + 21.71 + 24
17. 31.62 + 14.15 + 13.57
18. 26.87 + 71.81 + 0.04
19. 53.42 + 16.53 + 21
20. 18.43 + 21.07 + 13.01

Add across. Add down.

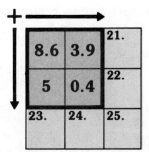

8.6	3.9	21.
5	0.4	22.
23.	24.	25.

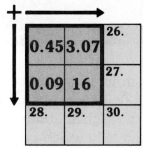

0.45	3.07	26.
0.09	16	27.
28.	29.	30.

Add.

31. 5.36
   $+\ 2.78$

32. 0.19
   $+\ 3.04$

33. 8.9
   $+\ 2.5$

34. 14.8
   $+\ 25.3$

35. 18.72
   $+\ 30.98$

36. 16.5
   $+\ \ 8.7$

37. 2.45
   0.16
   $+\ 0.89$

38. 16.7
   8.7
   $+\ \ 4.8$

39. 7.23
   4.58
   $+\ 8.15$

40. 12.68
   5.04
   $+\ \ 1.26$

41. 1.3
   4.6
   $+\ 9.5$

42. 14.9
   3.4
   $+\ \ 0.7$

Subtracting Tenths and Hundredths

A. The Apollo 11 astronauts brought back moon rocks that weigh about 22.3 kilograms on earth. On the moon, these rocks weighed about 3.7 kilograms. How much less did they weigh on the moon?

Find 22.3 − 3.7.

Line up the decimal points. Write the decimal point in the answer.

$$\begin{array}{r} 22.3 \\ -\ 3.7 \\ \hline \end{array}$$

You need more tenths. Rename to show 10 more tenths.

2 ones 3 tenths = 1 one 13 tenths

Subtract the tenths.

$$\begin{array}{r} {\overset{1}{2}}{\overset{13}{2}}.\overset{}{\cancel{3}} \\ -\ 3.7 \\ \hline .6 \end{array}$$

You need more ones. Rename to show 10 more ones.

2 tens 1 one = 1 ten 11 ones

Subtract the ones. Subtract the tens.

$$\begin{array}{r} {\overset{11}{\cancel{2}}}{\overset{1\ \cancel{1}\ 13}{2}}.\cancel{3} \\ -\ 3.7 \\ \hline 18.6 \end{array}$$

The rocks weighed about 18.6 kilograms less on the moon.

B. Find 16.73 − 4.

Write 4 as 4.00

$$\begin{array}{r} 16.73 \\ -\ 4.00 \\ \hline 12.73 \end{array}$$

Line up the decimal points. Write the decimal point in the answer. Subtract.

C. Find 5 − 1.72.

Write 5 as 5.00.

$$\begin{array}{r} \overset{9}{4\ \overset{}{\cancel{5}}.\overset{10}{\cancel{0}}\overset{10}{\cancel{0}}} \\ -\ 1.72 \\ \hline 3.28 \end{array}$$

Line up the decimal points. Write the decimal point in the answer. Subtract.

Subtract.

1. $\begin{array}{r}18.9\\-\ 7.6\end{array}$	**2.** $\begin{array}{r}37.5\\-16.2\end{array}$	**3.** $\begin{array}{r}6.4\\-2.7\end{array}$	**4.** $\begin{array}{r}9.8\\-6.2\end{array}$	**5.** $\begin{array}{r}7.5\\-1.8\end{array}$	**6.** $\begin{array}{r}23.2\\-\ 2.8\end{array}$

7. $\begin{array}{r}89.3\\-46.4\end{array}$	**8.** $\begin{array}{r}56.5\\-13.7\end{array}$	**9.** $\begin{array}{r}84.7\\-71.1\end{array}$	**10.** $\begin{array}{r}4.63\\-1.87\end{array}$	**11.** $\begin{array}{r}29.32\\-16.49\end{array}$	**12.** $\begin{array}{r}55.84\\-37.39\end{array}$

13. 38.59 − 16.77   **14.** 78.24 − 39.09   **15.** 85.36 − 79.18   **16.** 6 − 2.09

17. 47.62 − 18   **18.** 86.15 − 57.34   **19.** 63.54 − 27.36   **20.** 3 − 0.75

21. 8.3 − 5.8   **22.** 7.52 − 4.73   **23.** 99.91 − 88.88   **24.** 31.7 − 15

25. 16.1 − 2.2   **26.** 35 − 14.55   **27.** 12.2 − 0.5   **28.** 9.05 − 5.62

29. 53.91 − 39   **30.** 15.01 − 3.96   **★31.** 600 − 401.5   **★32.** 40 − 19.99

How much more does each person weigh on earth than on the moon?

33. Moon weight: 13.5 kilograms
Earth weight: 81 kilograms

34. Moon weight: 5.9 kilograms
Earth weight: 35.4 kilograms

35. Moon weight: 12.34 kilograms
Earth weight: 74.04 kilograms

36. Moon weight: 17.8 kilograms
Earth weight: 106.8 kilograms

More practice
Set 14, page 374

Using Subtraction of Decimals

Average Annual Precipitation

City	Precipitation (centimeters)
Albany, New York	84.73
Boston, Massachusetts	108.00
Burlington, Vermont	82.65
Cheyenne, Wyoming	38.25
Honolulu, Hawaii	58.17
Juneau, Alaska	138.86
Nashville, Tennessee	116.84
Omaha, Nebraska	76.66
Phoenix, Arizona	17.91
Salt Lake City, Utah	38.53

Which city gets more precipitation?

1. Boston or Nashville   2. Salt Lake City or Cheyenne
3. Albany or Burlington   4. Cheyenne or Honolulu

Find the difference in annual precipitation between

5. Honolulu and Salt Lake City.   6. Albany and Phoenix.
7. Juneau and Salt Lake City.   8. Omaha and Phoenix.
9. Burlington and Juneau.   10. Honolulu and Albany.
11. Cheyenne and Omaha.   12. Burlington and Nashville.
13. Phoenix and Juneau.   14. Honolulu and Juneau.
15. Boston and Nashville.   16. Burlington and Honolulu.
17. Omaha and Albany.   18. Phoenix and Salt Lake City.
19. Albany and Cheyenne.   20. Juneau and Cheyenne.

Subtract.

21. 64.8	22. 55.3	23. 136.1	24. 529.4	25. 64.06	26. 0.60
− 13.4	− 47.5	− 93.5	− 346.8	− 30.08	− 0.37

27. 157.8	28. 632.5	29. 0.53	30. 80.71	31. 8.46	32. 17.9
− 31.9	− 17.8	− 0.28	− 29.53	− 3.97	− 9.8

33. 429.3	34. 876.2	35. 26.3	36. 32.5	37. 500.6	38. 45.07
− 247.6	− 187.1	− 4.8	− 17.8	− 128.3	− 18.35

39. 0.83 − 0.29   40. 48 − 25.04   41. 146 − 35.63   42. 67.4 − 25.7
43. 493.2 − 287.5   44. 18 − 12.7   45. 25 − 3.24   46. 570.8 − 126.9
47. 58.3 − 19   48. 295.6 − 78   49. 99 − 80.91   50. 75 − 50.25

Using Addition and Subtraction of Decimals

Model 43276

Bells and horns may be ordered at extra cost.

Model 43276	$17.90				
Model 65829	$16.63		Bell $0.59		Horn $0.86
Model 34751	$14.75				

This catalog ad shows a three-wheel cycle from the year 1890.

Find each answer.

1. How much more does model 43276 cost than model 65829?

2. How much more does model 65829 cost than model 34751?

Find the cost of each cycle.

3. Model 43276 with a bell

4. Model 65829 with a horn

5. Model 34751 with a bell and a horn

6. Model 43276 with a bell and a horn

Add or subtract.

7. 34.7
 +27.9

8. 4.5
 − 1.3

9. 142.8
 + 29.5

10. 23.7
 −18.8

11. 298.3
 +429.6

12. 45.76
 −39.85

13. 18.6
 +37.7

14. 564.3
 −258.5

15. 465.4
 −439.8

16. 56.64
 −28.32

17. 19.8
 +26.8

18. 34.06
 + 9.47

19. 142.7
 − 76.4

20. 3.89
 +8.36

21. 28.85
 −19.93

22. 238.6
 16.4
 + 3.8

23. 5.96
 4.72
 +2.05

24. 37.45
 4.61
 +26.13

25. 19 − 7.65

26. 11.65 + 0.68

27. 91.53 + 6.87

28. 532.4 − 16.5

29. 0.49 + 3.83

30. 6.34 − 3.57

31. 57 − 2.86

32. 34.6 + 17

33. 1.02 + 0.06

34. 16.35 − 14.81

35. 42.3 + 78.8

36. 64.3 − 5

37. 37.5 − 18.2

38. 3.25 + 0.65

39. 56.64 + 3.25 + 18

40. 814.6 + 38 + 120.5

Copy these dots on your paper.

Draw four straight lines that go through all the dots. Do not lift your pencil or retrace a line.

Now try it with six lines going through sixteen dots.

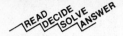

Problem Solving: Choosing the Operation

These are the ten most popular foods in the United States. The amounts show the average number of kilograms eaten by each person per year.

Milk and cream
132.36 kilograms

Potatoes
54.68 kilograms

Sugar
39.86 kilograms

Fresh citrus fruit
13 kilograms

Canned vegetables
24.18 kilograms

Eggs
16.05 kilograms

Chicken
18.32 kilograms

Beef
40.41 kilograms

Fresh noncitrus fruit
23.82 kilograms

Pork
18.63 kilograms

READ   **A.** How much beef and chicken are eaten?

DECIDE   Add the weight of the beef and the weight of the chicken. Use this equation.

$$40.41 + 18.32 = n$$

SOLVE

$$\begin{array}{r} \mathbf{40.41} \\ \mathbf{+\,18.32} \\ \hline \mathbf{58.73} \end{array}$$

ANSWER $n = 58.73$

58.73 kilograms

READ   **B.** The amount of potatoes a person eats is how much more than the amount of sugar?

DECIDE   Subtract the weight of the sugar from the weight of the potatoes. Use this equation.

$$54.68 - 39.86 = n$$

SOLVE

$$\begin{array}{r} {\scriptstyle 13} \\ {\scriptstyle 4\ \ 3\ 16} \\ \cancel{5}\cancel{4}.\cancel{6}8 \\ -\,39.86 \\ \hline 14.82 \end{array}$$

ANSWER $n = 14.82$

14.82 kilograms

Write an equation for each problem. Give the answer.

1. Find the total amount of citrus and noncitrus fruit eaten by each person.

2. The amount of potatoes eaten by each person is how much more than the amount of canned vegetables?

3. Find the total amount of sugar and citrus fruit each person eats.

4. A person eats how much more pork than chicken?

5. The weight of chicken eaten by each person is how much more than the weight of eggs eaten?

6. What is the total weight of beef and potatoes each person eats?

7. Find the total weight of beef, pork, and chicken eaten by each person.

8. How many kilograms of eggs and canned vegetables are eaten in all?

9. A person eats how much more noncitrus fruit than citrus fruit?

*10. How much less beef, pork, and chicken is eaten than the total amount of milk and cream?

*11. Find the total amount of the top ten foods eaten by each person.

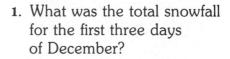

Meteorologist

Anita Perez is a meteorologist. She forecasts the
weather and keeps records of weather information.

Date	Dec. 1	Dec. 2	Dec. 3
Wind speed (kilometers per hour)	12.5	21.9	19.0
Snowfall (centimeters)	0.13	2.56	0.96

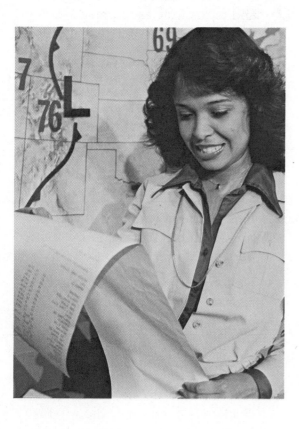

1. What was the total snowfall for the first three days of December?

2. How much greater was the snowfall on December 2 than on December 3?

How much faster did the wind blow

3. on December 2 than on December 1?

4. on December 3 than on December 1?

5. on December 2 than on December 3?

Anita's records show that it rained 10.82 centimeters in March and 15.71 centimeters in April.

6. How much more rain fell in April than in March?

7. What was the total rainfall for March and April?

It rained 11.73 centimeters in May, 9.75 centimeters in June, and 10.00 centimeters in July.

8. What was the total rainfall for May and June?

9. What was the total rainfall for May, June, and July?

Chapter 5 Test
Decimals, pages 84–106

How much is shaded?
Give the decimal.

1.

2.

Give each decimal.

3. seven and eight tenths

4. 9 and 84 hundredths

Tell what each 5 means.

5. 4.56   **6.** 75.43

7. 83.45   **8.** 563.41

Compare the decimals.
Use <, >, or =.

9. 0.4 ● 0.3

10. 0.8 ● 0.80

11. 2.46 ● 2.49

12. 3.56 ● 3.26

Add.

13. $\begin{array}{r} 0.86 \\ +\,0.35 \\ \hline \end{array}$ **14.** $\begin{array}{r} 5.52 \\ +\,8.64 \\ \hline \end{array}$

15. 5.6 + 3

16. 7.49 + 8.62

17. 21.8 + 3.4

18. 91.4 + 3.2 + 18

Subtract.

19. $\begin{array}{r} 0.47 \\ -\,0.29 \\ \hline \end{array}$ **20.** $\begin{array}{r} 13.65 \\ -\;\;8.92 \\ \hline \end{array}$

21. 0.28 − 0.17

22. 18.47 − 9

23. 628.3 − 286.4

24. 48 − 3.62

Find the answer.

25. In a year each person eats about 18.32 kilograms of chicken and about 16.05 kilograms of eggs. What is the total weight of these foods?

Points on a Grid

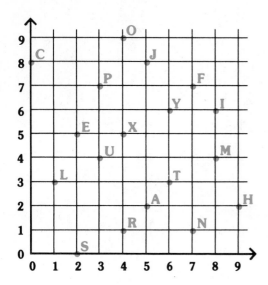

Which letter names each point?

1. (5, 2) **2.** (7, 7) **3.** (3, 7)

4. (2, 0) **5.** (7, 1) **6.** (9, 2)

7. (8, 4) **8.** (2, 5) **9.** (6, 6)

10. (0, 8) **11.** (3, 4) **12.** (1, 3)

Give the number pair for each point.

13. M **14.** U **15.** T **16.** J

17. E **18.** S **19.** L **20.** A

21. F **22.** N **23.** R **24.** Y

The **number pair** (4, 5) names the location of point X on the **grid.**

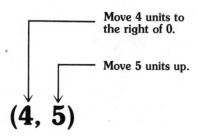

To find the answer to these riddles, give the letter that is located at each point.

What do you call a seven-foot-tall prizefighter with a big club?

25. (2, 0) **26.** (8, 6) **27.** (4, 1)

How can you spell *dried grass* with just three letters?

28. (9, 2) **29.** (5, 2) **30.** (6, 6)

• **Discuss** Are (2, 5) and (5, 2) locations of the same point?

How did the patient get to the hospital so fast?

31. (7, 7) **32.** (1, 3) **33.** (3, 4)

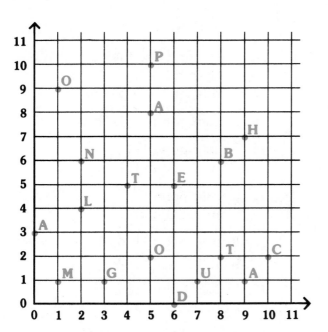

Student A goes to school A. Student B goes to school B. Student C goes to school C. Student D goes to school D.

How does each student walk to school without crossing another's path, and without going outside the rectangle?

Trace the drawing. Find each student's path to school.

To find the answer to these riddles, give the letter that is located at each point.

Mr. Ham, a butcher, is six feet tall. He wears a forty-six-inch belt and shoes that are size eleven. What does he weigh?

34. (1, 1)   **35.** (6, 5)   **36.** (9, 1)   **37.** (4, 5)

What kind of dog has no tail?

38. (9, 7)   **39.** (5, 2)   **40.** (4, 5)
41. (6, 0)   **42.** (1, 9)   **43.** (3, 1)

What fish can tune a piano?

44. (5, 8)

45. (8, 2)   **46.** (7, 1)   **47.** (2, 6)   **48.** (0, 3)

Locating Points on a Grid

This is how Janice located (5, 3) on a grid. She began at (0, 0).

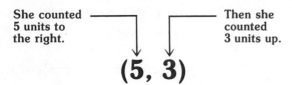

She counted 5 units to the right. → (5, 3) ← Then she counted 3 units up.

She made a dot and used the letter Z to name the point.

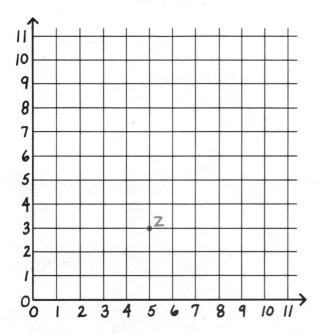

Number a grid like the one above. Then locate each point. Use the letter to name the point.

1. A (3, 7)   2. B (7, 0)

3. C (2, 1)   4. D (6, 5)

5. E (0, 6)   6. F (4, 4)

7. G (1, 7)   8. H (5, 2)

Number a grid like the one on this page. Then mark and label each point with the letter given.

9. Locate point A (1, 7).

10. Locate point B (2, 4).
    Connect A and B.

11. Locate point C (3, 5).
    Connect B and C.

12. Locate point D (4, 4).
    Connect C and D.

13. Locate point E (5, 7).
    Connect D and E.

14. What letter have you drawn?

Number a grid. Then mark and label each point with the letter given.

15. Locate point A (2, 6).

16. Locate point B (2, 2).
    Connect A and B.

17. Locate point C (5, 6).

18. Locate point D (5, 2).
    Connect C and D.

19. Locate point E (2, 4).

20. Locate point F (5, 4).
    Connect E and F.

21. What letter have you drawn?

*22. Give directions for drawing the letter A.

110

When the March wind blows, what time is it?

To find the answer, number a grid. For each exercise, locate and connect the points. Use a straightedge.

23. (0, 7) and (0, 4)
24. (3, 0) and (3, 3)
25. (7, 2) and (8, 2)
26. (0, 3) and (2, 3)
27. (5, 4) and (5, 7)
28. (7, 6) and (8, 6)
29. (1, 0) and (1, 3)
30. (7, 4) and (7, 7)
31. (5, 2) and (6, 3)
32. (7, 0) and (9, 0)
33. (7, 7) and (9, 7)
34. (0, 6) and (2, 7)
35. (6, 0) and (6, 3)
36. (3, 4) and (3, 7)
37. (4, 0) and (4, 3)
38. (7, 3) and (9, 3)
39. (7, 0) and (7, 3)
40. (7, 4) and (9, 4)
41. (4, 3) and (5, 2)
42. (0, 6) and (2, 4)
43. (4, 7) and (6, 7)

Keeping Skillful

Add.

1. 823 + 128
2. 674 + 19
3. 5286 + 417
4. $36.48 + $20.88
5. $17.39 + $20.76
6. $21.12 + $90.09

Subtract.

7. 783 − 16
8. 513 − 44
9. 342 − 59
10. $5.65 − $3.98
11. $9.49 − $8.92
12. $35.18 − $27.09

Add or subtract.

13. 1111 − 39
14. 107 + 97
15. 208 − 19
16. 97 + 97
17. $1.05 − $0.98
18. $9.07 + $9.07
19. $36.95 − $34.98
20. $18.81 + $80.19

111

Line Graphs

This line graph shows how much Casey earns delivering newspapers.

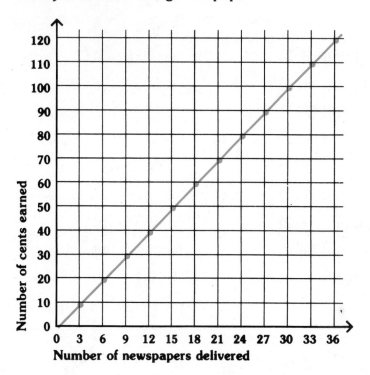

Number of newspapers delivered

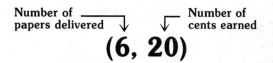

Number of papers delivered ↓ ↓ Number of cents earned

(6, 20)

The point (6, 20) shows that Casey delivered 6 newspapers to earn 20 cents.

Use the graph to answer each question.

How much money will Casey earn if she delivers

1. 24 newspapers?

2. 15 newspapers?

3. 36 newspapers?

4. 18 newspapers?

5. 9 newspapers?

6. 3 newspapers?

7. 21 newspapers?

8. 30 newspapers?

9. 12 newspapers?

How many newspapers must Casey deliver to earn

10. 60 cents?

11. 10 cents?

12. 50 cents?

13. 40 cents?

14. 80 cents?

15. 30 cents?

16. 70 cents?

17. 20 cents?

18. 90 cents?

Carol sells boxes of greeting cards. The line graph
shows how much she earns.

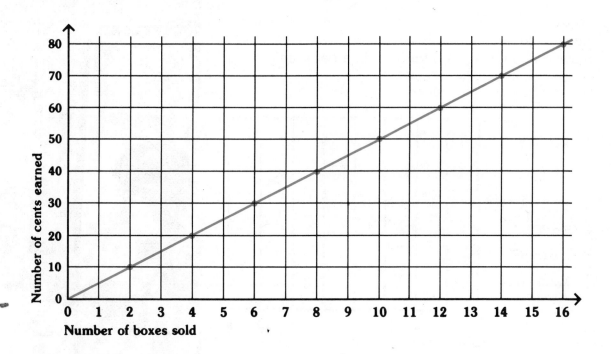

How many boxes of cards must Carol sell to earn

19. 40 cents? **20.** 60 cents? **21.** 50 cents? **22.** 10 cents?

23. 70 cents? **24.** 30 cents? **25.** 20 cents? **26.** 80 cents?

How much will she earn if she sells

27. 4 boxes? **28.** 6 boxes? **29.** 14 boxes? **30.** 8 boxes?

31. 10 boxes? **32.** 2 boxes? **33.** 16 boxes? **34.** 12 boxes?

If Carol sells 5 boxes of greeting cards, she will
earn 25 cents. This amount is half-way between
20 cents and 30 cents. How much will she earn
if she sells

*35. 9 boxes? ***36.** 13 boxes? ***37.** 3 boxes? ***38.** 7 boxes?

Bar Graphs

The students in Ms. Whitewing's class live in North America. They selected the continents they would like to visit. Each student was allowed one vote. Then they made a **bar graph** to show their choices.

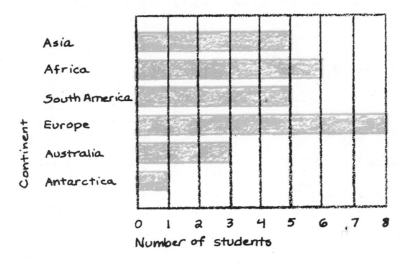

The number of students is shown at the bottom of the graph. The names of the continents are shown at the left of the graph. The graph shows that 5 students want to visit Asia.

How many students want to visit

1. South America? 2. Europe? 3. Africa?

How many students chose either

4. Europe or Australia? 5. Antarctica or Africa?

How many more students chose

6. Africa than Asia? 7. Europe than Antarctica?

114

This graph shows the number of absences in Ms. Whitewing's class last week. The height of the bar above each day shows the number of absences for the day.

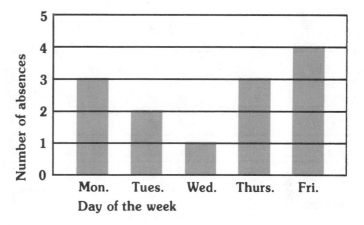

On which day were there

8. the fewest absences?

9. the most absences?

On which days of the week were there

10. more than 2 absences?

11. fewer than 3 absences?

How many absences were there

12. on Thursday?

13. on Tuesday?

14. on Monday and Friday?

15. during the entire week?

Pictographs

The fourth-grade students at Hillrise School
made a pictograph to show how many students
are learning to play each instrument.

Each ♩ means 1 student.

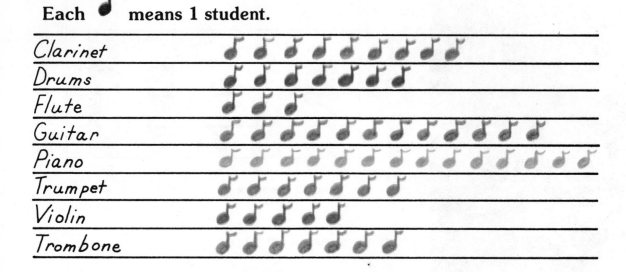

Which instrument is being studied by the

1. fewest students?   2. most students?

How many instruments are being studied by

3. more than 8 students?   4. fewer than 6 students?

Tell how many students are learning to play the

5. piano.   6. clarinet.   7. trombone.   8. drums.   9. trumpet.

How many more students are studying

10. the guitar than the flute?   11. the trombone than the violin?

12. the clarinet than the trumpet?   13. the guitar than the drums?

The students voted for the dogs
they liked best. Then they made
a pictograph to show the results.

Each **means 2 votes.**

Poodle	
German shepherd	
Doberman pinscher	
Irish setter	
Cocker spaniel	
Beagle	
Labrador retriever	
Dachshund	

Which dog got the

14. most votes?　　**15.** fewest votes?

Which dogs got

16. fewer than 14 votes?　　**17.** more than 10 votes?

Tell how many students voted for each dog.

18. Poodle　　**19.** Irish setter　　**20.** Cocker spaniel　　**21.** Labrador retriever

22. Beagle　　**23.** Dachshund　　**24.** German shepherd　　**25.** Doberman pinscher

Tell how many more students voted for the poodle
than for the

26. Doberman pinscher.　　**27.** Dachshund.　　**28.** Irish setter.

Using Graphs

Bill sells small note pads. The amount he earns is shown by this line graph.

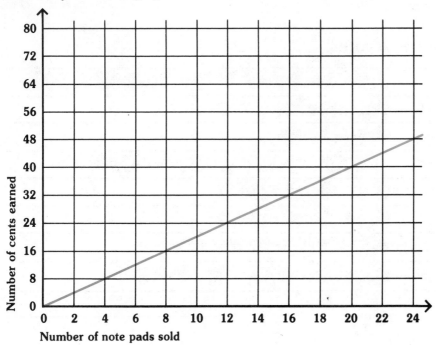

How much will Bill earn if he sells

1. 4 note pads?　　2. 24 note pads?　　3. 16 note pads?

4. 8 note pads?　　5. 20 note pads?　　6. 12 note pads?

How many note pads must Bill sell to earn

7. 48 cents?　　8. 32 cents?　　9. 16 cents?

10. 24 cents?　　★11. 28 cents?　　★12. 44 cents?

This bar graph shows the number of talent-show tickets Mary sold each day last week.

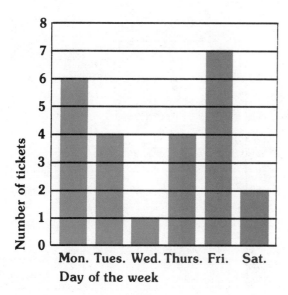

Day of the week

On which day did Mary sell

13. the most tickets?

14. the fewest tickets?

On which days did Mary sell

15. more than 5 tickets?

16. fewer than 4 tickets?

17. the same number of tickets?

How many tickets did Mary sell

18. Monday?

19. Thursday?

20. Wednesday and Saturday?

21. all week?

This pictograph shows how many kilograms of newspapers Anthony collected for each of the last 6 months.

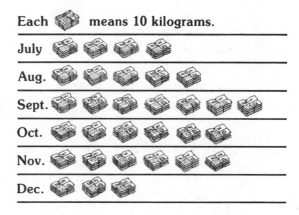

During what month were the

22. most kilograms collected?

23. fewest kilograms collected?

How many kilograms of newspapers were collected during

24. August?

25. October?

26. December?

27. September?

28. Give the total number of kilograms of newspapers collected in September, October, and November.

*29. How many kilograms of newspapers were collected in all?

Making Line and Bar Graphs

Jackie sat quietly and counted the number of breaths she took in one minute. She breathed 15 times in 1 minute. Jackie made this table showing the number of breaths she would take in different amounts of time.

Jackie used the table to make this graph.

Number of minutes	Number of breaths	
1	15	
2	30	← Add 15.
3	45	← Add 15.
4	60	← Add 15.
5	75	← Add 15.
6	90	← Add 15.

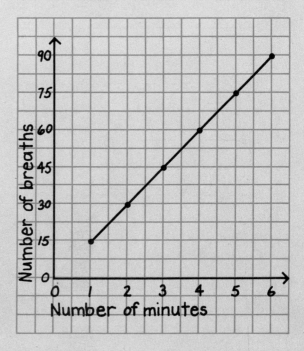

Tell how many times Jackie breathed in

1. 5 minutes.   2. 4 minutes.   3. 3 minutes.   4. 2 minutes.

5. Sit quietly and measure the number of times you breathe in one minute. Make a table to show your results. Then make a line graph.

6. Make a table to show the number of birthdays in your class for each month. Use tally marks.

Month	Number of birthdays	Month	Number of birthdays
Jan.		July	
Feb.		Aug.	
Mar.		Sept.	
Apr.		Oct.	
May		Nov.	
June		Dec.	

7. Make a bar graph. Use these labels and the information in your table.

Chapter 6 Test
Graphing, Pages 108–121

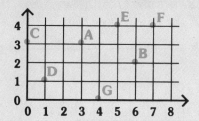

Which letter names each point?

1. (6, 2)   **2.** (1, 1)   **3.** (7, 4)

Give the number pair for each point.

4. E   **5.** A   **6.** G   **7.** C

Rosa made this line graph to show the cost of pencils.

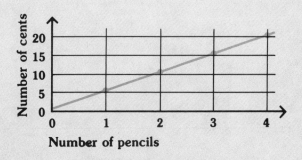

Tell how many pencils Rosa can buy for

8. 20 cents.   **9.** 5 cents.

How much must she pay for

10. 3 pencils?   **11.** 2 pencils?

Several students made this graph to show their favorite colors.

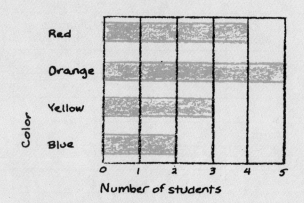

Tell how many students chose

12. blue.   **13.** red.   **14.** yellow.

Tell which color was chosen

15. most often.   **16.** least often.

This pictograph shows how much money 4 students earned last week. Each ● means 10 cents.

Bill	● ● ● ● ●
Jean	● ● ● ●
Frank	● ● ●
Susan	● ● ● ● ● ●

How much money was earned by

17. Bill?   **18.** Frank?   **19.** Jean?

20. Who earned the most money?

Problems Around Us

1. An infant's heart beats about 140 times a minute. An adult's heart beats about 80 times a minute. An infant's heart beats about how many more times a minute than an adult's heart?

2. Samuel Morse invented a telegraph system in 1837. He sent his first Morse Code message 7 years later. In what year was this message sent?

3. A bristlecone pine tree is about 4900 years old. A giant redwood tree is about 3800 years old. The bristlecone pine is about how many years older than the redwood?

4. Clara Barton founded the American Red Cross and became its president in 1881. She remained its president until 1904. How many years was she president?

5. The first hour, a train traveled 80.45 kilometers. It traveled 82.86 kilometers the second hour, and 81.77 kilometers the third hour. How far did the train travel in all?

6. Martin Luther King, Jr., was born in 1929. 35 years later, he was awarded the Nobel Peace Prize. In what year did he receive this prize?

7. An ostrich, the world's tallest bird, may grow to be 2.74 meters tall. A giraffe, the tallest land animal, may grow to be 5.49 meters tall. A giraffe is about how much taller than an ostrich?

8. A spine-tailed swift flew 170.5 kilometers the first hour and 151.6 kilometers the second hour. How far did the swift fly in two hours?

9. A pony express rider earned $25.00 a week in 1860. If he spent $4.79 for food during the week, how much money would he have left?

10. An astronaut needs 0.95 kilograms of oxygen, 0.73 kilograms of food, and 2.22 kilograms of water for each day in space. How many kilograms of food and water does an astronaut need for one day?

Individualized Skills Maintenance

Diagnose

A *pages 30–38*

238 + 475

1562 + 3983

7136 + 253 + 9248

B *pages 50–58*

916 − 287

5394 − 1765

7003 − 5461

Practice

A

1. 365
   + 138

2. 627
   + 493

3. 5783
   + 1409

4. 3894
   + 2763

5. 4805
   + 9672

6. 2589
   + 1368

7. 842
   + 739

8. 457
   + 196

9. 4765
   + 3917

10. 5462
    + 3851

11. 7516
    + 3478

12. 7589
    + 2375

13. 65
    38
    + 79

14. 27
    84
    + 39

15. 723
    589
    + 634

16. 219
    376
    + 854

17. 7058
    4136
    + 9274

18. 5926
    3804
    + 1639

B

19. 418
    − 395

20. 325
    − 148

21. 3176
    − 1947

22. 7058
    − 2174

23. 5732
    − 2475

24. 6008
    − 5287

25. 871
    − 367

26. 900
    − 345

27. 4259
    − 1387

28. 5001
    − 3761

29. 7618
    − 3709

30. 6025
    − 3582

31. 407
    − 218

32. 324
    − 178

33. 5934
    − 1678

34. 9300
    − 2184

35. 8516
    − 2135

36. 7125
    − 3682

Unit 2 Review

Chapter 4, pages 68–82
Add or subtract. Watch the signs.

1. $3.89
  + 0.65

2. $0.68
  − 0.39

3. 58
  +97

Find n.

4. $16 + n = 23$ **5.** $n + 9 = 88$

Find each answer.

6. Eric collected 254 cans one week and 329 cans the next week. How many did he collect in all?

7. 327 students attended a concert on Monday. 932 attended on Tuesday. How many more students attended the concert on Tuesday?

Chapter 5, pages 84–106
Give each decimal.

8. twenty-one hundredths

9. six and one tenth

Tell what each 2 means.

10. 156.02   **11.** 38.29

Compare the decimals. Use < or >.

12. 3.79 ● 3.80   **13.** 5.6 ● 5.9

Add or subtract. Watch the signs.

14. 7.2
  − 3.9

15. 6.7
  +4.9

16. 3.56
  +0.81

17. $37.9 + 6.2 + 29$

18. $86 − 27.4$

Chapter 6, pages 108–121
Shannon made this graph to show the cost of erasers.

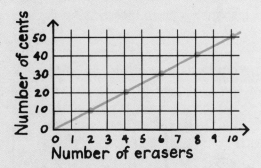

How many erasers could she buy for

19. 40 cents?   **20.** 10 cents?

Some students made this graph to show their favorite subjects.

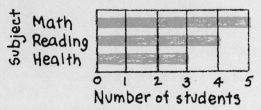

Tell how many students chose

21. reading.   **22.** math.   **23.** health.

Unit 2 Test
Chapters 4–6, pages 68–122

Lynne made this graph to show the cost of roller-skating lessons.

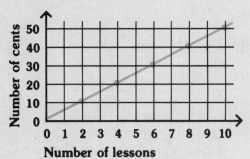

Number of lessons

How much must she pay for

1. 6 lessons?   **2.** 10 lessons?

Some students made this graph to show their favorite birds.

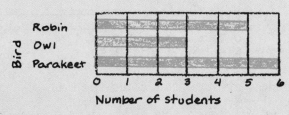

Tell how many students chose the

3. robin.   **4.** owl.

Give each decimal.

5. eighty-nine hundredths

6. eleven and seven tenths

Tell what each 9 means.

7. 235.49   **8.** 56.91

Compare the decimals. Use < or >.

9. 3.6 ● 3.9   **10.** 2.89 ● 2.56

11. 1.2 ● 1.1   **12.** 0.68 ● 0.63

Add.

13. 284
       + 77

14. $4.78
       + 5.17

15. 6.31
       +0.89

16. 21.4 + 5.9 + 1

17. 83 + 2.90 + 5.74

Subtract.

18. 817
       − 64

19. $0.73
       − 0.35

20. 3.58
       −2.90

21. 27.4 − 19.6

22. 89 − 26.9

23. Group A made 138 greeting cards for senior citizens. Group B made 157 cards. How many more cards did Group B make?

Find n.

24. $28 + n = 93$

25. $n + 11 = 64$

Unit 3

Meaning of Multiplication

You can use an addition sentence and a
multiplication sentence for each picture.

A. 5 groups of arrowheads

3 in each group

How many in all?

B. 3 groups of arrowheads

5 in each group

How many in all?

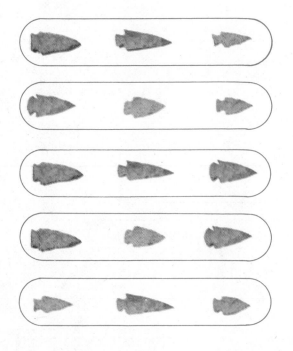

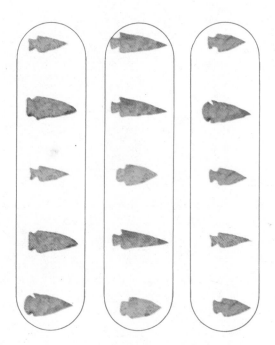

$3 + 3 + 3 + 3 + 3 = 15$

5 groups of 3 = 15

$5 \times 3 = 15$

Number of groups ↑   ↑ Number in each group

$5 + 5 + 5 = 15$

3 groups of 5 = 15

$3 \times 5 = 15$

Number of groups ↑   ↑ Number in each group

128

Copy and complete the addition sentence and
multiplication sentence for each picture.

Here's how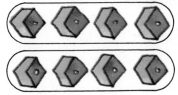

$2 + 2 + 2 = 6$

$3 \times 2 = 6$

1.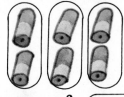

$4 + 4 = $ ▦

$2 \times 4 = $ ▦

2.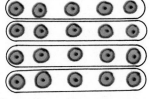

$5 + 5 + 5 + 5 = $ ▦

$4 \times 5 = $ ▦

3.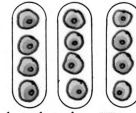

$4 + 4 + 4 = $ ▦

$3 \times 4 = $ ▦

4.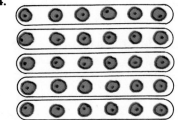

$6 + 6 + 6 + 6 + 6 = $ ▦

$5 \times 6 = $ ▦

5.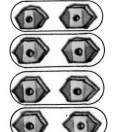

$5 + 5 + 5 + 5 + 5 = $ ▦

$5 \times 5 = $ ▦

6.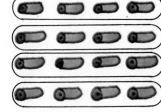

$4 + 4 + 4 + 4 = $ ▦

$4 \times 4 = $ ▦

7.

$4 + 4 + 4 + 4 + 4 + 4 = $ ▦

$6 \times 4 = $ ▦

8.

$2 + 2 + 2 + 2 = $ ▦

$4 \times 2 = $ ▦

9.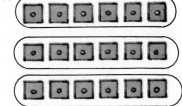

$6 + 6 + 6 = $ ▦

$3 \times 6 = $ ▦

129

2 and 3 in Multiplication

You can write a multiplication sentence for each
picture. 2 and 6 are *factors.* 12 is the *product.*

A. 6 groups of 2

B. 2 groups of 6

6 × 2 = 12

Factor ↑   ↑   ↑ *Product*

2 × 6 = 12

Factor ↑   ↑   ↑ *Product*

C. David drew a picture to find
3 × 3.

D. Carol used addition to find
3 × 3.

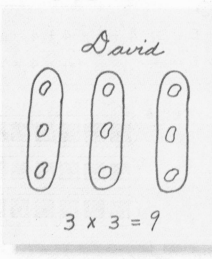

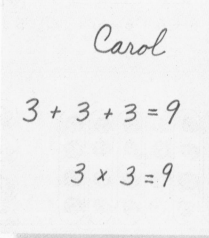

130

Copy and complete the multiplication sentence
for each picture.

1.

6 × 2 = ▦

2.
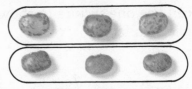
2 × 3 = ▦

3.
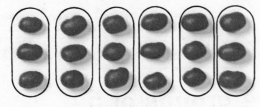
6 × 3 = ▦

4.
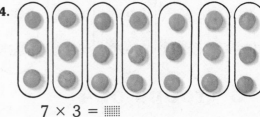
7 × 3 = ▦

5.

7 × 2 = ▦

6.

4 × 3 = ▦

Give each answer.

7. 2 × 2   **8.** 3 × 2   **9.** 4 × 2   **10.** 5 × 2   **11.** 6 × 2   **12.** 7 × 2

13. 8 × 2   **14.** 9 × 2   **15.** 2 × 3   **16.** 2 × 4   **17.** 2 × 5   **18.** 2 × 6

19. 2 × 7   **20.** 2 × 8   **21.** 2 × 9   **22.** 2 × 3   **23.** 3 × 3   **24.** 4 × 3

25. 5 × 3   **26.** 6 × 3   **27.** 7 × 3   **28.** 8 × 3   **29.** 9 × 3   **30.** 3 × 2

31. 3 × 4   **32.** 3 × 5   **33.** 3 × 6   **34.** 3 × 7   **35.** 3 × 8   **36.** 3 × 9

37. There are 4 drum players.
Each player has 3 drums. How
many drums are there in all?

38. There are 4 drum players. Each
player has 2 drumsticks. How
many drumsticks are there in all?

131

4 and 5 in Multiplication

A. You can use one picture to show one
multiplication fact.

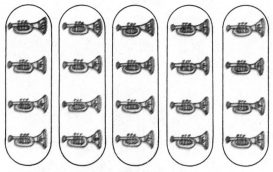

5 groups of 4
5 × 4 = 20

4 groups of 5
4 × 5 = 20

B. You can use a picture like this to show
two multiplication facts.

Think of 5 groups of 4.
5 × 4 = 20

Think of 4 groups of 5.
4 × 5 = 20

C. You can write these multiplication facts
in another way.

5	⟵ Factor ⟶	**4**
×4	⟵ Factor ⟶	**×5**
20	⟵ Product ⟶	**20**

Give two multiplication sentences for each picture.

Here's how

$2 \times 5 = 10$

$5 \times 2 = 10$

1.

2.

3.

Give each answer.

4. 2 $\times 4$	5. 3 $\times 4$	6. 4 $\times 4$	7. 5 $\times 4$	8. 6 $\times 4$	9. 7 $\times 4$	10. 8 $\times 4$	11. 9 $\times 4$

12. 4 $\times 2$	13. 4 $\times 3$	14. 4 $\times 4$	15. 4 $\times 5$	16. 4 $\times 6$	17. 4 $\times 7$	18. 4 $\times 8$	19. 4 $\times 9$

20. 2 $\times 5$	21. 3 $\times 5$	22. 4 $\times 5$	23. 5 $\times 5$	24. 6 $\times 5$	25. 7 $\times 5$	26. 8 $\times 5$	27. 9 $\times 5$

28. 5 $\times 2$	29. 5 $\times 3$	30. 5 $\times 4$	31. 5 $\times 5$	32. 5 $\times 6$	33. 5 $\times 7$	34. 5 $\times 8$	35. 5 $\times 9$

36. The marching band has 5 rows of trumpets. There are 3 trumpets in each row. How many trumpets are there in all?

37. The marching band has 4 rows of flag carriers. There are 6 flag carriers in each row. How many flag carriers are there in all?

**More practice
Set 15, page 374**

133

Using Multiplication Facts

Give each answer.

1. Ryan brought 4 boxes of bottles to the recycling center. 9 bottles were in each box. How many bottles did he bring?

2. The Youngbear family makes 3 trips to the center each week. How many trips do they make in 8 weeks?

3. Corinne brought 5 bags of cans to the center. 7 cans were in each bag. How many cans did she bring?

4. 6 different people work each day at the center. How many people work there in 5 days?

5. 9 people came to the center. Each brought 3 boxes of bottles. How many boxes did they bring in all?

6. Maria can fill 4 plastic bags in one minute. How many bags can she fill in 4 minutes?

7. There were 7 stacks of newspaper. 3 bundles of newspaper were in each stack. How many bundles of newspaper were there in all?

8. Lamar makes 5 trips to the center each month. How many trips does he make in 5 months?

9. A bundle of newspaper weighs 5 kilograms. How much do 4 bundles of newspaper weigh?

10. Each student on team C brought 8 bags of cans to the center. There are 5 students on team C. How many bags of cans did they bring?

Give each answer.

11. $\begin{array}{r} 4 \\ \times 6 \\ \hline \end{array}$	**12.** $\begin{array}{r} 3 \\ \times 3 \\ \hline \end{array}$	**13.** $\begin{array}{r} 6 \\ \times 3 \\ \hline \end{array}$	**14.** $\begin{array}{r} 2 \\ \times 2 \\ \hline \end{array}$
15. $\begin{array}{r} 5 \\ \times 4 \\ \hline \end{array}$	**16.** $\begin{array}{r} 2 \\ \times 9 \\ \hline \end{array}$	**17.** $\begin{array}{r} 7 \\ \times 5 \\ \hline \end{array}$	**18.** $\begin{array}{r} 4 \\ \times 4 \\ \hline \end{array}$
19. $\begin{array}{r} 5 \\ \times 9 \\ \hline \end{array}$	**20.** $\begin{array}{r} 2 \\ \times 8 \\ \hline \end{array}$	**21.** $\begin{array}{r} 9 \\ \times 3 \\ \hline \end{array}$	**22.** $\begin{array}{r} 3 \\ \times 8 \\ \hline \end{array}$
23. $\begin{array}{r} 2 \\ \times 3 \\ \hline \end{array}$	**24.** $\begin{array}{r} 6 \\ \times 5 \\ \hline \end{array}$	**25.** $\begin{array}{r} 8 \\ \times 5 \\ \hline \end{array}$	**26.** $\begin{array}{r} 8 \\ \times 2 \\ \hline \end{array}$
27. $\begin{array}{r} 4 \\ \times 8 \\ \hline \end{array}$	**28.** $\begin{array}{r} 4 \\ \times 3 \\ \hline \end{array}$	**29.** $\begin{array}{r} 9 \\ \times 5 \\ \hline \end{array}$	**30.** $\begin{array}{r} 6 \\ \times 2 \\ \hline \end{array}$
31. $\begin{array}{r} 9 \\ \times 2 \\ \hline \end{array}$	**32.** $\begin{array}{r} 5 \\ \times 2 \\ \hline \end{array}$	**33.** $\begin{array}{r} 8 \\ \times 4 \\ \hline \end{array}$	**34.** $\begin{array}{r} 7 \\ \times 3 \\ \hline \end{array}$
35. $\begin{array}{r} 2 \\ \times 6 \\ \hline \end{array}$	**36.** $\begin{array}{r} 7 \\ \times 4 \\ \hline \end{array}$	**37.** $\begin{array}{r} 5 \\ \times 6 \\ \hline \end{array}$	**38.** $\begin{array}{r} 9 \\ \times 4 \\ \hline \end{array}$
39. $\begin{array}{r} 4 \\ \times 2 \\ \hline \end{array}$	**40.** $\begin{array}{r} 3 \\ \times 6 \\ \hline \end{array}$	**41.** $\begin{array}{r} 7 \\ \times 2 \\ \hline \end{array}$	**42.** $\begin{array}{r} 2 \\ \times 5 \\ \hline \end{array}$
43. $\begin{array}{r} 6 \\ \times 4 \\ \hline \end{array}$	**44.** $\begin{array}{r} 5 \\ \times 3 \\ \hline \end{array}$	**45.** $\begin{array}{r} 8 \\ \times 4 \\ \hline \end{array}$	**46.** $\begin{array}{r} 4 \\ \times 7 \\ \hline \end{array}$

Keeping Skillful

1. $\begin{array}{r} 1.2 \\ +3.8 \\ \hline \end{array}$	**2.** $\begin{array}{r} 32.1 \\ +16.3 \\ \hline \end{array}$	**3.** $\begin{array}{r} 36.42 \\ +25.07 \\ \hline \end{array}$
4. $\begin{array}{r} 0.3 \\ +2.9 \\ \hline \end{array}$	**5.** $\begin{array}{r} 0.78 \\ +3.65 \\ \hline \end{array}$	**6.** $\begin{array}{r} 14.77 \\ +11.23 \\ \hline \end{array}$
7. $\begin{array}{r} 9.2 \\ +6.9 \\ \hline \end{array}$	**8.** $\begin{array}{r} 25.7 \\ +\ 0.8 \\ \hline \end{array}$	**9.** $\begin{array}{r} 13.09 \\ +\ 6.45 \\ \hline \end{array}$
10. $\begin{array}{r} 0.5 \\ +0.5 \\ \hline \end{array}$	**11.** $\begin{array}{r} 7.31 \\ +2.26 \\ \hline \end{array}$	**12.** $\begin{array}{r} 35.75 \\ +31.75 \\ \hline \end{array}$
13. $\begin{array}{r} 3.91 \\ +1.09 \\ \hline \end{array}$	**14.** $\begin{array}{r} 2.07 \\ +3.08 \\ \hline \end{array}$	**15.** $\begin{array}{r} 9.9 \\ +1.1 \\ \hline \end{array}$

16. $0.8 + 1.2 + 6$

17. $1.42 + 9 + 2.56$

18. $10 + 3.7 + 5.9$

19. $11.89 + 2 + 4.11$

20. $13.06 + 7.35 + 21$

21. $78.8 + 29 + 6.5$

22. $57.36 + 26.93 + 1$

23. $10.86 + 5 + 13.47$

24. $0.9 + 0.2 + 2$

25. $9.99 + 1.11 + 4$

0 and 1 in Multiplication

A. There are 3 canoes.

There are 2 people in each canoe.

There are 6 people in all.

$3 \times 2 = 6$

B. There are 3 canoes.

There is 1 person in each canoe.

There are 3 people in all.

$3 \times 1 = 3$

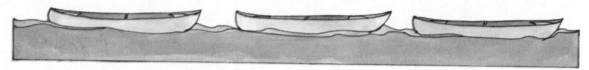

C. There are 3 canoes.

There are 0 people in each canoe.

There are 0 people in all.

$3 \times 0 = 0$

•*Discuss*   What is the answer when you multiply 1 and a number?

•*Discuss*   What is the answer when you multiply 0 and a number?

Give each answer.

1. 4×0
   0×4

2. 6×0
   0×6

3. 2×0
   0×2

4. 8×0
   0×8

5. 5×0
   0×5

6. 9×0
   0×9

7. 3×1
   1×3

8. 7×1
   1×7

9. 9×1
   1×9

10. 5×1
    1×5

11. 8×1
    1×8

12. 4×1
    1×4

13. 8×4
14. 2×7
15. 0×7
16. 7×0
17. 3×0
18. 8×3
19. 6×2
20. 2×4
21. 3×3
22. 1×1
23. 2×8
24. 0×1
25. 4×7
26. 4×3
27. 9×2
28. 0×0
29. 2×2
30. 9×4
31. 6×5
32. 2×1
33. 9×5
34. 3×9
35. 0×3
36. 4×5
37. 5×8
38. 5×6
39. 6×1
40. 1×6
41. 7×3
42. 6×4
43. 1×0
44. 5×3
45. 7×5
46. 3×6
47. 1×2
48. 4×9

Time Out

Martie used pins to hang pictures. She followed these rules.

a. Use 4 pins for each picture.
b. Place pins only at the corners of a picture.
c. The pictures may touch at one edge, but one picture may not cover part of another.

You may hang
3 pictures
this way with
8 pins.

You may not hang
3 pictures this
way with 9 pins.

Show how you would hang

1. 3 pictures with 9 pins.
2. 3 pictures with 10 pins.
3. 4 pictures with 9 pins.
4. 4 pictures with 10 pins.
5. 4 pictures with 11 pins.
6. 4 pictures with 12 pins.
7. 4 pictures with 13 pins.
8. 5 pictures with the greatest possible number of pins.
9. 5 pictures with the least possible number of pins.

6, 7, 8, and 9 in Multiplication

A.

$6 \times 8 = 48$

$8 \times 6 = 48$

B.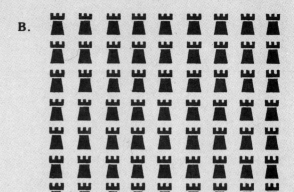

$7 \times 9 = 63$

$9 \times 7 = 63$

Give one multiplication sentence for each picture.

1.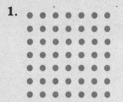

2.

3.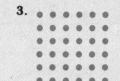

4.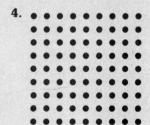

Give two multiplication sentences for each picture.

5.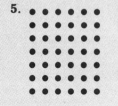

6.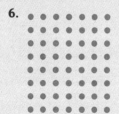

7.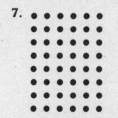

8.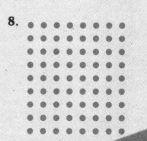

Give each answer.

| 9. $\begin{array}{r} 6 \\ \times 2 \end{array}$ | 10. $\begin{array}{r} 6 \\ \times 3 \end{array}$ | 11. $\begin{array}{r} 6 \\ \times 4 \end{array}$ | 12. $\begin{array}{r} 6 \\ \times 5 \end{array}$ | 13. $\begin{array}{r} 6 \\ \times 6 \end{array}$ | 14. $\begin{array}{r} 6 \\ \times 7 \end{array}$ | 15. $\begin{array}{r} 6 \\ \times 8 \end{array}$ | 16. $\begin{array}{r} 6 \\ \times 9 \end{array}$ |

| 17. $\begin{array}{r} 2 \\ \times 7 \end{array}$ | 18. $\begin{array}{r} 3 \\ \times 7 \end{array}$ | 19. $\begin{array}{r} 4 \\ \times 7 \end{array}$ | 20. $\begin{array}{r} 5 \\ \times 7 \end{array}$ | 21. $\begin{array}{r} 6 \\ \times 7 \end{array}$ | 22. $\begin{array}{r} 7 \\ \times 7 \end{array}$ | 23. $\begin{array}{r} 8 \\ \times 7 \end{array}$ | 24. $\begin{array}{r} 9 \\ \times 7 \end{array}$ |

| 25. $\begin{array}{r} 8 \\ \times 2 \end{array}$ | 26. $\begin{array}{r} 8 \\ \times 3 \end{array}$ | 27. $\begin{array}{r} 8 \\ \times 4 \end{array}$ | 28. $\begin{array}{r} 8 \\ \times 5 \end{array}$ | 29. $\begin{array}{r} 8 \\ \times 6 \end{array}$ | 30. $\begin{array}{r} 8 \\ \times 7 \end{array}$ | 31. $\begin{array}{r} 8 \\ \times 8 \end{array}$ | 32. $\begin{array}{r} 8 \\ \times 9 \end{array}$ |

| 33. $\begin{array}{r} 2 \\ \times 9 \end{array}$ | 34. $\begin{array}{r} 3 \\ \times 9 \end{array}$ | 35. $\begin{array}{r} 4 \\ \times 9 \end{array}$ | 36. $\begin{array}{r} 5 \\ \times 9 \end{array}$ | 37. $\begin{array}{r} 6 \\ \times 9 \end{array}$ | 38. $\begin{array}{r} 7 \\ \times 9 \end{array}$ | 39. $\begin{array}{r} 8 \\ \times 9 \end{array}$ | 40. $\begin{array}{r} 9 \\ \times 9 \end{array}$ |

41. The Robot game has 8 cards. How many cards are in 6 games?

42. There are 6 markers in a game. How many markers are in 9 games?

43. Each chess set has 4 castles. How many castles are in 8 sets?

44. Each box holds 8 games. How many games are in 7 boxes?

45. The Fly to the Moon game has 6 markers. How many markers are in 7 games?

46. The Star game has 8 cards. How many cards are in 9 games?

47. There are 2 kings in a chess set. How many kings are in 6 sets?

**More practice
Set 16, page 375**

Using Multiplication Facts

Give each answer. Use the code to help you find
the missing words in the limerick.

There was a young lady named Mabel,
Who at math was really quite able.
The "times" facts she wrote, and

<u>Word 1</u> <u>Word 2</u> <u>Word 3</u> <u>Word 4</u> <u>Word 5</u> <u>Word 6</u>

Made a multiplication table.

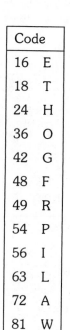

Code	
16	E
18	T
24	H
36	O
42	G
48	F
49	R
54	P
56	I
63	L
72	A
81	W

Word 1	Word 2	Word 3	Word 4	Word 5	Word 6
1. 9×9	**5.** 9×2	**8.** 3×8	**12.** 6×6	**14.** 4×6	**17.** 7×6
2. 7×8	**6.** 6×4	**9.** 4×4	**13.** 8×6	**15.** 2×8	**18.** 9×4
3. 6×3	**7.** 8×2	**10.** 7×9		**16.** 7×7	**19.** 8×9
4. 8×3		**11.** 6×9			**20.** 3×6

Complete each table.

	× 6
4	24
21. 1	
22. 9	
23. 2	
24. 5	

	× 3
25. 3	
26. 5	
27. 2	
28. 9	
29. 7	

	× 8
30. 5	
31. 8	
32. 6	
33. 4	
34. 9	

	× 0
35. 4	
36. 0	
37. 5	
38. 1	
39. 7	

	× 7
40. 5	
41. 9	
42. 6	
43. 3	
44. 8	

	× 1
45. 3	
46. 9	
47. 2	
48. 8	
49. 6	

	× 5
50. 6	
51. 8	
52. 5	
53. 7	
54. 9	

	× 9
55. 2	
56. 4	
57. 5	
58. 3	
59. 0	

Find each answer.

60. There are 8 boxes of pencils. Each box holds 4 pencils. How many pencils are there in all?

61. There are 4 packages of erasers. Each package holds 7 erasers. How many erasers are there in all?

62. There are 7 bags of paper clips. There are 8 paper clips in each bag. How many paper clips are there in all?

63. There is 1 package of rulers. There are 6 rulers in the package. How many rulers are there in all?

64. There are 5 boxes of pens. Each box holds 4 pens. How many pens are there in all?

65. There are 9 cartons of tape. Each carton holds 9 rolls of tape. How many rolls of tape are there in all?

Basic Facts Spinners

Brian, Mindy, Peggy, and Todd made two spinners like these.

Each player spun one of the spinners to decide who would play first, second, third, and fourth. Todd got the highest number, so he was the first player.

Todd spun both spinners. One pointer stopped on 8, and the other pointer stopped on 6. Todd wrote the multiplication sentence 8 × 6 = 48. He multiplied correctly, so 48 was his score for the first round.

Mindy was next. The pointers stopped on 2 and 9. Mindy wrote the multiplication sentence 2 × 9 = 18. Her score was 18 for the first round.

Brian was third. The pointers stopped on 6 and 4. Brian wrote the multiplication sentence 6 × 4 = 30. He did not multiply correctly, so his score was 0.

Peggy was last. The pointers stopped on 7 and 7. Peggy wrote the multiplication sentence 7 × 7 = 49. Her score was 49. Peggy won the first round because her score was the highest.

Todd started the next round.

Make two spinners. Find one or more players and play four rounds. Add to find your total score at the end of four rounds. The player with the highest total wins the game.

Chapter 7 Test
Multiplication Basic Facts, pages 128–142

Copy and complete the addition
sentence and multiplication
sentence for the picture.

(★ ★ ★ ★ ★)
(★ ★ ★ ★ ★)
(★ ★ ★ ★ ★)
(★ ★ ★ ★ ★)

1. $5 + 5 + 5 + 5 = $ ▦

2. $4 \times 5 = $ ▦

Give each answer.

3. $\begin{array}{r} 2 \\ \times 4 \\ \hline \end{array}$ 4. $\begin{array}{r} 8 \\ \times 2 \\ \hline \end{array}$

5. $\begin{array}{r} 9 \\ \times 3 \\ \hline \end{array}$ 6. $\begin{array}{r} 3 \\ \times 7 \\ \hline \end{array}$

7. $\begin{array}{r} 4 \\ \times 8 \\ \hline \end{array}$ 8. $\begin{array}{r} 6 \\ \times 4 \\ \hline \end{array}$

9. $\begin{array}{r} 5 \\ \times 5 \\ \hline \end{array}$ 10. $\begin{array}{r} 8 \\ \times 5 \\ \hline \end{array}$

11. $\begin{array}{r} 7 \\ \times 1 \\ \hline \end{array}$ 12. $\begin{array}{r} 1 \\ \times 3 \\ \hline \end{array}$

13. $\begin{array}{r} 0 \\ \times 6 \\ \hline \end{array}$ 14. $\begin{array}{r} 4 \\ \times 0 \\ \hline \end{array}$

15. $\begin{array}{r} 6 \\ \times 7 \\ \hline \end{array}$ 16. $\begin{array}{r} 7 \\ \times 8 \\ \hline \end{array}$

17. $\begin{array}{r} 9 \\ \times 9 \\ \hline \end{array}$ 18. $\begin{array}{r} 9 \\ \times 8 \\ \hline \end{array}$

19. $\begin{array}{r} 4 \\ \times 3 \\ \hline \end{array}$ 20. $\begin{array}{r} 7 \\ \times 5 \\ \hline \end{array}$

21. $\begin{array}{r} 9 \\ \times 6 \\ \hline \end{array}$ 22. $\begin{array}{r} 6 \\ \times 6 \\ \hline \end{array}$

23. $\begin{array}{r} 7 \\ \times 9 \\ \hline \end{array}$ 24. $\begin{array}{r} 8 \\ \times 6 \\ \hline \end{array}$

25. $\begin{array}{r} 2 \\ \times 9 \\ \hline \end{array}$ 26. $\begin{array}{r} 5 \\ \times 9 \\ \hline \end{array}$

27. $\begin{array}{r} 8 \\ \times 8 \\ \hline \end{array}$ 28. $\begin{array}{r} 8 \\ \times 3 \\ \hline \end{array}$

29. $\begin{array}{r} 9 \\ \times 4 \\ \hline \end{array}$ 30. $\begin{array}{r} 5 \\ \times 6 \\ \hline \end{array}$

Chapter 8 Multiplication: One-Digit Multipliers

Multiplying with 10, 100, and 1000

A. Edmond has 6 dollars in pennies.
How many pennies does he have?
Remember, 1 dollar = 100 pennies.

You can add to find the answer.

$$
\begin{array}{r}
100 \\
100 \\
100 \\
100 \\
100 \\
+100 \\
\hline
600
\end{array}
$$

You can also multiply to find the answer.

$$6 \times 100 = 600$$

Edmond has 600 pennies.

Study these patterns.

B. $1 \times 36 = 36$
   $10 \times 36 = 360$
   $100 \times 36 = 3600$
   $1000 \times 36 = 36,000$

C. $12 \times 1 = 12$
   $12 \times 10 = 120$
   $12 \times 100 = 1200$
   $12 \times 1000 = 12,000$

Multiply.
Study each pattern.

1. 9×1

2. 9×10

3. 9×100

4. 9×1000

5. 24×1

6. 24×10

7. 24×100

8. 24×1000

9. 1×67

10. 10×67

11. 100×67

12. 1000×67

13. 10×1

14. 10×10

15. 10×100

16. 10×1000

• **Discuss** What is the answer when you multiply 1 and a number?

• **Discuss** What is an easy way to multiply a number by 10? By 100? By 1000?

144

Multiply.

17. 3×10 **18.** 8×10 **19.** 46×10 **20.** 78×10

21. 10×132 **22.** 10×361 **23.** 5×100 **24.** 100×9

25. 100×55 **26.** 21×100 **27.** 7×1000 **28.** 2×1000

29. 36×1000 **30.** 72×1000 **31.** 80×10 **32.** 100×34

33. 10×93 **34.** 70×100 **35.** 425×10 **36.** 237×10

37. 375×100 **38.** 653×100 **39.** 10×951 **40.** 10×670

41. 75×1000 **42.** 87×1000 **43.** 50×1000 **44.** 37×1000

There are 10 pennies in a dime.
How many pennies can you get for

45. 6 dimes?   **46.** 84 dimes?   **47.** 100 dimes?   **48.** 93 dimes?

There are 100 pennies in a dollar.
How many pennies can you get for

49. 8 dollars?   **50.** 37 dollars?   **51.** 60 dollars?   **52.** 87 dollars?

How many dimes can you get for

★53. 10 dollars?   **★54.** 30 dollars?   **★55.** 100 dollars?   **★56.** 130 dollars?

145

Multiplying with Multiples of 10, 100, and 1000

A. Sara jogs 30 minutes each day around Sunset Park. How much time does she spend jogging in 4 days?

You can add to find the answer.

$$\begin{array}{r} 30 \\ 30 \\ 30 \\ +30 \\ \hline 120 \end{array}$$

You can also multiply to find the answer.

$$4 \times 30 = 120$$

Sara jogs 120 minutes in 4 days.

B. $500 \times 8 = 4000$

C. $7 \times 6000 = 42{,}000$

• **Discuss**   When you find 4×800, what do you multiply? How many zeros do you write?

Multiply. Study each pattern.

1. 3×2
2. 3×20
3. 3×200
4. 3×2000

5. 7×8
6. 7×80
7. 7×800
8. 7×8000

9. 5×4
10. 5×40
11. 5×400
12. 5×4000

13. 6×3
14. 60×3
15. 600×3
16. 6000×3

Multiply.

17. 8×30
18. 4×70
19. 90×7
20. 40×9
21. 60×5
22. 50×2
23. 6×900
24. 9×300
25. 700×5
26. 7×200
27. 4×6000
28. 2×8000
29. 7000×7
30. 6000×6
31. 8×900
32. 5×500
33. 90×5
34. 70×3
35. 9×9000
36. 8×8000
★37. $5 \times 80,000$
★38. $6 \times 300,000$

A swimming pool is 50 meters long. How many meters would you travel if you swam

39. 5 lengths?
40. 8 lengths?
41. 3 lengths?

A jogging path is 300 meters long. How many meters would you jog if you went around the path

42. 3 times?
43. 5 times?
44. 8 times?

A bicycle trail is 9000 meters long. How many meters would you travel if you rode your bicycle around the trail

45. 2 times?
46. 5 times?
47. 7 times?

147

Multiplication: No Renaming

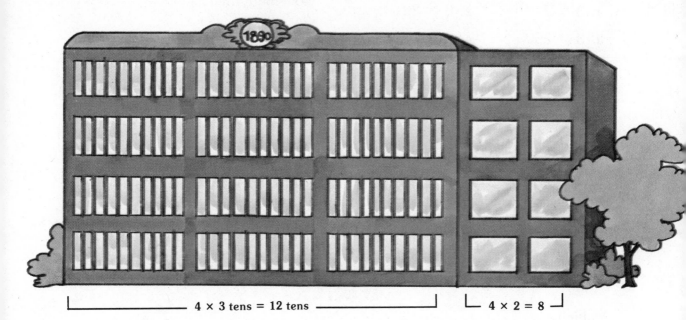

4 × 3 tens = 12 tens   4 × 2 = 8

A. The Midland Office Building has 4 stories. On the side that faces the street, each story has 32 windows. How many windows are on that side?

Find 4 × 32.

$$\begin{array}{r} 3\mathbf{2} \\ \times\ \ \mathbf{4} \\ \hline \mathbf{8} \end{array}$$

Multiply the ones.
4 × 2 = 8

Show 8 ones.

$$\begin{array}{r} \mathbf{3}2 \\ \times\ \ 4 \\ \hline \mathbf{12}8 \end{array}$$

Multiply the tens.
4 × 3 tens = 12 tens

Show 12 tens.

There are 128 windows on that side.

B. Tell how to find 3 × 512.

$$\begin{array}{r} 51\mathbf{2} \\ \times\ \ \ \mathbf{3} \\ \hline \mathbf{6} \end{array}$$

$$\begin{array}{r} 5\mathbf{1}2 \\ \times\ \ \ 3 \\ \hline \mathbf{3}6 \end{array}$$

$$\begin{array}{r} \mathbf{5}12 \\ \times\ \ \ 3 \\ \hline 1\mathbf{5}36 \end{array}$$

Multiply.

1. 12 × 4	**2.** 43 × 2	**3.** 11 × 8	**4.** 33 × 3	**5.** 72 × 3	**6.** 51 × 4	**7.** 41 × 5
8. 93 × 2	**9.** 61 × 7	**10.** 82 × 4	**11.** 73 × 3	**12.** 31 × 9	**13.** 42 × 4	**14.** 64 × 2
15. 213 × 3	**16.** 431 × 2	**17.** 112 × 4	**18.** 231 × 3	**19.** 123 × 3	**20.** 134 × 2	**21.** 411 × 8
22. 413 × 2	**23.** 233 × 3	**24.** 321 × 3	**25.** 512 × 4	**26.** 423 × 3	**27.** 721 × 4	**28.** 611 × 5

There are 4 panes of glass in each window.
How many panes of glass are in

29. 22 windows?   **30.** 32 windows?   **31.** 30 windows?

32. 40 windows?   **33.** 52 windows?   **34.** 62 windows?

Time Out

There are fifteen toothpicks. Can you take
six of them away and still have ten left?

Multiplication: One Renaming

A. A dog team pulling a sled can travel about 32 kilometers a day. How far can this team travel in 7 days?

Find 7 × 32.

$$\begin{array}{r} \overset{1}{3}2 \\ \times\ 7 \\ \hline 4 \end{array}$$

Multiply the ones.
7 × 2 = 14

Show 1 ten 4 ones.

$$\begin{array}{r} \overset{1}{3}2 \\ \times\ 7 \\ \hline 224 \end{array}$$

Multiply the tens.
7 × 3 tens = 21 tens.
Add the 1 ten.

Show 22 tens.

This dog team can travel 224 kilometers in 7 days.

B. Tell how to find 4 × 15.

$$\begin{array}{r} \overset{2}{1}5 \\ \times\ 4 \\ \hline 0 \end{array} \qquad \begin{array}{r} \overset{2}{1}5 \\ \times\ 4 \\ \hline 60 \end{array}$$

C. Tell how to find 9 × 47.

$$\begin{array}{r} \overset{6}{4}7 \\ \times\ 9 \\ \hline 3 \end{array} \qquad \begin{array}{r} \overset{6}{4}7 \\ \times\ 9 \\ \hline 423 \end{array}$$

Multiply.

1. $\begin{array}{r} 23 \\ \times\ 4 \end{array}$
2. $\begin{array}{r} 37 \\ \times\ 2 \end{array}$
3. $\begin{array}{r} 29 \\ \times\ 3 \end{array}$
4. $\begin{array}{r} 48 \\ \times\ 2 \end{array}$
5. $\begin{array}{r} 13 \\ \times\ 6 \end{array}$
6. $\begin{array}{r} 17 \\ \times\ 5 \end{array}$
7. $\begin{array}{r} 31 \\ \times\ 3 \end{array}$

8. $\begin{array}{r} 32 \\ \times\ 8 \end{array}$
9. $\begin{array}{r} 24 \\ \times\ 7 \end{array}$
10. $\begin{array}{r} 32 \\ \times\ 5 \end{array}$
11. $\begin{array}{r} 53 \\ \times\ 8 \end{array}$
12. $\begin{array}{r} 57 \\ \times\ 6 \end{array}$
13. $\begin{array}{r} 26 \\ \times\ 5 \end{array}$
14. $\begin{array}{r} 43 \\ \times\ 7 \end{array}$

15. $\begin{array}{r} 12 \\ \times\ 8 \end{array}$
16. $\begin{array}{r} 73 \\ \times\ 6 \end{array}$
17. $\begin{array}{r} 64 \\ \times\ 8 \end{array}$
18. $\begin{array}{r} 14 \\ \times\ 7 \end{array}$
19. $\begin{array}{r} 19 \\ \times\ 5 \end{array}$
20. $\begin{array}{r} 28 \\ \times\ 9 \end{array}$
21. $\begin{array}{r} 68 \\ \times\ 3 \end{array}$

22. 4×65
23. 5×16
24. 34×7
25. 38×9
26. 4×73

27. 26×3
28. 87×2
29. 9×12
30. 59×6
31. 6×14

32. 9×15
33. 2×49
34. 8×25
35. 21×4
36. 84×3

37. A dog sled team had 6 dogs. Each dog weighed about 68 kilograms. What was the total weight of the dogs?

38. There were 8 dogs on a team. If each dog pulled a load of 92 kilograms, how much was the total weight of the load?

More practice
Set 17, page 375

Multiplication: One Renaming

A. Stellaria I can travel at a speed of 761 kilometers per minute. How far can Stellaria I go in 5 minutes?

Find 5 × 761.

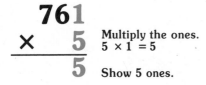

$$\begin{array}{r} 76\mathbf{1} \\ \times\ \ \ 5 \\ \hline 5 \end{array}$$

Multiply the ones.
$5 \times 1 = 5$

Show 5 ones.

$$\begin{array}{r} {}^{3}\ \\ 761 \\ \times\ \ \ 5 \\ \hline 05 \end{array}$$

Multiply the tens.
5×6 tens $= 30$ tens

Show 3 hundreds 0 tens.

$$\begin{array}{r} {}^{3}\ \\ 761 \\ \times\ \ \ 5 \\ \hline 3805 \end{array}$$

Multiply the hundreds.
5×7 hundreds $= 35$ hundreds
Add the 3 hundreds.

Show 38 hundreds.

Stellaria I can go 3805 kilometers in 5 minutes.

B. Tell how to find 4 × 1219.

$$
\begin{array}{r}
\overset{3}{12\overset{}{1}9} \\
\times \quad 4 \\
\hline
6
\end{array}
\qquad
\begin{array}{r}
\overset{3}{12\overset{}{1}9} \\
\times \quad 4 \\
\hline
76
\end{array}
\qquad
\begin{array}{r}
\overset{3}{12\overset{}{1}9} \\
\times \quad 4 \\
\hline
876
\end{array}
\qquad
\begin{array}{r}
\overset{3}{12\overset{}{1}9} \\
\times \quad 4 \\
\hline
4876
\end{array}
$$

Multiply.

1. $\begin{array}{r} 171 \\ \times\ 5 \\ \hline \end{array}$
2. $\begin{array}{r} 283 \\ \times\ 2 \\ \hline \end{array}$
3. $\begin{array}{r} 327 \\ \times\ 3 \\ \hline \end{array}$
4. $\begin{array}{r} 124 \\ \times\ 4 \\ \hline \end{array}$
5. $\begin{array}{r} 463 \\ \times\ 3 \\ \hline \end{array}$
6. $\begin{array}{r} 251 \\ \times\ 7 \\ \hline \end{array}$

7. $\begin{array}{r} 312 \\ \times\ 8 \\ \hline \end{array}$
8. $\begin{array}{r} 214 \\ \times\ 6 \\ \hline \end{array}$
9. $\begin{array}{r} 261 \\ \times\ 4 \\ \hline \end{array}$
10. $\begin{array}{r} 512 \\ \times\ 5 \\ \hline \end{array}$
11. $\begin{array}{r} 315 \\ \times\ 6 \\ \hline \end{array}$
12. $\begin{array}{r} 141 \\ \times\ 9 \\ \hline \end{array}$

13. $\begin{array}{r} 1216 \\ \times\ 4 \\ \hline \end{array}$
14. $\begin{array}{r} 2117 \\ \times\ 3 \\ \hline \end{array}$
15. $\begin{array}{r} 2311 \\ \times\ 7 \\ \hline \end{array}$
16. $\begin{array}{r} 3621 \\ \times\ 4 \\ \hline \end{array}$
17. $\begin{array}{r} 4163 \\ \times\ 3 \\ \hline \end{array}$
18. $\begin{array}{r} 3241 \\ \times\ 4 \\ \hline \end{array}$

19. 421 × 8
20. 431 × 9
21. 2 × 715
22. 623 × 4

23. 3 × 928
24. 2263 × 3
25. 1732 × 2
26. 4 × 4181

27. 4 × 4116
28. 3 × 4319
*29. 3 × 612,124
*30. 726,134 × 2

31. Robot model RBA has 115 moving parts. How many moving parts would 6 of these robots have?

32. Starship I can travel 514 kilometers per minute. How far can it travel in 3 minutes?

**More practice
Set 18, page 375**

Using Multiplication

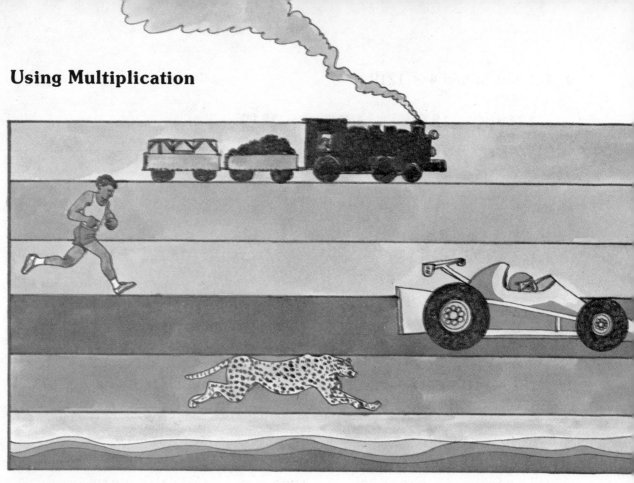

Find each answer.

A human can run 6 meters per second. How many meters can a human run in

1. 20 seconds? 2. 70 seconds?

3. 10 seconds? 4. 100 seconds?

5. 1000 seconds? 6. 40 seconds?

A cheetah can run 26 meters per second. How many meters can a cheetah run in

7. 7 seconds? 8. 3 seconds?

9. 10 seconds? 10. 5 seconds?

11. 100 seconds? 12. 9 seconds?

A train can travel 38 meters per second. How many meters can a train travel in

13. 10 seconds? 14. 2 seconds?

15. 100 seconds? 16. 7 seconds?

17. 1000 seconds? 18. 5 seconds?

A racing car can travel 85 meters per second. How many meters can a racing car travel in

19. 8 seconds? 20. 3 seconds?

21. 9 seconds? 22. 7 seconds? .

23. 5 seconds? 24. 10 seconds?

A tidal wave can travel 214 meters per second. How many meters can a tidal wave travel in

25. 2 seconds?   **26.** 10 seconds?

27. 5 seconds?   **28.** 7 seconds?

29. 4 seconds?   **30.** 3 seconds?

Sound can travel 331 meters per second. How many meters can sound travel in

31. 8 seconds?   **32.** 2 seconds?

33. 3 seconds?   **34.** 5 seconds?

35. 10 seconds?   **36.** 4 seconds?

Keeping Skillful

1. 4.8 − 2.5	**2.** 5.3 − 1.7	**3.** 6.0 − 2.3
4. 85.9 − 26.4	**5.** 157.2 − 85.6	**6.** 384.7 − 239.7
7. 0.98 − 0.56	**8.** 1.74 − 0.49	**9.** 8.83 − 2.34
10. 5.06 − 3.25	**11.** 11.75 − 7.82	**12.** 36.41 − 18.23
13. 58.7 − 29.1	**14.** 139.5 − 86.5	**15.** 0.73 − 0.26
16. 9.22 − 0.43	**17.** 36.19 − 15.55	**18.** 280.3 − 148.4
19. 4.02 − 1.95	**20.** 426.3 − 189.2	**21.** 63.04 − 42.93

22. 8.7 − 2.9   **23.** 1.6 − 0.7

24. 9.1 − 3.5   **25.** 23.4 − 9.3

26. 0.53 − 0.46   **27.** 6.45 − 2.08

28. 82.4 − 15   **29.** 32.54 − 26

30. 47.9 − 8   **31.** 90.06 − 75

32. 6 − 1.7   **33.** 8 − 4.92

34. 23 − 11.64   **35.** 14 − 3.26

Multiplication: Factors with Zeros

A. A supersonic jet flew from Paris to Washington in 3 hours. The jet flew at a speed of 2060 kilometers per hour. How many kilometers did the jet fly?

Find 3 × 2060.

$$\begin{array}{r} 2060 \\ \times \quad 3 \\ \hline 0 \end{array}$$ 3 × 0 = 0
Show 0 ones.

$$\begin{array}{r} {}^{1}\ \ \\ 2060 \\ \times \quad 3 \\ \hline 80 \end{array}$$ 3 × 6 tens = 18 tens
Show 1 hundred 8 tens.

$$\begin{array}{r} {}^{1}\ \ \\ 2060 \\ \times \quad 3 \\ \hline 180 \end{array}$$ 3 × 0 hundreds = 0 hundreds
Add the 1 hundred.
Show 1 hundred.

$$\begin{array}{r} {}^{1}\ \ \\ 2060 \\ \times \quad 3 \\ \hline 6180 \end{array}$$ 3 × 2 thousands = 6 thousands
Show 6 thousands.

The jet flew 6180 kilometers.

B. Tell how to find 8 × 607.

$$
\begin{array}{r}
\overset{5}{6}07 \\
\times\ \ 8 \\
\hline
6
\end{array}
\qquad
\begin{array}{r}
\overset{5}{6}07 \\
\times\ \ 8 \\
\hline
56
\end{array}
\qquad
\begin{array}{r}
\overset{5}{6}07 \\
\times\ \ 8 \\
\hline
4856
\end{array}
$$

Multiply.

1. $\begin{array}{r} 107 \\ \times\ 5 \\ \hline \end{array}$
2. $\begin{array}{r} 206 \\ \times\ 3 \\ \hline \end{array}$
3. $\begin{array}{r} 350 \\ \times\ 2 \\ \hline \end{array}$
4. $\begin{array}{r} 240 \\ \times\ 5 \\ \hline \end{array}$

5. $\begin{array}{r} 308 \\ \times\ 4 \\ \hline \end{array}$
6. $\begin{array}{r} 406 \\ \times\ 6 \\ \hline \end{array}$
7. $\begin{array}{r} 800 \\ \times\ 9 \\ \hline \end{array}$
8. $\begin{array}{r} 902 \\ \times\ 3 \\ \hline \end{array}$

9. $\begin{array}{r} 601 \\ \times\ 7 \\ \hline \end{array}$
10. $\begin{array}{r} 700 \\ \times\ 8 \\ \hline \end{array}$
11. $\begin{array}{r} 670 \\ \times\ 4 \\ \hline \end{array}$
12. $\begin{array}{r} 430 \\ \times\ 5 \\ \hline \end{array}$

13. $\begin{array}{r} 3045 \\ \times\ 2 \\ \hline \end{array}$
14. $\begin{array}{r} 1014 \\ \times\ 5 \\ \hline \end{array}$
15. $\begin{array}{r} 2310 \\ \times\ 4 \\ \hline \end{array}$
16. $\begin{array}{r} 1430 \\ \times\ 3 \\ \hline \end{array}$

17. $\begin{array}{r} 5007 \\ \times\ 9 \\ \hline \end{array}$
18. $\begin{array}{r} 7008 \\ \times\ 6 \\ \hline \end{array}$
★19. $\begin{array}{r} 30{,}060 \\ \times\ 7 \\ \hline \end{array}$
★20. $\begin{array}{r} 80{,}004 \\ \times\ 3 \\ \hline \end{array}$

How far did each airplane fly?

21. 3 hours at 605 kilometers per hour

22. 2 hours at 360 kilometers per hour

23. 4 hours at 950 kilometers per hour

24. 5 hours at 1020 kilometers per hour

**More practice
Set 19, page 376**

157

Multiplication: More Than One Renaming

A. One of the largest airplanes has a seating capacity of 396 people. What is the seating capacity of 4 of these planes?

Find 4 × 396.

$$\begin{array}{r} {\scriptstyle 2} \\ 396 \\ \times\ \ 4 \\ \hline 4 \end{array}$$

4 × 6 = 24

Show 2 tens 4 ones.

$$\begin{array}{r} {\scriptstyle 3\ 2} \\ 396 \\ \times\ \ 4 \\ \hline 84 \end{array}$$

4 × 9 tens = 36 tens
Add the 2 tens.
Show 3 hundreds 8 tens.

$$\begin{array}{r} {\scriptstyle 3\ 2} \\ 396 \\ \times\ \ 4 \\ \hline 1584 \end{array}$$

4 × 3 hundreds =
12 hundreds
Add the 3 hundreds.
Show 15 hundreds.

The seating capacity of 4 of these planes is 1584 people.

B. Tell how to find 4 × 1680.

```
  1680        3         2 3         2 3
             1680      1680        1680
×    4      ×    4     ×    4      ×    4
─────      ──────     ──────      ──────
     0         20        720        6720
```

Multiply.

1. 176
   × 2

2. 249
   × 3

3. 158
   × 4

4. 135
   × 7

5. 662
   × 5

6. 355
   × 4

7. 229
   × 4

8. 134
   × 6

9. 177
   × 5

10. 238
    × 3

11. 985
    × 2

12. 752
    × 6

13. 1825
    × 3

14. 1517
    × 5

15. 1149
    × 6

16. 2178
    × 4

17. 2045
    × 9

18. 3062
    × 8

19. 8379
    × 2

20. 3246
    × 4

21. 6950
    × 3

22. 2870
    × 5

23. 4171
    × 7

24. 6412
    × 8

25. Another large airplane has 264 passenger seats
    in it. The airline maintenance crew cleaned 5 of
    these planes. How many seats did they clean?

26. A medium-sized airplane can seat 127 passengers.
    If all the planes are full, how many meals would
    be needed to serve 7 of these planes?

*27. A small airplane can seat 14 people in first class
    and 133 people in coach. How many people can
    be seated in 3 of these planes?

**More practice
Set 20, page 376**

Using Multiplication

Multiply. Use the code to find the answer to the riddle.

Why are dinosaurs and chickens alike?

Code	
136	U
312	O
432	R
576	B
600	A
692	H
720	E
828	C
972	S
1743	M
2448	T
3423	Y
4675	N
5528	F
18,972	G

Word 1

1. 6×96
2. 240×3
3. 2×414
4. 3×200
5. 17×8
6. 108×9
7. 72×10

Word 2

8. 816×3
9. 2×346
10. 120×6
11. 1141×3

Word 3

12. 72×8
13. 2×156
14. 408×6
15. 173×4

Word 4

16. 207×4
17. 75×8
18. 3×581
19. 9×80

Word 5

20. 1382×4
21. 144×3
22. 78×4
23. 7×249

Word 6

24. 4×150
25. 935×5

Word 7

26. 180×4
27. 6×3162
28. 9486×2

Multiply across.
Multiply down.

× →		
3	**3**	29.
2	**8**	30.
31.	32.	33.

× →		
3	**4**	34.
5	**2**	35.
36.	37.	38.

× →		
6	**9**	39.
1	**8**	40.
41.	42.	43.

Multiplication: Money

A. Bernie's Beach Shop rents surfboards for $3.25 each day. How much would it cost to rent a surfboard for 5 days?

Find 5 × $3.25.

$$\begin{array}{r} \mathbf{\$3.25} \\ \times \qquad \mathbf{5} \\ \hline \end{array}$$

Multiply as you would whole numbers.

$$\begin{array}{r} \mathbf{\$3.25} \\ \times \qquad \mathbf{5} \\ \hline \mathbf{\$16.25} \end{array}$$

$$\begin{array}{r} \text{1 2} \\ 325 \\ \times \quad 5 \\ \hline 1625 \end{array}$$

Write the answer in dollars and cents.

It would cost $16.25.

Tell how to find each answer.

B.
$$\begin{array}{r} \text{3 7} \\ \mathbf{\$0.49} \\ \times \qquad \mathbf{8} \\ \hline \mathbf{\$3.92} \end{array}$$

C.
$$\begin{array}{r} \mathbf{\$0.04} \\ \times \qquad \mathbf{2} \\ \hline \mathbf{\$0.08} \end{array}$$

Multiply.

1. $0.09 × 5	**2.** $0.07 × 6	**3.** $0.19 × 4	**4.** $0.28 × 3	**5.** $0.03 × 3	**6.** $0.04 × 2
7. $0.83 × 7	**8.** $0.59 × 5	**9.** $2.15 × 3	**10.** $1.32 × 4	**11.** $1.53 × 9	**12.** $1.44 × 8
13. $4.50 × 7	**14.** $3.90 × 6	**15.** $6.25 × 4	**16.** $3.75 × 4	**17.** $4.06 × 8	**18.** $2.08 × 7

19. 4 × $0.57   **20.** 8 × $0.39   **21.** 3 × $3.40   **22.** 9 × $2.45

23. 5 × $3.19   **24.** 2 × $6.97   **25.** 7 × $4.30   **26.** 5 × $3.71

27. Beach umbrellas rent for $1.75 per day. How much would it cost to rent an umbrella for 7 days?

28. Surf mats rent for $0.85 per hour. How much would it cost to rent a mat for 3 hours?

29. Paddleboats rent for $6.50 per hour. How much would it cost to rent a paddleboat for 5 hours?

★30. Beach chairs cost $7.95 and rent for $1.25 per day. If you needed a chair for a week, would it be cheaper to buy or rent the chair? (1 week is 7 days.)

163

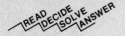

Problem Solving: Choosing the Operation

READ   Brighton Electric Company put
light switches in 319 hotel rooms.
They put 3 switches in each room.
How many switches is this in all?

DECIDE   Multiply the number of rooms by
the number of switches in each room.

$3 \times 319 = n$

SOLVE

$$
\begin{array}{r}
319 \\
\times\ \ \ 3 \\
\hline
957
\end{array}
$$

ANSWER $n = 957$

957 light switches

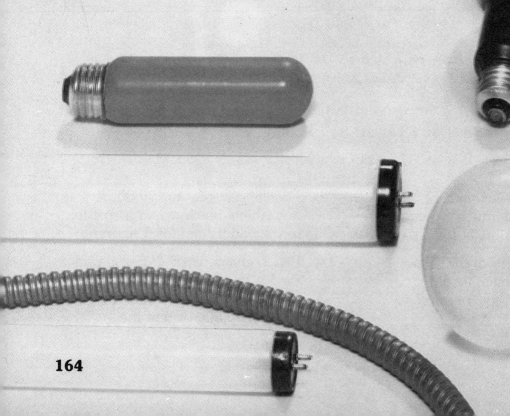

Write an equation for each problem.
Give each answer.

1. A light switch costs $2.39 and a cover plate costs $0.59. What is the total cost?
($2.39 + $0.59 = n)

2. Steve joined 426 centimeters of electrical tubing and 379 centimeters of tubing. Then how much tubing did he have?
(426 + 379 = n)

3. Tony needs 640 centimeters of electrical tubing. He has 328 centimeters. How much more tubing does he need?

4. The ballroom has 128 sets of lights. There are 7 bulbs in each set. How many bulbs are there in all?

5. It costs $6 to wire a light switch. How much does it cost to wire 256 switches?

6. The lights in a meeting room use 3600 watts. The lights in a snack shop use 2550 watts. How much more power do the lights in the meeting room use?

7. Virlean used 306 meters of electrical wire to wire a room. She wired 5 rooms the same way. How much wire did she use in all five rooms?

8. Isabel used 375 meters of wire in one room and 250 meters in another room. How much wire did she use in all?

9. A floodlight uses 2325 watts. How many watts would 2 of these lights use?

10. A ceiling lamp costs $26.25. A floor lamp costs $45.70. How much more does the floor lamp cost?

Three Factors

Find $8 \times 3 \times 7$.

Here is one way to multiply.   Here is another way to multiply.

$$8 \times 3 \times 7$$

$$24 \times 7$$

$$168$$

$$8 \times 3 \times 7$$

$$8 \times 21$$

$$168$$

Multiply.

1. $2 \times 2 \times 9$ 2. $8 \times 1 \times 7$ 3. $3 \times 2 \times 8$ 4. $4 \times 7 \times 3$

5. $9 \times 2 \times 3$ 6. $4 \times 7 \times 6$ 7. $6 \times 5 \times 9$ 8. $3 \times 0 \times 5$

9. $6 \times 6 \times 6$ 10. $7 \times 3 \times 8$ 11. $3 \times 6 \times 1$ 12. $5 \times 2 \times 9$

13. $4 \times 0 \times 8$ 14. $6 \times 5 \times 7$ 15. $3 \times 7 \times 2$ 16. $5 \times 8 \times 3$

Multiply across. Multiply down.

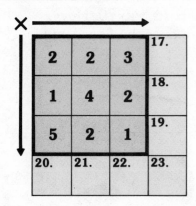

×			
2	2	3	17.
1	4	2	18.
5	2	1	19.
20.	21.	22.	23.

×			
5	3	5	24.
4	2	1	25.
5	10	2	26.
27.	28.	29.	30.

Chapter 8 Test
Multiplication: One-Digit Multipliers, pages 144–166

Multiply.

1. 64×10

2. 1000×8

3. 25×100

4. 52×10

5. 7×30

6. 5×400

7. 2000×8

8. 6×900

9. $\begin{array}{r} 42 \\ \times\ 3 \\ \hline \end{array}$ 10. $\begin{array}{r} 124 \\ \times\ \ 2 \\ \hline \end{array}$

11. $\begin{array}{r} 17 \\ \times\ 4 \\ \hline \end{array}$ 12. $\begin{array}{r} 45 \\ \times\ 2 \\ \hline \end{array}$

13. $\begin{array}{r} 65 \\ \times\ 7 \\ \hline \end{array}$ 14. $\begin{array}{r} 228 \\ \times\ \ 3 \\ \hline \end{array}$

15. $\begin{array}{r} 431 \\ \times\ \ 6 \\ \hline \end{array}$ 16. $\begin{array}{r} 841 \\ \times\ \ 5 \\ \hline \end{array}$

17. $\begin{array}{r} 250 \\ \times\ \ 3 \\ \hline \end{array}$ 18. $\begin{array}{r} 406 \\ \times\ \ 8 \\ \hline \end{array}$

19. $\begin{array}{r} 148 \\ \times\ \ 4 \\ \hline \end{array}$ 20. $\begin{array}{r} 517 \\ \times\ \ 7 \\ \hline \end{array}$

21. $\begin{array}{r} \$0.63 \\ \times\ \ \ \ 2 \\ \hline \end{array}$ 22. $\begin{array}{r} \$3.51 \\ \times\ \ \ \ 5 \\ \hline \end{array}$

Find each answer.

23. There are 48 cans of soup in a case. How many cans are there in 7 cases?

24. There are 171 cans of beef soup and 243 cans of tomato soup on a grocery store shelf. How many more cans of tomato soup are there?

25. A can of beef soup costs $0.36. How much do 6 cans cost?

Chapter 9 Multiplication: Two-Digit Multipliers

Multiples of 10 as Factors

A. On a trip from Chicago to Miami, a car traveled about 80 kilometers per hour. The trip took 30 hours. How many kilometers did the car travel?

Find 30 × 80.

30 × 80 = 2400 $3 \times 8 = 24$

The car traveled 2400 kilometers.

Study these patterns.

B. $1 \times 60 = 60$

$10 \times 60 = 600$

$100 \times 60 = 6000$

C. $50 \times 4 = 200$

$50 \times 40 = 2000$

$50 \times 400 = 20,000$

Multiply. Study each pattern.

1. 1×70
2. 10×70
3. 100×70

4. 3×60
5. 30×60
6. 300×60

7. 20×4
8. 20×40
9. 20×400

10. 8×50
11. 80×50
12. 800×50

13. 9×30
14. 90×30
15. 900×30

Multiply.

16. 40 × 60   17. 20 × 90   18. 80 × 90   19. 60 × 80

20. 70 × 70   21. 90 × 40   22. 10 × 40   23. 100 × 40

24. 900 × 70   25. 500 × 50   26. 700 × 60   27. 20 × 700

28. 90 × 800   29. 60 × 50   30. 30 × 300   31. 10 × 800

32. 10 × 10   33. 100 × 10   ★34. 900 × 900   ★35. 8000 × 40

36. On a one-week bicycle trip, the cyclists rode 30 hours. They traveled 20 kilometers per hour. How many kilometers did they travel during the trip?

37. A train traveled 70 kilometers per hour. How far did the train travel in 50 hours?

38. An ocean liner crossed the Atlantic Ocean in 90 hours. It traveled 60 kilometers per hour. How many kilometers did the ocean liner travel?

39. One month a pilot flew 40 hours. The pilot traveled about 400 kilometers per hour. About how many kilometers did the pilot fly that month?

Estimating Products

A. A school needs 38 new desks. The desks cost $92 each.

Ms. Adkins, the principal, thought, "These desks will cost about $3600."

Ms. Adkins **estimated** the product of 38 and 92. This is what she did.

38 × 92

40 × 90 = 3600

Round both 38 and 92 to the nearest ten. Then multiply.

Round each two-digit number to the nearest ten. Estimate each product.

B. 23 × 8

20 × 8 = 160

C. 56 × 86

60 × 90 = 5400

D. 31 × 84

30 × 80 = 2400

Estimate each product.

1. 2 × 53
   (2 × 50)

2. 6 × 58
   (6 × 60)

3. 19 × 47
   (20 × 50)

4. 49 × 71
   (50 × 70)

5. 89 × 29
   (90 × 30)

6. 18 × 83
   (20 × 80)

7. 9 × 51

8. 8 × 78

9. 57 × 6

10. 39 × 8

11. 3 × 67

12. 82 × 9

13. 61 × 21

14. 22 × 43

15. 89 × 72

16. 63 × 74

17. 58 × 34

18. 41 × 54

19. 69 × 32

20. 32 × 42

21. 52 × 67

22. 82 × 13

23. 17 × 28

24. 29 × 88

Estimate the total cost.

25. 77 film strips, $7 each

26. 38 globes, $42 each

27. 49 band uniforms, $79 each

28. 51 science kits, $29 each

29. 38 dictionaries, $5 each

30. 12 basketballs, $17 each

Time Out

This football park has 10 lettered exits and 16 numbered gates.

You are inside the park. In how many different ways can you leave through a lettered exit and a numbered gate?

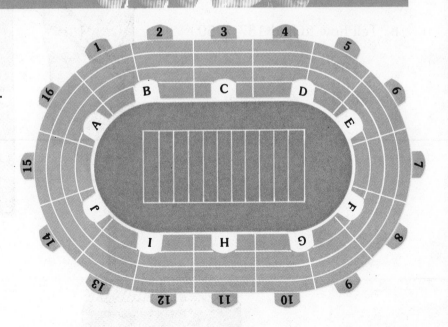

171

Multiplying with a Multiple of 10

A. Alicia's heart beats about 85 times
per minute. How many times does
it beat in one hour? Remember,
1 hour is 60 minutes.

Find 60 × 85.

$$\begin{array}{r} 85 \\ \times\,60 \\ \hline 0 \end{array}$$ Multiply by 0 ones.

$$\begin{array}{r} 85 \\ \times\,60 \\ \hline 5100 \end{array}$$ Then multiply by 6 tens.

Her heart beats about
5100 times in one hour.

B. Tell how to find 137 × 50.

$$\begin{array}{r} 137 \\ \times\ \ 50 \\ \hline 6850 \end{array}$$

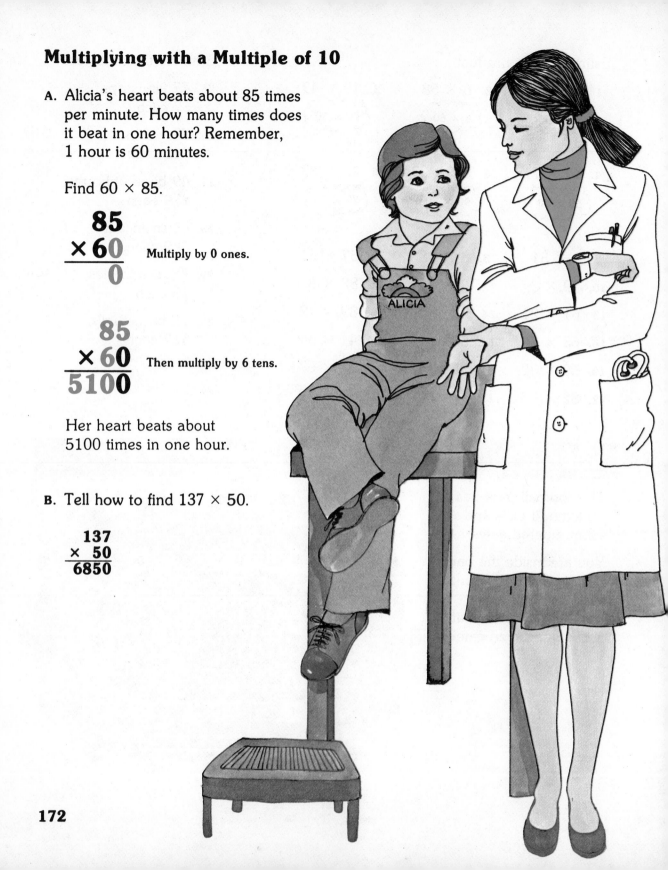

172

Give each answer.

1. $4 \times 21 = 84$
   $40 \times 21 = $ ▦

2. $3 \times 82 = 246$
   $30 \times 82 = $ ▦

3. $7 \times 45 = 315$
   $70 \times 45 = $ ▦

4. $5 \times 98 = 490$
   $50 \times 98 = $ ▦

5. $6 \times 157 = 942$
   $60 \times 157 = $ ▦

6. $8 \times 471 = 3768$
   $80 \times 471 = $ ▦

Multiply.

7. $\begin{array}{r} 34 \\ \times 20 \\ \hline \end{array}$

8. $\begin{array}{r} 31 \\ \times 30 \\ \hline \end{array}$

9. $\begin{array}{r} 72 \\ \times 40 \\ \hline \end{array}$

10. $\begin{array}{r} 53 \\ \times 30 \\ \hline \end{array}$

11. $\begin{array}{r} 62 \\ \times 90 \\ \hline \end{array}$

12. $\begin{array}{r} 73 \\ \times 50 \\ \hline \end{array}$

13. $\begin{array}{r} 96 \\ \times 60 \\ \hline \end{array}$

14. $\begin{array}{r} 75 \\ \times 90 \\ \hline \end{array}$

15. $\begin{array}{r} 69 \\ \times 40 \\ \hline \end{array}$

16. $\begin{array}{r} 87 \\ \times 50 \\ \hline \end{array}$

17. $\begin{array}{r} 58 \\ \times 90 \\ \hline \end{array}$

18. $\begin{array}{r} 79 \\ \times 80 \\ \hline \end{array}$

19. $\begin{array}{r} 213 \\ \times 40 \\ \hline \end{array}$

20. $\begin{array}{r} 141 \\ \times 30 \\ \hline \end{array}$

21. $\begin{array}{r} 329 \\ \times 30 \\ \hline \end{array}$

22. $\begin{array}{r} 178 \\ \times 50 \\ \hline \end{array}$

23. $\begin{array}{r} 145 \\ \times 80 \\ \hline \end{array}$

24. $\begin{array}{r} 258 \\ \times 40 \\ \hline \end{array}$

25. $\begin{array}{r} 316 \\ \times 60 \\ \hline \end{array}$

26. $\begin{array}{r} 224 \\ \times 90 \\ \hline \end{array}$

*27. $\begin{array}{r} 1267 \\ \times 20 \\ \hline \end{array}$

*28. $\begin{array}{r} 3123 \\ \times 60 \\ \hline \end{array}$

*29. $\begin{array}{r} 784 \\ \times 500 \\ \hline \end{array}$

*30. $\begin{array}{r} 565 \\ \times 800 \\ \hline \end{array}$

31. Nikki blinks about 12 times per minute. How many times does she blink in 1 hour? Remember, 1 hour is 60 minutes.
($60 \times 12 = $ ▦)

32. Len breathes about 23 times per minute. How many times does he breathe in 1 hour?
($60 \times 23 = $ ▦)

**More practice
Set 21, page 376**

Multiplication: Two-Digit Numbers

A. Farmer Farmington collected 28 dozen eggs. How many eggs did the farmer collect? Remember, 1 dozen is 12.

Find 28 × 12.

$$\begin{array}{r} 12 \\ \times 28 \\ \hline 96 \end{array}$$ 20 + 8

8 × 12

$$\begin{array}{r} 12 \\ \times 28 \\ \hline 96 \\ 240 \end{array}$$ 20 × 12

$$\begin{array}{r} 12 \\ \times 28 \\ \hline 96 \\ 240 \\ \hline 336 \end{array}$$ 96 + 240

The farmer collected 336 eggs.

There are 28 groups of 12 eggs. Think of 28 as 8 + 20.

8 × 12

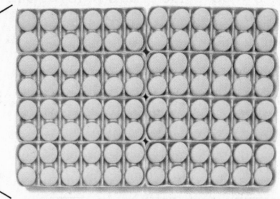

20 × 12

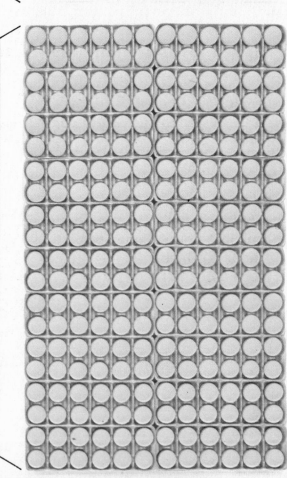

Tell how to find each answer.

B.
$$\begin{array}{r} 32 \\ \times 41 \\ \hline 32 \\ 1280 \\ \hline 1312 \end{array}$$

C.
$$\begin{array}{r} 84 \\ \times 72 \\ \hline 168 \\ 5880 \\ \hline 6048 \end{array}$$

Multiply.

1. $\begin{array}{r} 22 \\ \times 41 \end{array}$ 2. $\begin{array}{r} 31 \\ \times 23 \end{array}$ 3. $\begin{array}{r} 53 \\ \times 12 \end{array}$ 4. $\begin{array}{r} 72 \\ \times 13 \end{array}$ 5. $\begin{array}{r} 41 \\ \times 23 \end{array}$ 6. $\begin{array}{r} 23 \\ \times 14 \end{array}$ 7. $\begin{array}{r} 18 \\ \times 12 \end{array}$

8. $\begin{array}{r} 34 \\ \times 42 \end{array}$ 9. $\begin{array}{r} 78 \\ \times 21 \end{array}$ 10. $\begin{array}{r} 81 \\ \times 43 \end{array}$ 11. $\begin{array}{r} 24 \\ \times 72 \end{array}$ 12. $\begin{array}{r} 58 \\ \times 13 \end{array}$ 13. $\begin{array}{r} 25 \\ \times 15 \end{array}$ 14. $\begin{array}{r} 26 \\ \times 14 \end{array}$

15. $\begin{array}{r} 96 \\ \times 13 \end{array}$ 16. $\begin{array}{r} 64 \\ \times 17 \end{array}$ 17. $\begin{array}{r} 43 \\ \times 28 \end{array}$ 18. $\begin{array}{r} 49 \\ \times 19 \end{array}$ 19. $\begin{array}{r} 37 \\ \times 18 \end{array}$ 20. $\begin{array}{r} 79 \\ \times 21 \end{array}$ 21. $\begin{array}{r} 23 \\ \times 32 \end{array}$

22. $\begin{array}{r} 65 \\ \times 31 \end{array}$ 23. $\begin{array}{r} 52 \\ \times 33 \end{array}$ 24. $\begin{array}{r} 83 \\ \times 52 \end{array}$ 25. $\begin{array}{r} 61 \\ \times 68 \end{array}$ 26. $\begin{array}{r} 94 \\ \times 25 \end{array}$ 27. $\begin{array}{r} 74 \\ \times 32 \end{array}$ 28. $\begin{array}{r} 59 \\ \times 41 \end{array}$

29. A cow gives 85 kilograms of milk each week. How much milk does this cow give in one year? Remember, 1 year is 52 weeks.

30. A farmer sells 72 eggs per day. How many eggs has he sold in 15 days?

Multiplication: Two-Digit Numbers

There were 25 busloads of people who
came to the Cougars game. Each bus
brought 48 people. How many people
came to the game on the buses?

Find 25 × 48.

$$\begin{array}{r} 48 \\ \times\,25 \\ \hline 240 \\ 960 \\ \hline 1200 \end{array}$$

240   5×48

960   20×48

1200 $240 + 960$

1200 people came on the buses.

Multiply.

1. 36 ×24	**2.** 43 ×16	**3.** 78 ×12	**4.** 35 ×25	**5.** 42 ×36	**6.** 53 ×27	**7.** 46 ×29

8. 74 ×18	**9.** 65 ×19	**10.** 68 ×32	**11.** 83 ×34	**12.** 85 ×45	**13.** 67 ×63	**14.** 57 ×24

15. 88 ×79	**16.** 97 ×55	**17.** 69 ×52	**18.** 74 ×28	**19.** 79 ×47	**20.** 58 ×46	**21.** 87 ×68

22. 49 × 17   **23.** 87 × 15   **24.** 98 × 23   **25.** 83 × 57   **26.** 57 × 37

27. 94 × 77   **28.** 79 × 56   **29.** 96 × 37   **30.** 84 × 66   **31.** 83 × 53

32. 89 × 89   **33.** 75 × 38   **34.** 76 × 46   **35.** 95 × 95   **36.** 98 × 86

37. It costs $85 to rent a bus. How much would it cost to rent 27 buses?

38. There are 42 rows of box seats with 45 seats in each row. How many box seats are there?

39. About 38 baseballs are used in a game. How many baseballs are used in 96 games?

*40. Station XTZ gives away 35 tickets to each of 48 games. Each ticket is worth $4. How much are all the tickets worth?

More practice
Set 22, page 377

Multiplication: Two-Digit and Three-Digit Numbers

A. The submarine *Nautilus* can travel at a speed of 32 kilometers per hour. At this speed, how far can it travel in a week? 1 week is 168 hours.

Find 32 × 168.

$$
\begin{array}{r}
168 \\
\times\ 32 \\
\hline
336 \\
5040 \\
\hline
5376
\end{array}
$$

336   2 × 168

5040   30 × 168

5376   336 + 5040

The submarine can travel 5376 kilometers in a week.

B. Tell how to find 74 × 103.

$$
\begin{array}{r}
103 \\
\times\ 74 \\
\hline
412 \\
7210 \\
\hline
7622
\end{array}
$$

Multiply.

1. 212
× 34

2. 331
× 23

3. 525
× 12

4. 436
× 15

5. 135
× 45

6. 172
× 28

7. 445
× 13

8. 271
× 17

9. 318
× 36

10. 243
× 29

11. 195
× 52

12. 168
× 43

13. 351
× 27

14. 775
× 35

15. 275
× 84

16. 245
× 44

17. 960
× 16

18. 840
× 26

19. 234
× 77

20. 918
× 53

21. 508
× 92

22. 809
× 47

*23. 1388
× 37

*24. 819
×162

25. In 1958, the *Nautilus* crossed the Atlantic Ocean in 156 hours. At a speed of 32 kilometers per hour, how far could the *Nautilus* travel in 156 hours?

26. In 1960, the submarine *Triton* went around the world in 84 days. If it traveled 790 kilometers per day, how many kilometers did it travel in all?

**More practice
Set 23, page 377**

Multiplication: Money

A. An admission ticket to the Mountain Trails Nature Center costs $0.45. How much did the science club pay for 28 tickets?

Find 28 × $0.45.

Think of $0.45 as 45 cents. Multiply 45 cents by 28.

$$
\begin{array}{r}
45 \\
\times 28 \\
\hline
360 \\
900 \\
\hline
1260
\end{array}
$$

1260 cents can be written as $12.60

The science club paid $12.60.

B. Tell how to find 19 × $2.16.

$$
\begin{array}{r}
216 \longrightarrow \$2.16 \\
\times\ 19 \\
\hline
1944 \\
2160 \\
\hline
4104 \longrightarrow \$41.04
\end{array}
$$

Multiply.

1. $0.32 × 24	**2.** $0.41 × 12	**3.** $0.37 × 15	**4.** $0.53 × 17
5. $2.11 × 42	**6.** $1.22 × 67	**7.** $1.20 × 14	**8.** $2.40 × 18
9. $1.07 × 25	**10.** $1.05 × 36	**11.** $3.68 × 32	**12.** $4.27 × 24
13. $0.73 × 61	**14.** $4.36 × 31	**15.** $6.15 × 13	**16.** $0.34 × 52

17. 48 × $0.29   **18.** 35 × $0.37

19. 23 × $2.48   **20.** 29 × $0.63

21. 57 × $0.92   **22.** 82 × $1.46

★23. 76 × $15.85   **★24.** 54 × $24.55

25. There are 27 nature books in a set. Each book costs $1.50. How much does the set cost?

26. A set of slides costs $0.95. How much do 12 sets cost?

27. Last spring, the nature center planted 72 trees. Each tree cost $6.98. How much did the trees cost?

28. Bird seed costs $2.95 a bag. One winter the nature center used 45 bags of seed. How much did the seed cost?

Using Multiplication

Multiply. Use the code to find
the answer to the riddle.

What occurs once in every minute,
twice in every moment, but never
in a thousand years?

Code	
884	E
1236	L
2990	M
3612	I
5152	R
6696	H
8112	T
9200	S

Word 1

1. 84 × 43

2. 208 × 39

Word 2

3. 42 × 86

4. 200 × 46

Word 3

5. 624 × 13

6. 18 × 372

7. 34 × 26

Word 4

8. 103 × 12

9. 52 × 17

10. 104 × 78

11. 312 × 26

12. 68 × 13

13. 92 × 56

Word 5

14. 130 × 23

There are 60 seconds in 1 minute.
How many seconds in

15. 10 minutes?   **16.** 60 minutes?

17. 90 minutes?   **18.** 120 minutes?

There are 60 minutes in 1 hour.
How many minutes in

19. 12 hours?   **20.** 24 hours?

21. 72 hours?   **22.** 168 hours?

There are 24 hours in 1 day.
How many hours in

23. 28 days?   **24.** 60 days?

25. 180 days?   **26.** 365 days?

There are 12 months in 1 year.
How many months in

27. 15 years?   **28.** 25 years?

29. 75 years?   **30.** 125 years?

There are 52 weeks in 1 year.
How many weeks in

31. 18 years?   **32.** 48 years?

33. 65 years?   **34.** 120 years?

There are 365 days in 1 year.
How many days in

35. 12 years?   **36.** 35 years?

37. 48 years?   **38.** 72 years?

Keeping Skillful

Add.

1. $\begin{array}{r} 4.8 \\ +3.1 \end{array}$	**2.** $\begin{array}{r} 6.7 \\ +2.8 \end{array}$	**3.** $\begin{array}{r} 8.71 \\ +3.42 \end{array}$
4. $\begin{array}{r} 4.05 \\ +3.26 \end{array}$	**5.** $\begin{array}{r} 58.5 \\ +\ 3.1 \end{array}$	**6.** $\begin{array}{r} 14.25 \\ +37.64 \end{array}$

Subtract.

7. $\begin{array}{r} 8.9 \\ -5.6 \end{array}$	**8.** $\begin{array}{r} 7.2 \\ -2.8 \end{array}$	**9.** $\begin{array}{r} 62.4 \\ -\ 9.5 \end{array}$
10. $\begin{array}{r} 9.31 \\ -4.17 \end{array}$	**11.** $\begin{array}{r} 6.55 \\ -0.74 \end{array}$	**12.** $\begin{array}{r} 86.19 \\ -41.37 \end{array}$

Add or subtract.

13. $15.9 - 8.4$

14. $48.1 - 37.6$

15. $1.76 + 3.89$

16. $2.67 - 1.39$

17. $37.6 + 8$

18. $6.79 + 3.11$

19. $8.65 - 0.46$

20. $37 - 13.19$

21. $63.4 + 0.7$

22. $31.87 + 9.04$

23. $159.3 + 760.4$

24. $26.03 - 19.52$

Problem Solving: Choosing the Operation

READ In 1860, it cost about $160 per pound to send mail by Pony Express. How much was collected for 18 pounds of mail?

DECIDE Multiply $160 by 18.

$18 \times \$160 = n$

SOLVE

```
   160
 ×  18
  1280
  1600
  2880
```

ANSWER $n = 2880$

$2880

Write an equation. Give each answer.

1. By 1861, the cost of sending mail by Pony Express was down to $32 per pound. How much money was collected for 18 pounds of mail? $(32 \times 18 = n)$

2. A Pony Express rider weighed 125 pounds and carried about 28 pounds of mail and supplies. What was the total weight? $(125 + 28 = n)$

3. When most horses cost about $48 each, Pony Express horses cost about $150. How much more did a Pony Express horse cost? $(150 - 48 = n)$

4. In 1776, it cost $0.25 to send a one-page letter from Boston to Richmond. How much did it cost to send 12 one-page letters?

5. In 1776, there were 28 post offices in the United States. By 1795, there were 425 more. How many post offices were there in 1795?

6. In 1975, it cost $0.31 to send a letter from the United States to England. How much did it cost to send 36 letters?

7. Laverne could send a package first class for $3.10 or by parcel post for $1.28. How much more would it cost to send the package first class?

8. A company bought 225 sheets of stamps. There were 50 stamps on each sheet. How many stamps did the company buy?

9. A company shipped 148 cartons of books. Each carton weighed 35 pounds. What was the total weight of the cartons of books?

10. A postal worker delivered 398 pieces of mail in the morning and 245 pieces in the afternoon. How many pieces did the worker deliver that day?

*11. In 1901, there were 76,945 post offices in the United States. In 1976, there were 30,521 post offices. How many more post offices were there in 1901?

*12. Pony Express horses cost about $150 each. What was the cost of 500 of these horses?

Shipping Clerk

John Lehman is a shipping clerk for a
record company. With each shipment
he includes a packing slip like the
one shown below.

To find the total cost for 20 albums
of Marty Martin's Hits, John multiplied
$3.29 by 20.

$$\begin{array}{r} \$\ 3.29 \\ \times\ \ 20 \\ \hline \$65.80 \end{array}$$

John wrote the total
amount in the last
column of the
packing slip.

For each exercise, find the total cost.

Jupiter Record Company
Recordville, USA

Ship To: Red Spot Music Shop
Music City, Canada

Number	Album	Price Each	Total
20	Marty Martin's Hits	$3.29	**$65.80**
12	Favorites of Yesterday	$1.79	**1.**
18	Sing Along with Kim	$2.50	**2.**
75	Art Asher Plays the Guitar	$0.79	**3.**
4	Classical Favorites	$12.25	**4.**
25	Broadway's Top Tunes	$4.15	**5.**
35	Music for Disco Dancing	$1.98	**6.**

What's in an Age?

Tammy is 12 years old today.

A. About how many days old is she?

12 × 365 = 4380
Years Days in
1 year

She is about 4380 days old.

B. About how many hours old is she?

4380 × 24 = 105,120
Days Hours in
1 day

She is about 105,120 hours old.

C. About how many minutes old is she?

105,120 × 60 = 6,307,200
Hours Minutes in
1 hour

She is about 6,307,200 minutes old.

Complete the table.

Years	Days	Hours	Minutes
1	1.	2.	3.
2	4.	5.	6.
8	7.	8.	9.
9	10.	11.	12.
10	13.	14.	15.
11	16.	17.	18.
25	19.	20.	21.
50	22.	23.	24.
100	25.	26.	27.

George Washington was alive 200 years ago. About how long ago was this in

28. days?   **29.** hours?

Christopher Columbus was alive 500 years ago. About how long ago was this in

30. days?   **31.** hours?

On your last birthday, about how old were you in

32. days?   **33.** hours?

34. minutes?

Chapter 9 Test
Multiplication: Two-Digit Multipliers, pages 168–187

Multiply.

1. 60×40

2. 20×900

3. 700×80

4. 40×50

Estimate each product.

5. 4×29

6. 38×71

Multiply.

7. $\begin{array}{r} 83 \\ \times 60 \\ \hline \end{array}$

8. $\begin{array}{r} 97 \\ \times 40 \\ \hline \end{array}$

9. $\begin{array}{r} 148 \\ \times 20 \\ \hline \end{array}$

10. $\begin{array}{r} 271 \\ \times 70 \\ \hline \end{array}$

11. $\begin{array}{r} 39 \\ \times 15 \\ \hline \end{array}$

12. $\begin{array}{r} 94 \\ \times 23 \\ \hline \end{array}$

13. $\begin{array}{r} 28 \\ \times 81 \\ \hline \end{array}$

14. $\begin{array}{r} 37 \\ \times 35 \\ \hline \end{array}$

15. $\begin{array}{r} 67 \\ \times 46 \\ \hline \end{array}$

16. $\begin{array}{r} 95 \\ \times 72 \\ \hline \end{array}$

17. $\begin{array}{r} 122 \\ \times 43 \\ \hline \end{array}$

18. $\begin{array}{r} 308 \\ \times 83 \\ \hline \end{array}$

19. $\begin{array}{r} 214 \\ \times 27 \\ \hline \end{array}$

20. $\begin{array}{r} 432 \\ \times 56 \\ \hline \end{array}$

21. $\begin{array}{r} \$0.75 \\ \times 29 \\ \hline \end{array}$

22. $\begin{array}{r} \$1.08 \\ \times 64 \\ \hline \end{array}$

Find each answer.

23. A store charged $5.98 for a lilac bush. How much would 12 bushes cost?

24. A tree farmer planted 24 rows of trees with 36 trees in each row. How many trees did he plant?

25. A city planted 147 maple trees and 284 pine trees. What is the total number of trees that were planted?

Problems Around Us

1. A baby blue whale gains about 4 kilograms per hour. How many kilograms would the whale gain in one day? (1 day is 24 hours.)

2. An African elephant drank 177.9 liters of water one day and 158.7 liters the next day. How many liters did it drink in the two days?

3. A marine crocodile weighed 1814 kilograms. How much would 6 of these crocodiles weigh?

4. A giant earthworm of Australia measures about 3.5 meters long when resting. It can stretch out to measure 6.4 meters. How much longer is the earthworm when it is stretched out?

5. A white oak uses 57 liters of water per day during its growing season. How much water would it use during a 20-day growing season?

6. In one hour a garden snail moved 58.42 centimeters, and the next hour it moved 53.34 centimeters. How far did it move?

7. A three-toed sloth of South America travels about 2 meters per minute. How many meters does the sloth travel in 1 hour? (1 hour is 60 minutes.)

8. A frog jumped 3.96 meters in one jump. A person jumped 3.66 meters in one jump. How much farther did the frog jump?

9. A gold brick weighs 0 kilograms at the earth's center. How much would 5 gold bricks weigh at the earth's center?

10. The first hour a greyhound ran 64.36 kilometers, and the second hour it ran 61.14 kilometers. How far did it run?

11. An African elephant eats about 113 kilograms of plants per day. How many kilograms of plants would the elephant eat in 30 days?

12. A hummingbird beats its wings about 85 times per second. How many times does the hummingbird beat its wings in 1 minute? (1 minute is 60 seconds.)

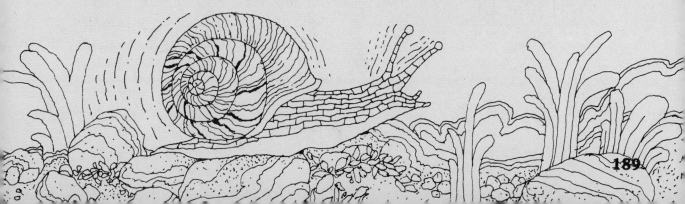

Individualized Skills Maintenance

Diagnose

A *pages 94–97*

17.2 + 48.9

13.92 + 58.73

0.38 + 3.95 + 6

B *pages 98–101*

25.3 − 16.4

38.42 − 15.87

12 − 7.34

Practice

A

1. $\begin{array}{r} 7.3 \\ +\,0.2 \\ \hline \end{array}$
2. $\begin{array}{r} 36.4 \\ +\,13.7 \\ \hline \end{array}$
3. $\begin{array}{r} 1.42 \\ +\,3.77 \\ \hline \end{array}$
4. $\begin{array}{r} 22.9 \\ +\,83.5 \\ \hline \end{array}$
5. $\begin{array}{r} 16.58 \\ +\,25.37 \\ \hline \end{array}$
6. $\begin{array}{r} 27.31 \\ +\,16.92 \\ \hline \end{array}$

7. $\begin{array}{r} 9.1 \\ +\,3.5 \\ \hline \end{array}$
8. $\begin{array}{r} 46.3 \\ +\,87.2 \\ \hline \end{array}$
9. $\begin{array}{r} 7.65 \\ +\,3.24 \\ \hline \end{array}$
10. $\begin{array}{r} 0.86 \\ +\,2.97 \\ \hline \end{array}$
11. $\begin{array}{r} 12.64 \\ +\,9.08 \\ \hline \end{array}$
12. $\begin{array}{r} 34.75 \\ +\,10.38 \\ \hline \end{array}$

13. 0.6 + 0.8
14. 4.3 + 2.9 + 5.8
15. 6 + 3.2 + 0.8
16. 4.82 + 1.09
17. 7.25 + 3 + 4.87
18. 0.76 + 1.35 + 2.19
19. 7.38 + 2.91
20. 3.26 + 48.73 + 6
21. 9.16 + 0.34 + 2

B

22. $\begin{array}{r} 6.3 \\ -\,0.8 \\ \hline \end{array}$
23. $\begin{array}{r} 47.2 \\ -\,38.9 \\ \hline \end{array}$
24. $\begin{array}{r} 3.65 \\ -\,1.72 \\ \hline \end{array}$
25. $\begin{array}{r} 46.3 \\ -\,25.6 \\ \hline \end{array}$
26. $\begin{array}{r} 75.34 \\ -\,18.92 \\ \hline \end{array}$
27. $\begin{array}{r} 62.51 \\ -\,38.24 \\ \hline \end{array}$

28. $\begin{array}{r} 7.5 \\ -\,3.9 \\ \hline \end{array}$
29. $\begin{array}{r} 38.5 \\ -\,24.6 \\ \hline \end{array}$
30. $\begin{array}{r} 3.96 \\ -\,0.57 \\ \hline \end{array}$
31. $\begin{array}{r} 5.38 \\ -\,2.47 \\ \hline \end{array}$
32. $\begin{array}{r} 36.27 \\ -\,18.19 \\ \hline \end{array}$
33. $\begin{array}{r} 48.51 \\ -\,24.76 \\ \hline \end{array}$

34. 0.7 − 0.4
35. 6.2 − 4.7
36. 2.18 − 0.35
37. 3.56 − 1.29
38. 8 − 3.2
39. 25.9 − 6
40. 76.1 − 25.4
41. 80.2 − 31.9
42. 8.3 − 2.7
43. 3 − 1.8
44. 7.31 − 4.28
45. 12.6 − 9

Unit 3 Review

Chapter 7, pages 128–142

Copy and complete the addition sentence and the multiplication sentence for this picture.

1.

$2 + 2 + 2 + 2 + 2 + 2 =$ ▦
$6 × 2 =$ ▦

Multiply.

2.	6 ×2	3.	8 ×3	4.	5 ×2	5.	7 ×5
6.	9 ×4	7.	6 ×5	8.	2 ×1	9.	4 ×0
10.	8 ×6	11.	9 ×8	12.	8 ×7	13.	9 ×9
14.	7 ×1	15.	6 ×9	16.	9 ×0	17.	7 ×6

Chapter 8, pages 144–166

Multiply.

18. $8 × 100$ 19. $72 × 10$

20. $24 × 1000$ 21. $5 × 600$

22. $6 × 80$ 23. $7 × 2000$

24.	11 × 7	25.	72 × 4	26.	37 × 6
27.	48 × 3	28.	282 × 4	29.	1141 × 6
30.	109 × 6	31.	230 × 5	32.	176 × 3
33.	265 × 2	34.	$3.75 × 5	35.	$12.49 × 3

Chapter 9, pages 168–187

Multiply.

36. $60 × 40$ 37. $500 × 70$

38.	95 ×60	39.	138 × 40	40.	28 ×16
41.	49 ×23	42.	525 × 13	43.	243 × 17
44.	$1.09 × 26	45.	$2.98 × 12	46.	$0.75 × 6

47. Josh charges $0.25 to sweep a sidewalk. How much will he earn if he sweeps 13 sidewalks?

Unit 3 Test
Chapters 7-9, pages 128-188

Multiply.

1. 9
    × 2

2. 4
    × 3

3. 8
    × 3

4. 7
    × 4

5. 8
    × 5

6. 3
    × 5

7. 4
    × 6

8. 6
    × 7

9. 9
    × 6

10. 2
     × 9

11. 9
     × 8

12. 9
     × 9

13. 5
     × 0

14. 1
     × 1

15. 24 × 10

16. 11 × 1000

17. 17 × 100

18. 4 × 3000

19. 7 × 600

20. 50 × 30

21.   63
    × 2

22. 1323
    ×   3

23.   27
    × 5

24. 361
    ×   8

25. 407
    ×   8

26. 384
    ×   3

27. 599
    ×   6

28. $3.27
    ×   8

29. $4.98
    ×   9

30.   63
    × 30

31. 596
    × 40

32.   16
    × 27

33. 827
    × 55

34. $0.99
    ×   34

35. A farmer collected 145 eggs per day for 16 days. How many eggs did he collect in all?

Unit 4

Chapter 10 Measurement

Time

A. Each clock shows that the time is fifteen minutes after six.

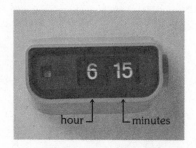 

6:15
six-fifteen

6:15 A.M. is between **midnight** and **noon.**

6:15 P.M. is between **noon** and **midnight.**

B. The calendar shows days, weeks, and months in a year.

March						
Sun.	Mon.	Tues.	Wed.	Thurs.	Fri.	Sat.
			1	2	3	4
5	6	7	8	9	10	11
12	13	14	15	16	17	18
19	20	21	22	23	24	25
26	27	28	29	30	31	

The days of the week are Sunday, Monday, Tuesday, Wednesday, Thursday, Friday, and Saturday.

The months of the year are January, February, March, April, May, June, July, August, September, October, November, and December.

On this calendar, the third of March is a Friday.
One week from March 3 is Friday, March 10.

The twenty-ninth of March is a Wednesday.
One week before March 29 is Wednesday, March 22.

The fifth of March is a Sunday.
Three weeks from March 5 is Sunday, March 26.

c. Here is a chart to help you measure time.

60 seconds = 1 minute	12 months = 1 year
60 minutes = 1 hour	365 days = 1 year
24 hours = 1 day	366 days = 1 leap year
7 days = 1 week	100 years = 1 century

Write each time as A.M. or P.M.

1. Eat breakfast at 7:45 ▦
2. Practice piano at 4:30 ▦
3. Play outside at 2:00 ▦
4. Deliver papers at 6:30 ▦
5. Watch TV at 4:00 ▦
6. Eat lunch at 11:45 ▦
7. Wake up at 8:00 ▦
8. Practice soccer at 5:45 ▦
9. Eat dinner at 6:15 ▦
10. Go bike riding at 3:30 ▦
11. Go to the library at 10:30 ▦
12. Go shopping at 12:15 ▦

Use the calendar on page 194.
Write the day and date that is

13. 2 weeks from March 2.
14. 1 week before March 20.
15. 3 weeks from March 4.
16. 4 weeks from March 3.

Complete each sentence. Use seconds, minutes, or hours.

17. Mary slept 10 (?) last night.
18. Sam's violin lesson lasts 30 (?).
19. Dee rides to school in 15 (?).
20. Bill can wash his face in 45 (?).

Complete each sentence.
Use days, weeks, months, years, or centuries.

21. Pat's grandfather is 58 (?) old.
22. October has 31 (?).
23. America was discovered about 5 (?) ago.
24. There are about 4 (?) in 1 month.

Centimeter and Decimeter

The **centimeter** (cm) and **decimeter** (dm) are metric units of length.

A. The width of your little finger is about 1 centimeter.

B. The width of this hand is about 1 decimeter.

1 dm = 10 cm

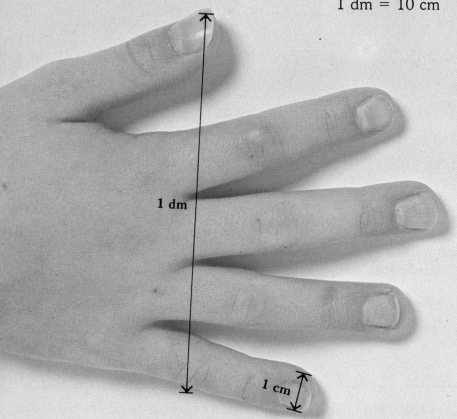

1 dm

1 cm

Estimate the length of each object to the nearest centimeter. Then measure each object.

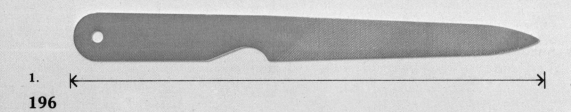

1.

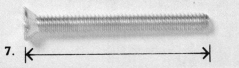

2. |←————————————→| 3. |←————→|

4. |←————→| 5. |←————————→|

6. |←————————————————→|

7. |←————————————→| 8. |←————→|

9. |←————————————————→|

Tell if each measure is sensible.
Use yes or no.

10. A pencil is about 1 dm long.

11. A book is about 2 cm long.

12. A carton of milk is about 10 dm high.

13. A cup is about 8 cm high.

Keeping Skillful

1. 6 ×7   2. 2 ×4   3. 6 ×3

4. 8 ×5   5. 4 ×6   6. 3 ×4

7. 5 ×5   8. 3 ×8   9. 8 ×4

10. 4 ×4   11. 3 ×7   12. 5 ×4

13. 7 ×4   14. 3 ×9   15. 6 ×5

16. 7 ×7   17. 6 ×6   18. 7 ×5

19. 9 ×9   20. 9 ×5   21. 8 ×6

22. 9 ×7   23. 4 ×9   24. 8 ×8

25. 8 ×9   26. 7 ×8   27. 6 ×9

28. 5 ×3   29. 6 ×8   30. 7 ×6

Meter and Kilometer

The **meter** (m) and **kilometer** (km) are also metric units of length.

A. A passenger seat on a school bus is about 1 meter long.

$$1 \text{ m} = 100 \text{ cm}$$

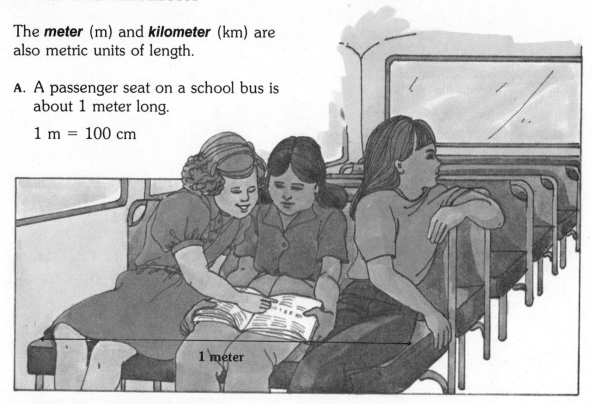

1 meter

B. The total length of 90 school buses is about 1 kilometer.

$$1 \text{ km} = 1000 \text{ m}$$

Which unit would you use to measure each object?
Use meter or kilometer.

1.

2.

3.

4.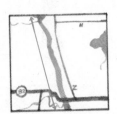

5.

6.

Choose the more sensible measure.

7. Length of a baseball bat:
1 meter or 1 kilometer

8. Length of a railroad train:
2 meters or 2 kilometers

9. Height of a man:
2 meters or 2 kilometers

10. Height of a room:
4 meters or 4 kilometers

11. Height of a basketball hoop:
3 meters or 3 kilometers

12. Length of a curtain:
2 meters or 2 kilometers

13. Length of a football field:
96 meters or 96 kilometers

14. Height of a sunflower:
2 meters or 2 kilometers

15. Width of a door:
1 meter or 1 kilometer

16. Depth of a swimming pool:
4 meters or 4 kilometers

17. Length of a car:
5 meters or 5 kilometers

18. Distance walked in 15 minutes:
1 meter or 1 kilometer

19. Length of a river:
40 meters or 40 kilometers

20. Length of a long-jump:
7 meters or 7 kilometers

21. Distance traveled by a letter
in two days:
360 meters or 360 kilometers

22. Distance a car travels in
one hour:
88 meters or 88 kilometers

Using Measures of Length

Which unit would you use to measure these objects?
Use centimeter, meter, or kilometer.

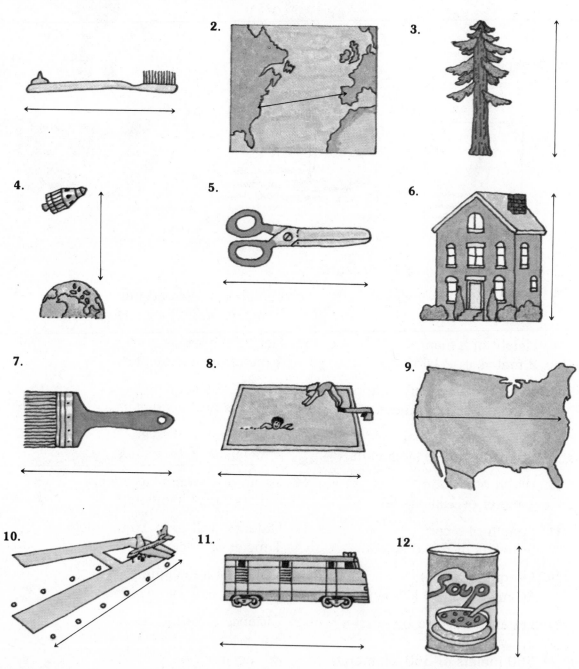

2.

3.

4.

5.

6.

7.

8.

9.

10.

11.

12.

Choose the most sensible measure.

13. Width of a nickel:
    2 cm   2 dm   2 m

14. Height of a dog:
    75 cm   75 dm   75 km

15. Length of a hammer:
    3 cm   3 dm   3 m

16. Height of a room:
    3 dm   3 m   3 km

17. Width of a TV screen:
    5 cm   5 dm   5 km

18. Length of a dinner fork:
    20 cm   20 m   20 km

19. Length of a wagon:
    1 dm   1 m   1 km

20. Width of a shoe:
    8 cm   8 m   8 km

21. Length of a whale:
    22 cm   22 dm   22 m

22. Length of a soccer field:
    100 cm   100 m   100 km

23. Length of a 72-car train:
    1 dm   1 m   1 km

24. Width of a book:
    15 cm   15 dm   15 m

25. Length of a stapler:
    15 cm   15 m   15 km

26. Distance from home to school:
    2 cm   2 dm   2 km

27. Height of a table:
    8 dm   8 m   8 km

28. Length of a saw:
    7 cm   7 dm   7 km

Find each answer.

29. Nadia and her parents drove 325 kilometers before lunch and 272 kilometers after lunch. How far did they drive that day?

30. The swimming pool at the motel was 25 meters long. Nadia swam this distance 6 times. How many meters did she swim?

31. Nadia is 112 centimeters tall. Her father is 200 centimeters tall. How much taller is her father?

32. Each day for a week Nadia biked 17 kilometers. How many kilometers did she bike during the week? (1 week is 7 days.)

Gram and Kilogram

The **gram** (g) and **kilogram** (kg) are
metric units for measuring weight.

A. A bean weighs about 1 gram.

B. A cantaloupe weighs
about 1 kilogram.

$$1 \text{ kg} = 1000 \text{ g}$$

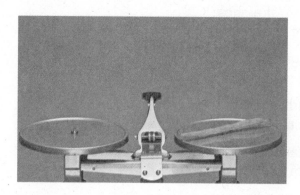

Which unit of weight would you use for each object?
Use gram or kilogram.

1.

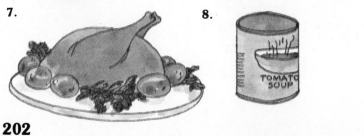

2.

3.

4.

5.

6.

7.

8.

9.

202

Choose the more sensible measure.

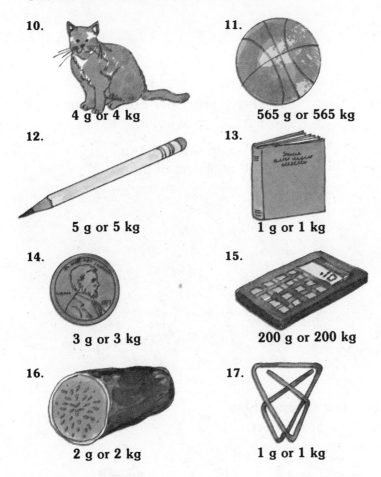

10.
4 g or 4 kg

11.
565 g or 565 kg

12.
5 g or 5 kg

13.
1 g or 1 kg

14.
3 g or 3 kg

15.
200 g or 200 kg

16.
2 g or 2 kg

17.
1 g or 1 kg

18. Bowling ball: 7 g or 7 kg

19. Dime: 2 g or 2 kg

20. Car: 1500 g or 1500 kg

21. Bag of potatoes: 5 g or 5 kg

22. Eraser: 3 g or 3 kg

23. Can of nuts: 370 g or 370 kg

24. 9-year-old girl: 37 g or 37 kg

25. Man: 80 g or 80 kg

26. Scissors: 60 g or 60 kg

Time Out

At least nine math words are hidden in this maze.

To find a word, start in any square and move one space in any direction until a word is made.

Do not use the same square twice for the same word.

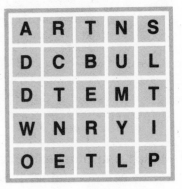

A	R	T	N	S
D	C	B	U	L
D	T	E	M	T
W	N	R	Y	I
O	E	T	L	P

Liter and Milliliter

The *liter* (L) and *milliliter* (mL) are metric units of *capacity.*

A. This milk carton holds about 1 liter of milk.

1 L = 1000 mL

B. This eyedropper holds about 1 milliliter of liquid.

This cup holds about 250 milliliters of liquid.

Which unit of measure would you use to show how much each container holds? Use liter or milliliter.

1.

2.

3.

4.

5.

6.

Choose the more sensible measure.

7.

2 mL or 2 L

8.

250 mL or 250 L

9.

15 mL or 15 L

10.

1 mL or 1 L

11.

5 mL or 5 L

12.

4 mL or 4 L

13.

200 mL or 200 L

14.

4 mL or 4 L

15. Washing machine: 40 mL or 40 L

16. Car's gas tank: 80 mL or 80 L

17. Water pail: 8 mL or 8 L

18. Can of soup: 250 mL or 250 L

19. Teapot: 700 mL or 700 L

20. Large flower vase: 1 mL or 1 L

21. Bowl of soup: 100 mL or 100 L

22. Mixing bowl: 3 mL or 3 L

23. Carton of cream: 125 mL or 125 L

Keeping Skillful

1. $\begin{array}{r} 57 \\ \times\ 6 \\ \hline \end{array}$
2. $\begin{array}{r} 43 \\ \times\ 8 \\ \hline \end{array}$

3. $\begin{array}{r} 68 \\ \times\ 7 \\ \hline \end{array}$
4. $\begin{array}{r} 23 \\ \times\ 9 \\ \hline \end{array}$

5. $\begin{array}{r} 451 \\ \times\ 7 \\ \hline \end{array}$
6. $\begin{array}{r} 780 \\ \times\ 3 \\ \hline \end{array}$

7. $\begin{array}{r} 716 \\ \times\ 5 \\ \hline \end{array}$
8. $\begin{array}{r} 312 \\ \times\ 8 \\ \hline \end{array}$

9. $\begin{array}{r} 379 \\ \times\ 4 \\ \hline \end{array}$
10. $\begin{array}{r} 532 \\ \times\ 9 \\ \hline \end{array}$

11. $\begin{array}{r} 487 \\ \times\ 6 \\ \hline \end{array}$
12. $\begin{array}{r} 5603 \\ \times\ 8 \\ \hline \end{array}$

13. $\begin{array}{r} 9837 \\ \times\ 2 \\ \hline \end{array}$
14. $\begin{array}{r} 2713 \\ \times\ 5 \\ \hline \end{array}$

15. $\begin{array}{r} 6473 \\ \times\ 3 \\ \hline \end{array}$
16. $\begin{array}{r} 6179 \\ \times\ 4 \\ \hline \end{array}$

17. $\begin{array}{r} 3409 \\ \times\ 7 \\ \hline \end{array}$
18. $\begin{array}{r} 1341 \\ \times\ 9 \\ \hline \end{array}$

19. $\begin{array}{r} 4193 \\ \times\ 5 \\ \hline \end{array}$
20. $\begin{array}{r} 6415 \\ \times\ 6 \\ \hline \end{array}$

Temperature

The degree **Celsius** (°C) is used to measure temperature.

This thermometer shows a temperature of 10 degrees Celsius (10°C).

100	Water boils
90	
80	
70	
60	
50	
40	
30	Very warm day
20	Room temperature
10	Cool day
0	Water freezes
−10	Ice skating weather
−20	
−30	

Choose the more sensible temperature.

1.

35°C or 10°C

2.

⁻10°C or 10°C

3.

20°C or ⁻15°C

4.

20°C or 90°C

5. Hot soup: 80°C or 20°C

6. Warm summer day: 75°C or 25°C

7. Snowstorm : ⁻10°C or 30°C

8. Fall day: 45°C or 10°C

9. Swimming weather: 0°C or 32°C

10. Warm bread: 30°C or 0°C

11. Spring day: 15°C or 55°C

12. Falling rain: 60°C or 18°C

13. Sledding weather: 20°C or ⁻5°C

14. Baseball weather: 25°C or 75°C

Estimating and Measuring

Copy this chart and estimate each measure.
Measure each object, using a centimeter ruler
or a meter stick. Subtract to find the difference
between your estimate and the actual measurement
for each object. Add the differences.

Compare your chart with a friend's. The person
with the lower sum is the "Best Estimator."

Object	Estimate	Actual measurement	Difference
Width of your desk	_____ cm	_____ cm	_____
Length of your math book	_____ cm	_____ cm	_____
Height of your desk	_____ cm	_____ cm	_____
Length of a piece of chalk	_____ cm	_____ cm	_____
Length of a pencil	_____ cm	_____ cm	_____
Width of a door	_____ cm	_____ cm	_____
Width of a window	_____ m	_____ m	_____
Length of a chalkboard	_____ m	_____ m	_____
Length of a table	_____ m	_____ m	_____
Length of a bookshelf	_____ m	_____ m	_____
		Sum	_____

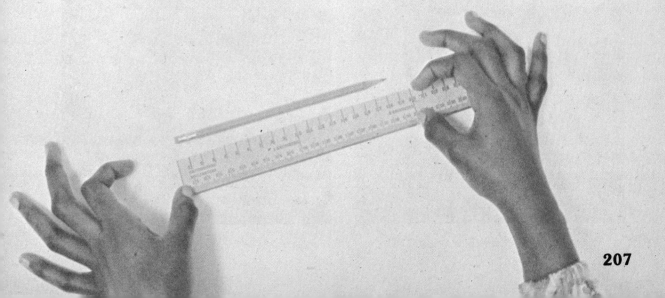

Customary Units of Length

A. The stamp is about
1 *inch* (in.) long.

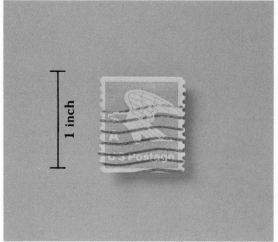

(actual size)

B. The record is about
1 *foot* (ft.) across.

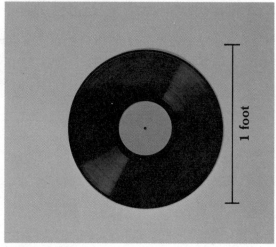

(not actual size)

C. The stove is about
1 *yard* (yd.) high.

1 yard = 3 feet

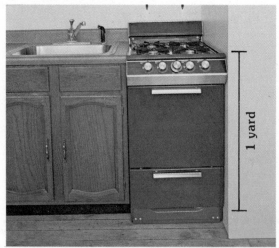

(not actual size)

D. The total length of 8 city
blocks is about 1 *mile* (mi.).

1 mile = 5280 feet

(not actual size)

Which unit would you use for each measure?
Use inches or feet.

1.

2.

3.

4.

5.

6.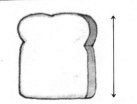

Which unit would you use for each measure?
Use yards or miles.

7.

8.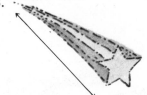

9.

Choose the more sensible measure.

10. Length of a mouse:
3 inches or 3 feet

11. Height of a table:
1 foot or 1 yard

12. Length of a car:
5 inches or 5 yards

13. Length of a river:
40 feet or 40 miles

14. Length of a room:
12 feet or 12 miles

15. Distance walked in 30 minutes:
1 yard or 1 mile

16. Height of a piano:
4 yards or 4 feet

17. Height of a building:
30 inches or 30 feet

18. Length of a bike path:
8 feet or 8 miles

19. Distance between bus stops:
1 yard or 1 mile

20. Length of a bicycle:
6 feet or 6 yards

21. Length of a baseball bat:
1 foot or 1 yard

Customary Units of Capacity and Weight

A. The **cup** (c.), the **pint** (pt.), the **quart** (qt.), and the **gallon** (gal.) are units for measuring liquids.

2 cups = 1 pint	2 pints = 1 quart	4 quarts = 1 gallon

B. The **ounce** (oz.), the **pound** (lb.), and the **ton** (T.) are units for measuring weight.

1 ounce   **1 pound**   **1 ton**

16 ounces = 1 pound   **2000 pounds = 1 ton**

Which unit would you use? Use cup, pint, quart, or gallon.

1. Car's gas tank: 20 ▦
2. Milk-shake glass: 3 ▦
3. Carton of cream: 1 ▦
4. Fish tank: 4 ▦
5. Coffeepot: 10 ▦
6. Juice pitcher: 2 ▦

Which unit would you use? Use ounce, pound, or ton.

7. Car: 2 ▦
8. Apple: 5 ▦
9. 10-year-old boy: 75 ▦
10. Moving van: 3 ▦
11. Watermelon: 5 ▦
12. Bag of potatoes: 10 ▦

Chapter 10 Test
Measurement, pages 194–210

Choose the more sensible measure.

1. Length of a pair of scissors:
   15 cm or 15 m

2. Length of a fishing rod:
   2 m or 2 km

3. Width of a kitchen table:
   1 cm or 1 m

4. Width of a book:
   15 cm or 15 m

5. Length of a desk:
   50 cm or 50 km

6. Width of a postage stamp:
   2 cm or 2 m

7. Length of an airport runway:
   1 dm or 1 km

8. Length of a dog:
   3 in. or 3 ft.

9. Height of a chair:
   1 yd. or 1 mi.

10. Width of a hallway:
    2 in. or 2 yd.

11. Length of a pencil:
    7 in. or 7 ft.

12.

20 g or 20 kg

13.

3 g or 3 kg

14. Weight of a slice of bread:
    2 oz. or 2 lb.

15. Weight of a can of beans:
    10 oz. or 10 lb.

16.

4 mL or 4 L

17.

950 mL or 950 L

18.

2 pt. or 2 gal.

19.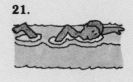

1 c. or 1 qt.

20.

−10°C or 20°C

21.

0°C or 32°C

22. Glass of iced tea:
    5°C or 50°C

Choose the better answer.

23. The team played baseball at
    3:30 A.M. or 3:30 P.M.

24. Jan held her breath for
    15 seconds or 15 minutes.

25. Summer vacation lasts
    2 months or 2 years.

Meaning of Division

A. Frank divided 8 keys into groups of 2. How many groups did he have?

B. Karen divided 8 keys into groups of 4. How many groups did she have?

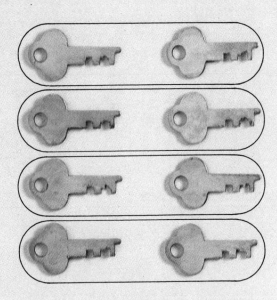

8 keys
2 keys in each group

$$8 \div 2 = 4$$

Divisor———↑   ↑———Quotient

8 keys
4 keys in each group

$$8 \div 4 = 2$$

Divisor———↑   ↑———Quotient

Copy and complete each division sentence.

1.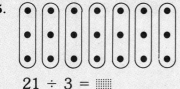

    $10 \div 5 = $ ▦

2.

    $6 \div 2 = $ ▦

3.

    $16 \div 4 = $ ▦

4.

    $24 \div 6 = $ ▦

5.

    $21 \div 3 = $ ▦

6.

    $15 \div 5 = $ ▦

7.

    $20 \div 4 = $ ▦

8.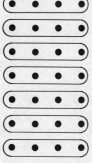

    $30 \div 6 = $ ▦

9.

    $28 \div 4 = $ ▦

10.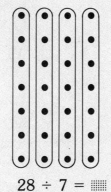

    $28 \div 7 = $ ▦

2 and 3 in Division

Bonnie wanted to find the quotient of 6 ÷ 2.

She drew 6 marks in all.

She divided them into groups of 2 marks each.

She counted to find how many groups of 2.

She wrote this division sentence.

6 ÷ 2 = 3

1.

12 ÷ 2 = ▦

2.

18 ÷ 3 = ▦

3.

21 ÷ 7 = ▦

4.

15 ÷ 3 = ▦

5.

10 ÷ 2 = ▦

6.

18 ÷ 9 = ▦

7.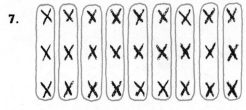

27 ÷ 3 = ▦

8.

9 ÷ 3 = ▦

9.

14 ÷ 7 = ▦

10.

16 ÷ 8 = ▦

11.

24 ÷ 8 = ▦

12.

12 ÷ 4 = ▦

Give each answer.

13. 4 ÷ 2   **14.** 6 ÷ 2   **15.** 8 ÷ 2   **16.** 10 ÷ 2   **17.** 12 ÷ 2

18. 14 ÷ 2   **19.** 16 ÷ 2   **20.** 18 ÷ 2   **21.** 4 ÷ 2   **22.** 6 ÷ 3

23. 8 ÷ 4   **24.** 10 ÷ 5   **25.** 12 ÷ 6   **26.** 14 ÷ 7   **27.** 16 ÷ 8

28. 18 ÷ 9   **29.** 6 ÷ 3   **30.** 9 ÷ 3   **31.** 12 ÷ 3   **32.** 15 ÷ 3

33. 18 ÷ 3   **34.** 21 ÷ 3   **35.** 24 ÷ 3   **36.** 27 ÷ 3   **37.** 6 ÷ 2

38. 9 ÷ 3   **39.** 12 ÷ 4   **40.** 15 ÷ 5   **41.** 18 ÷ 6   **42.** 21 ÷ 7

43. 24 ÷ 8   **44.** 27 ÷ 9   **45.** 18 ÷ 9   **46.** 24 ÷ 8   **47.** 14 ÷ 2

48. 12 ÷ 3   **49.** 16 ÷ 2   **50.** 10 ÷ 5   **51.** 21 ÷ 3   **52.** 27 ÷ 9

53. 18 ÷ 6   **54.** 12 ÷ 4   **55.** 14 ÷ 7   **56.** 16 ÷ 8   **57.** 8 ÷ 4

4 and 5 in Division

A. You can use one picture to show one division fact.

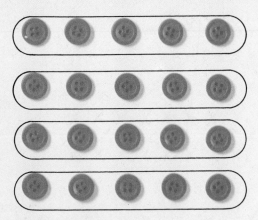

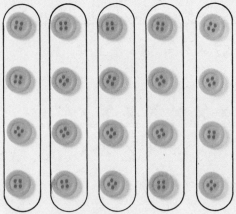

20 buttons
5 in each group
How many groups?

$20 \div 5 = 4$

20 buttons
4 in each group
How many groups?

$20 \div 4 = 5$

B. You can use a picture like this to show two division facts.

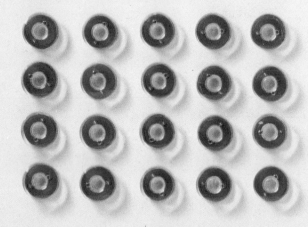

There are 20 bobbins.

Think of groups of 4.

$20 \div 4 = 5$

Think of groups of 5.

$20 \div 5 = 4$

C. You can show division in two ways.

$$36 \div 4 = 9 \qquad 4\overline{)36}^{\,9}$$

Give two division sentences for each picture.

Here's how   24 in all

$24 \div 6 = 4$
$24 \div 4 = 6$

1. 30 in all

2. 28 in all

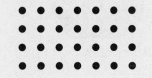

3. 32 in all

4. 45 in all

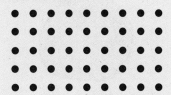

5. 35 in all

6. 40 in all

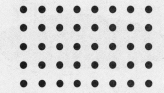

Give each answer.

7. $8 \div 4$ **8.** $12 \div 4$ **9.** $16 \div 4$ **10.** $20 \div 4$ **11.** $24 \div 4$

12. $28 \div 4$ **13.** $32 \div 4$ **14.** $36 \div 4$ **15.** $8 \div 2$ **16.** $12 \div 3$

17. $16 \div 4$ **18.** $20 \div 5$ **19.** $24 \div 6$ **20.** $28 \div 7$ **21.** $32 \div 8$

22. $36 \div 9$ **23.** $10 \div 5$ **24.** $15 \div 5$ **25.** $20 \div 5$ **26.** $25 \div 5$

27. $30 \div 5$ **28.** $35 \div 5$ **29.** $40 \div 5$ **30.** $45 \div 5$ **31.** $10 \div 2$

32. $3\overline{)15}$ **33.** $4\overline{)20}$ **34.** $5\overline{)25}$ **35.** $6\overline{)30}$ **36.** $7\overline{)35}$

37. $8\overline{)40}$ **38.** $9\overline{)45}$ **39.** $2\overline{)18}$ **40.** $3\overline{)21}$ **41.** $4\overline{)24}$

42. $2\overline{)16}$ **43.** $4\overline{)20}$ **44.** $3\overline{)12}$ **45.** $5\overline{)25}$ **46.** $3\overline{)18}$

More practice
Set 24, page 377

Using Division Facts

How many can you buy if you have

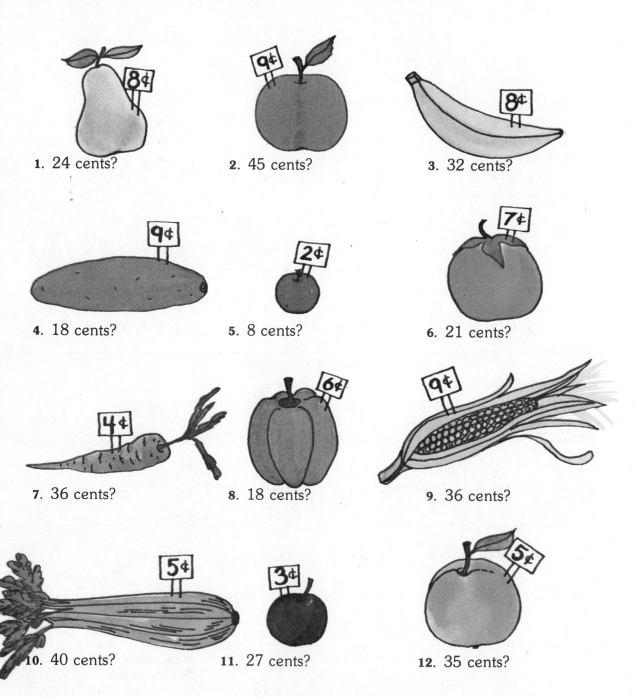

1. 24 cents?

2. 45 cents?

3. 32 cents?

4. 18 cents?

5. 8 cents?

6. 21 cents?

7. 36 cents?

8. 18 cents?

9. 36 cents?

10. 40 cents?

11. 27 cents?

12. 35 cents?

Complete each table.

	÷ 6
12	2
13. 30	
14. 18	
15. 24	

	÷ 3
16. 9	
17. 18	
18. 15	
19. 24	

	÷ 5
20. 10	
21. 45	
22. 35	
23. 20	

	÷ 4
24. 24	
25. 32	
26. 16	
27. 12	

	÷ 2
28. 18	
29. 6	
30. 12	
31. 4	

	÷ 7
32. 35	
33. 21	
34. 14	
35. 28	

	÷ 8
36. 40	
37. 16	
38. 24	
39. 32	

	÷ 9
40. 36	
41. 45	
42. 18	
43. 27	

Give each answer.

44. Nick bought 35 peaches. There were 7 peaches in each bag. How many bags of peaches did he buy?

45. Andrea bought 10 pounds of onions. How many 5-pound bags of onions did she buy?

46. Kendra bought 40 grapefruit. There were 8 grapefruit in each bag. How many bags of grapefruit did she buy?

47. Sally bought 15 bananas. There were 5 bananas in each bunch. How many bunches of bananas did she buy?

48. Mina bought 8 carrots. There were 4 carrots in each bunch. How many bunches of carrots did she buy?

49. Kyle bought 16 cucumbers. There were 4 cucumbers on each tray. How many trays of cucumbers did he buy?

0 and 1 in Division

The game of checkers is played by 2 people.

If 6 people want to play checkers, three checkerboards are needed.

$$6 \div 2 = 3$$

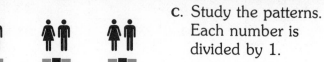

If 4 people want to play checkers, two checkerboards are needed.

$$4 \div 2 = 2$$

A. If 2 people want to play checkers, one checkerboard is needed.

$$2 \div 2 = 1$$

B. If 0 people want to play checkers, zero checkerboards are needed.

$$0 \div 2 = 0$$

C. Study the patterns. Each number is divided by 1.

$$1 \div 1 = 1$$
$$2 \div 1 = 2$$
$$3 \div 1 = 3$$
$$4 \div 1 = 4$$
$$5 \div 1 = 5$$
$$6 \div 1 = 6$$

D. Study the patterns. Zero is divided by other numbers.

$$0 \div 1 = 0$$
$$0 \div 2 = 0$$
$$0 \div 3 = 0$$
$$0 \div 4 = 0$$
$$0 \div 5 = 0$$
$$0 \div 6 = 0$$

Give each answer.

1. $0 \div 4$ 2. $0 \div 1$ 3. $0 \div 5$

4. $0 \div 8$ 5. $0 \div 6$ 6. $0 \div 9$

7. $0 \div 3$ 8. $0 \div 7$ 9. $0 \div 2$

10. $3 \div 1$ 11. $8 \div 1$ 12. $2 \div 1$

13. $6 \div 1$ 14. $6 \div 6$ 15. $7 \div 7$

16. $9 \div 9$ 17. $5 \div 1$ 18. $4 \div 1$

19. $7 \div 1$ 20. $2 \div 2$ 21. $9 \div 1$

22. $5 \overline{)5}$ 23. $8 \overline{)24}$ 24. $7 \overline{)14}$

25. $9 \overline{)45}$ 26. $5 \overline{)20}$ 27. $7 \overline{)0}$

28. $9 \overline{)36}$ 29. $2 \overline{)2}$ 30. $6 \overline{)18}$

31. $3 \overline{)15}$ 32. $4 \overline{)20}$ 33. $8 \overline{)0}$

34. Juanita built 2 birdhouses each week. How many weeks did it take her to build 18 birdhouses?

35. Each birdhouse holds 3 robins. How many birdhouses are needed for 3 robins?

• *Discuss*   What is the answer when you divide a number by 1? By itself?

• *Discuss*   What is the answer when you divide 0 by a number?

Keeping Skillful

1. $\begin{array}{r} 28 \\ \times\ 3 \\ \hline \end{array}$ 2. $\begin{array}{r} 52 \\ \times\ 5 \\ \hline \end{array}$ 3. $\begin{array}{r} 16 \\ \times\ 4 \\ \hline \end{array}$

4. $\begin{array}{r} 39 \\ \times\ 6 \\ \hline \end{array}$ 5. $\begin{array}{r} 55 \\ \times\ 4 \\ \hline \end{array}$ 6. $\begin{array}{r} 95 \\ \times\ 3 \\ \hline \end{array}$

7. $\begin{array}{r} 870 \\ \times\ 9 \\ \hline \end{array}$ 8. $\begin{array}{r} 214 \\ \times\ 5 \\ \hline \end{array}$ 9. $\begin{array}{r} 506 \\ \times\ 7 \\ \hline \end{array}$

10. $\begin{array}{r} 703 \\ \times\ 8 \\ \hline \end{array}$ 11. $\begin{array}{r} 192 \\ \times\ 2 \\ \hline \end{array}$ 12. $\begin{array}{r} 451 \\ \times\ 3 \\ \hline \end{array}$

13. $\begin{array}{r} 896 \\ \times\ 3 \\ \hline \end{array}$ 14. $\begin{array}{r} 194 \\ \times\ 4 \\ \hline \end{array}$ 15. $\begin{array}{r} 498 \\ \times\ 7 \\ \hline \end{array}$

16. $\begin{array}{r} 677 \\ \times\ 4 \\ \hline \end{array}$ 17. $\begin{array}{r} 348 \\ \times\ 6 \\ \hline \end{array}$ 18. $\begin{array}{r} 368 \\ \times\ 4 \\ \hline \end{array}$

19. $\begin{array}{r} 31 \\ \times 26 \\ \hline \end{array}$ 20. $\begin{array}{r} 84 \\ \times 30 \\ \hline \end{array}$ 21. $\begin{array}{r} 27 \\ \times 14 \\ \hline \end{array}$

22. $\begin{array}{r} 301 \\ \times\ 70 \\ \hline \end{array}$ 23. $\begin{array}{r} 215 \\ \times\ 21 \\ \hline \end{array}$ 24. $\begin{array}{r} 184 \\ \times\ 17 \\ \hline \end{array}$

25. $\begin{array}{r} 195 \\ \times\ 29 \\ \hline \end{array}$ 26. $\begin{array}{r} 486 \\ \times\ 67 \\ \hline \end{array}$ 27. $\begin{array}{r} 971 \\ \times\ 36 \\ \hline \end{array}$

28. $\begin{array}{r} 543 \\ \times\ 18 \\ \hline \end{array}$ 29. $\begin{array}{r} 608 \\ \times\ 35 \\ \hline \end{array}$ 30. $\begin{array}{r} 724 \\ \times\ 49 \\ \hline \end{array}$

6, 7, 8, and 9 in Division

Robert wanted to find the quotient of 56 ÷ 7.
Mr. Occom made 56 marks on the board.
Robert counted groups of 7 marks.

56 ÷ 7 = 8

• **Discuss**   How can you use the picture to find 56 ÷ 8?

Give two division sentences for each picture.

1. 48 in all

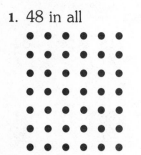

2. 35 in all

3. 27 in all

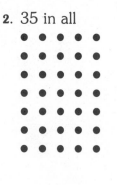

4. 42 in all

Give each answer.

5. $6\overline{)6}$ 6. $6\overline{)12}$ 7. $6\overline{)18}$ 8. $6\overline{)24}$ 9. $6\overline{)30}$ 10. $6\overline{)36}$

11. $6\overline{)42}$ 12. $6\overline{)48}$ 13. $6\overline{)54}$ 14. $7\overline{)7}$ 15. $7\overline{)14}$ 16. $7\overline{)21}$

17. $7\overline{)28}$ 18. $7\overline{)35}$ 19. $7\overline{)42}$ 20. $7\overline{)49}$ 21. $7\overline{)56}$ 22. $7\overline{)63}$

23. $8\overline{)8}$ 24. $8\overline{)16}$ 25. $8\overline{)24}$ 26. $8\overline{)32}$ 27. $8\overline{)40}$ 28. $8\overline{)48}$

29. $8\overline{)56}$ 30. $8\overline{)64}$ 31. $8\overline{)72}$ 32. $9\overline{)9}$ 33. $9\overline{)18}$ 34. $9\overline{)27}$

35. $9\overline{)36}$ 36. $9\overline{)45}$ 37. $9\overline{)54}$ 38. $9\overline{)63}$ 39. $9\overline{)72}$ 40. $9\overline{)81}$

41. $5\overline{)30}$ 42. $3\overline{)18}$ 43. $4\overline{)28}$ 44. $5\overline{)40}$ 45. $2\overline{)12}$ 46. $4\overline{)24}$

47. $3\overline{)21}$ 48. $4\overline{)32}$ 49. $5\overline{)45}$ 50. $4\overline{)36}$ 51. $3\overline{)24}$ 52. $5\overline{)25}$

53. There were 18 pupils in Marta's class. They formed teams of 2 pupils on each team for work at the chalkboard. How many teams were formed?

54. Marta had 48 pieces of chalk. There were 8 pieces of chalk in each box. How many boxes of chalk did Marta have?

More practice
Set 25, page 378

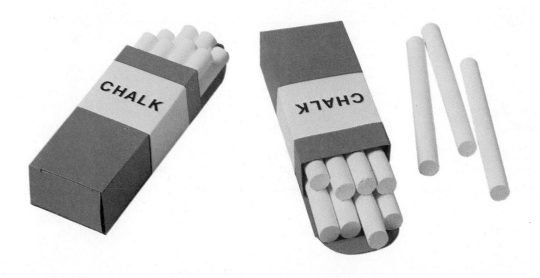

223

Using Division Facts

How many can you buy if you have

1. 36 cents?

2. 27 cents?

3. 42 cents?

4. 32 cents?

5. 81 cents?

6. 18 cents?

7. 0 cents?

8. 7 cents?

9. 72 cents?

10. 49 cents?

11. 35 cents?

12. 40 cents?

Complete each table.

	÷ 4
8	2
13. 20	
14. 4	
15. 36	

	÷ 7
16. 35	
17. 21	
18. 42	
19. 7	

	÷ 9
20. 72	
21. 27	
22. 63	
23. 36	

	÷ 1
24. 0	
25. 5	
26. 1	
27. 3	

	÷ 5
28. 40	
29. 15	
30. 30	
31. 25	

	÷ 8
32. 8	
33. 48	
34. 64	
35. 56	

	÷ 6
36. 0	
37. 42	
38. 36	
39. 54	

	÷ 3
40. 6	
41. 27	
42. 3	
43. 12	

Give each answer.

44. There are 48 tires. Each truck has 6 tires. How many trucks are there?

45. There are 18 eggs. Each plate has 2 eggs. How many plates are there?

46. Each box will hold 9 balls. How many boxes hold 81 balls?

47. There are 63 players. Each team has 9 players. How many teams are there?

48. Each committee has 7 students. How many committees can be formed with 49 students if no student is on more than one committee?

49. Each cage holds 7 canaries. How many cages hold 35 canaries?

Families of Facts

A. This picture can be used to show two multiplication facts and two division facts.

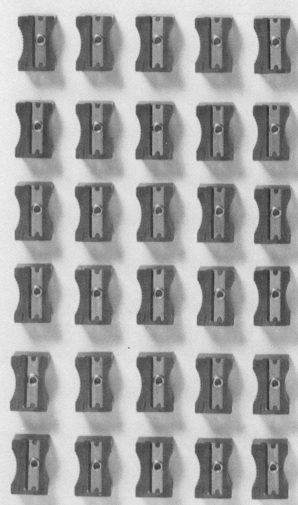

5 groups of 6 pencil sharpeners
5 × 6 = 30

Divide 30 into groups of 6.
30 ÷ 6 = 5

6 groups of 5 pencil sharpeners
6 × 5 = 30

Divide 30 into groups of 5.
30 ÷ 5 = 6

5 × 6 = 30   **30 ÷ 6 = 5**

6 × 5 = 30   **30 ÷ 5 = 6**

These four number sentences make up a *family of facts.*

B. These two number sentences also make up a family of facts.

4 × 4 = 16   **16 ÷ 4 = 4**

Copy and complete each sentence. Circle the one
that does not belong to the family of facts.

Here's how

$6 \times 8 = $ ▦ $6 \times 8 = 48$
$48 \div 8 = $ ▦ $48 \div 8 = 6$
$8 \times 6 = $ ▦ $8 \times 6 = 48$
$48 \div 6 = $ ▦ $48 \div 6 = 8$
$35 \div 7 = $ ▦ $(35 \div 7 = 5)$

1. $4 \times 8 = $ ▦
   $5 \times 5 = $ ▦
   $32 \div 8 = $ ▦
   $8 \times 4 = $ ▦
   $32 \div 4 = $ ▦

2. $3 \times 9 = $ ▦
   $27 \div 9 = $ ▦
   $12 \div 4 = $ ▦
   $9 \times 3 = $ ▦
   $27 \div 3 = $ ▦

3. $5 \times 6 = $ ▦
   $6 \times 7 = $ ▦
   $42 \div 7 = $ ▦
   $7 \times 6 = $ ▦
   $42 \div 6 = $ ▦

4. $5 \times 2 = $ ▦
   $10 \div 2 = $ ▦
   $2 \times 5 = $ ▦
   $40 \div 8 = $ ▦
   $10 \div 5 = $ ▦

5. $6 \times 6 = $ ▦
   $3 \times 6 = $ ▦
   $36 \div 6 = $ ▦

6. $9 \times 1 = $ ▦
   $9 \times 9 = $ ▦
   $81 \div 9 = $ ▦

7. $5 \times 5 = $ ▦
   $3 \times 9 = $ ▦
   $25 \div 5 = $ ▦

8. $4 \times 4 = $ ▦
   $16 \div 4 = $ ▦
   $4 \times 2 = $ ▦

For each exercise, write two multiplication sentences
and two division sentences.

Here's how

2, 9, 18 $2 \times 9 = 18$
          $9 \times 2 = 18$
          $18 \div 2 = 9$
          $18 \div 9 = 2$

9. 3, 6, 18   10. 5, 9, 45   11. 7, 8, 56   12. 7, 9, 63   13. 4, 6, 24

14. 1, 5, 5   15. 3, 8, 24   16. 2, 7, 14   17. 8, 9, 72   18. 5, 7, 35

For each exercise, write one multiplication sentence
and one division sentence.

19. 9, 9, 81   20. 3, 3, 9   21. 7, 7, 49   22. 8, 8, 64   23. 2, 2, 4

227

Using Multiplication and Division Facts

Multiply or divide. Use the codes to answer each riddle.

What is the best medicine for a pig with a sprained ankle?

Code	
0	M
4	K
8	T
18	N
32	I
42	E
72	O

1. 9×8

2. 8×4

3. 9×2

4. 4×1

5. 9×0

6. 6×7

7. 6×3

8. 4×2

What would you get if you crossed a hummingbird and a doorbell?

Code	
0	I
1	A
2	N
3	G
4	D
5	R
6	U
7	E
8	M
9	H

Word 1

9. $6 \div 6$

Word 2

10. $18 \div 2$

11. $24 \div 4$

12. $56 \div 7$

13. $36 \div 9$

14. $0 \div 4$

15. $4 \div 2$

16. $3 \div 1$

17. $49 \div 7$

18. $25 \div 5$

Complete each table. Watch the signs.

	÷ 6
19. 48	
20. 18	
21. 36	
22. 30	

	× 5
23. 8	
24. 4	
25. 7	
26. 1	

	× 9
27. 5	
28. 9	
29. 2	
30. 3	

	÷ 8
31. 56	
32. 32	
33. 16	
34. 64	

	× 3
35. 7	
36. 3	
37. 9	
38. 6	

	÷ 7
39. 28	
40. 56	
41. 0	
42. 49	

	÷ 4
43. 32	
44. 16	
45. 4	
46. 24	

	× 6
47. 8	
48. 0	
49. 3	
50. 7	

	÷ 3
51. 21	
52. 12	
53. 24	
54. 27	

	× 4
55. 3	
56. 7	
57. 2	
58. 6	

	÷ 5
59. 25	
60. 40	
61. 35	
62. 45	

	× 7
63. 4	
64. 8	
65. 6	
66. 9	

Remainders

A. Tony has 25 shells. How many displays of 6 shells each can he make? How many shells will be left over?

Find 25 ÷ 6.

$$6\overline{)25}$$

Divide. How many groups of 6 in 25? 4

$$\begin{array}{r} 4 \\ 6\overline{)25} \\ -24 \\ \hline 1 \end{array}$$

Write 4 above the 5.

Multiply. 4 × 6 = 24 Subtract. The remainder is 1.

$$\begin{array}{r} 4\ \text{R}1 \\ 6\overline{)25} \\ -24 \\ \hline 1 \end{array}$$

Write R1 in the answer.

When you divide 25 by 6, the answer is 4, remainder 1.

Quotient ⟶ **4 R1** ← Remainder
Divisor → 6)25 ⟵ Dividend

Tony can make 4 displays of 6 shells. 1 shell will be left over.

B. Find 59 ÷ 8.　　　**C.** Find 63 ÷ 7.

$$\begin{array}{r} 7 \text{ R3} \\ 8\overline{)59} \\ 56 \\ \hline 3 \end{array}$$

$$\begin{array}{r} 9 \\ 7\overline{)63} \\ 63 \\ \hline 0 \end{array}$$

Divide.

1. $6\overline{)35}$　　2. $3\overline{)21}$　　3. $2\overline{)11}$　　4. $5\overline{)27}$　　5. $9\overline{)38}$　　6. $7\overline{)25}$

7. $7\overline{)59}$　　8. $4\overline{)30}$　　9. $8\overline{)42}$　　10. $6\overline{)26}$　　11. $8\overline{)58}$　　12. $4\overline{)23}$

13. $4\overline{)13}$　　14. $3\overline{)17}$　　15. $9\overline{)75}$　　16. $6\overline{)44}$　　17. $7\overline{)49}$　　18. $5\overline{)19}$

19. 51 ÷ 9　　20. 16 ÷ 2　　21. 47 ÷ 5　　22. 86 ÷ 9　　23. 11 ÷ 3　　24. 68 ÷ 7

25. 45 ÷ 7　　26. 19 ÷ 2　　27. 18 ÷ 5　　28. 14 ÷ 6　　29. 21 ÷ 8　　30. 34 ÷ 9

Give each answer.

31. Doris had 46 grapefruit to put on trays. She put 6 grapefruit on each tray. How many trays did she fill? How many grapefruit were left over?

32. Steve had 23 eggs. He needed 3 eggs for each cake. How many cakes could he make? How many eggs would he have left?

33. Mark had 73 photographs to put in an album. He put 8 photographs on each page. How many pages did he fill? How many photographs were left?

34. Terry had 37 books. She put 7 on each shelf. How many shelves did she fill? How many books were left?

35. A librarian had 9 films. He gave the same number of films to each of 7 classes. How many films did he give each class? How many films were left?

36. A squirrel found 19 nuts and hid the same number of nuts in each of 9 trees. How many nuts were hidden in each tree? How many nuts were left?

Multiples

■ ■
■ ■ $1 \times 4 = 4$

■ ■ ■ ■
■ ■ ■ ■ $2 \times 4 = 8$

■ ■ ■ ■ ■ ■
■ ■ ■ ■ ■ ■ $3 \times 4 = 12$

■ ■ ■ ■ ■ ■ ■ ■
■ ■ ■ ■ ■ ■ ■ ■ $4 \times 4 = 16$

■ ■ ■ ■ ■ ■ ■ ■ ■ ■
■ ■ ■ ■ ■ ■ ■ ■ ■ ■ $5 \times 4 = 20$

The numbers 4, 8, 12, 16, and 20 are **multiples** of 4.

● **Discuss** What are the next four multiples of 4?

Complete each table.

1. Multiples of 5.

×	1	2	3	4	5	6	7	8	9
5									

2. Multiples of 8.

×	1	2	3	4	5	6	7	8	9
8									

Give each answer.

3. Give the next 6 multiples of 2.

2 4 6

4. Give the next 6 multiples of 6.

6 12 18

5. Give the next 6 multiples of 9.

9 18 27 ▦ ▦ ▦ ▦ ▦ ▦

6. Give the next 6 multiples of 7.

7 14 21 ▦ ▦ ▦ ▦ ▦ ▦

Chapter 11 Test
Division Facts, pages 212–232

Complete the division sentence for each picture.

1.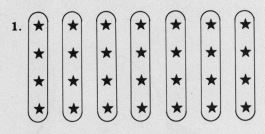

$$28 \div 4 = \text{\vrule}$$

2.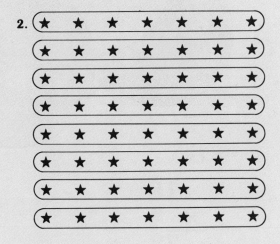

$$56 \div 7 = \text{\vrule}$$

Divide.

3. $6 \div 2$ 4. $18 \div 9$

5. $20 \div 5$ 6. $45 \div 9$

7. $36 \div 6$ 8. $32 \div 4$

9. $49 \div 7$ 10. $72 \div 8$

11. $0 \div 3$ 12. $7 \div 7$

13. $9\overline{)54}$ 14. $6\overline{)48}$ 15. $2\overline{)14}$

16. $1\overline{)9}$ 17. $4\overline{)16}$ 18. $7\overline{)21}$

19. $5\overline{)5}$ 20. $8\overline{)32}$ 21. $3\overline{)15}$

22. $7\overline{)46}$ 23. $2\overline{)7}$ 24. $8\overline{)60}$

25. $9\overline{)80}$ 26. $5\overline{)17}$ 27. $4\overline{)23}$

Copy and complete each sentence. Circle the one that does not belong to the family of facts.

28. $6 \times 7 = \text{\vrule}$
     $49 \div 7 = \text{\vrule}$
     $42 \div 7 = \text{\vrule}$
     $7 \times 6 = \text{\vrule}$
     $42 \div 6 = \text{\vrule}$

29. $3 \times 8 = \text{\vrule}$
     $24 \div 8 = \text{\vrule}$
     $8 \times 3 = \text{\vrule}$
     $21 \div 3 = \text{\vrule}$
     $24 \div 3 = \text{\vrule}$

For each exercise, write two multiplication sentences and two division sentences.

30. 3, 7, 21

Chapter 12 Division: One-Digit Divisors

Two-Digit Dividends and Two-Digit Quotients

A. Mrs. Lytton divided 75 fun-fair tickets equally among 4 students. How many tickets did each student get? How many were left over?

Find 75 ÷ 4.

$$\begin{array}{r} 1 \\ 4\overline{)75} \\ -4 \\ \hline 3 \end{array}$$

Divide. How many 4s in 7? *1*
Write 1 above the 7.

Multiply. 1 × 4 = 4
Subtract. The remainder must be less than the divisor. 3 is less than 4.

$$\begin{array}{r} 18 \text{ R3} \\ 4\overline{)75} \\ -4\downarrow \\ \hline 35 \\ -32 \\ \hline 3 \end{array}$$

Bring down the 5.

Divide. How many 4s in 35? *8*
Write 8 above the 5.

Multiply. 8 × 4 = 32

Subtract.
3 is less than 4.

There are no more digits to bring down. The remainder is 3. Write R3 in the answer.

Check

$$\begin{array}{r} 18 \\ \times\ 4 \\ \hline 72 \\ +\ 3 \\ \hline 75 \end{array}$$

Multiply the quotient and the divisor.

Add the remainder.
The result should be the dividend.

Each student got 18 tickets.
3 tickets were left over.

Check each answer. If the answer is wrong, give the correct answer.

1. $\overset{14\ R3}{5\overline{)73}}$ 2. $\overset{31}{2\overline{)72}}$ 3. $\overset{12\ R1}{4\overline{)59}}$

4. $\overset{27}{3\overline{)83}}$ 5. $\overset{15}{6\overline{)90}}$ 6. $\overset{33\ R1}{2\overline{)67}}$

Divide.

7. $3\overline{)57}$ 8. $4\overline{)84}$ 9. $2\overline{)46}$ 10. $5\overline{)70}$

11. $4\overline{)54}$ 12. $3\overline{)47}$ 13. $5\overline{)86}$ 14. $6\overline{)78}$

15. $4\overline{)97}$ 16. $2\overline{)95}$ 17. $7\overline{)90}$ 18. $8\overline{)93}$

19. $3\overline{)66}$ 20. $2\overline{)76}$ 21. $5\overline{)91}$ 22. $4\overline{)63}$

23. $6\overline{)84}$ 24. $9\overline{)99}$ 25. $6\overline{)73}$ 26. $3\overline{)94}$

27. $4\overline{)79}$ 28. $6\overline{)76}$ 29. $2\overline{)89}$ 30. $5\overline{)95}$

B. Tell how to find 96 ÷ 3.

$$\overset{3}{3\overline{)96}} \quad \overset{32}{3\overline{)96}}$$
$$\underline{-9} \qquad \underline{-9\downarrow}$$
$$\ \ 0 \qquad \ \ 06$$
$$\qquad\qquad \underline{-\ 6}$$
$$\qquad\qquad \ \ \ 0$$

Tell how to check the answer.

$$\begin{array}{r} 32 \\ \times\ 3 \\ \hline 96 \end{array}$$

31. Tammy has 55 balloons. She wants to put the same number of balloons on each of 4 booths. How many balloons will she put on each booth? How many balloons will she have left?

32. Terry has 84 prizes. He will give each of 7 game booths the same number of prizes. How many will he give to each booth?

*33. Ramon has 3 quarters, 4 nickels, and 3 pennies. How many 8¢ fun-fair tickets can he buy? How much money will Ramon have left?

Three-Digit Dividends and Three-Digit Quotients

A. Ginny loaded 920 milk cartons on 5 trucks.
She put the same number on each truck. How many
cartons did she put on each truck?

Find 920 ÷ 5.

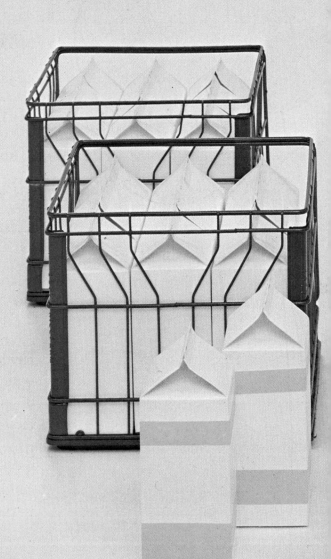

$$
\begin{array}{r}
1 \\
5\overline{)920} \\
-5 \\
\hline
4
\end{array}
$$

Divide. How many 5s in 9? *1*
Write 1 above the 9.

Multiply. 1 × 5 = 5

Subtract.
4 is less than 5.

$$
\begin{array}{r}
18 \\
5\overline{)920} \\
-5 \\
\hline
42 \\
-40 \\
\hline
2
\end{array}
$$

Bring down the 2.

Divide. How many 5s in 42? *8*
Write 8 above the 2.

Multiply. 8 × 5 = 40
Subtract.
2 is less than 5.

$$
\begin{array}{r}
184 \\
5\overline{)920} \\
-5 \\
\hline
42 \\
-40 \\
\hline
20 \\
-20 \\
\hline
0
\end{array}
$$

Bring down the 0.

Divide. How many 5s in 20? *4*
Write 4 above the 0.

Multiply. 4 × 5 = 20

Subtract.
0 is less than 5.

There are no more digits to
bring down. The remainder is 0.

She put 184 cartons on each truck.

B. Tell how to find
897 ÷ 2.

$$
\begin{array}{r}
4 \\
2\overline{)897} \\
-8 \\
\hline
0
\end{array}
$$

$$
\begin{array}{r}
44 \\
2\overline{)897} \\
-8\downarrow \\
\hline
09 \\
-8 \\
\hline
1
\end{array}
$$

$$
\begin{array}{r}
448\ R1 \\
2\overline{)897} \\
-8\downarrow \\
\hline
09 \\
-8\downarrow \\
\hline
17 \\
-16 \\
\hline
1
\end{array}
$$

Check each answer. If the answer is wrong,
give the correct answer.

1. $\overset{131\ R3}{6\overline{)789}}$ 　2. $\overset{221}{4\overline{)984}}$ 　3. $\overset{372\ R1}{2\overline{)745}}$

4. $\overset{116}{8\overline{)932}}$ 　5. $\overset{19\ R1}{3\overline{)580}}$ 　6. $\overset{29\ R1}{3\overline{)727}}$

Divide.

7. $3\overline{)936}$ 　　8. $2\overline{)842}$ 　　9. $4\overline{)468}$

10. $6\overline{)696}$ 　11. $5\overline{)762}$ 　12. $7\overline{)803}$

13. $6\overline{)830}$ 　14. $4\overline{)743}$ 　15. $2\overline{)671}$

16. $3\overline{)739}$ 　17. $4\overline{)849}$ 　18. $2\overline{)456}$

19. $942 \div 8$ 　20. $921 \div 5$ 　21. $945 \div 2$

22. $878 \div 3$ 　23. $797 \div 7$ 　24. $693 \div 6$

25. $898 \div 8$ 　26. $846 \div 6$ 　27. $500 \div 4$

28. $900 \div 8$ 　★29. $8739 \div 3$ 　★30. $48,533 \div 4$

31. The Yum-Yum Dairy has 900 liters of milk.
How many 4-liter bottles can be filled?

32. The dairy has 846 cartons of juice. How
many cases of 6 cartons each can be filled?

More practice
Set 26, page 378

Three-Digit Dividends and Two-Digit Quotients

A. Barney the Bull charged across the field after Sylvester and his friends. Barney traveled 120 meters in 8 seconds. How many meters per second did Barney travel?

Find 120 ÷ 8.

$8\overline{)120}$ Divide. How many 8s in 1? *None*

$8\overline{)120}$
$\underline{-8}$
4

Divide. How many 8s in 12? *1*
Write 1 above the 2.

Multiply. 1 × 8 = 8
Subtract.
4 is less than 8.

$\begin{array}{r}15\\8\overline{)120}\\-8\downarrow\\\hline 40\\-40\\\hline 0\end{array}$

Bring down the 0.
Divide. How many 8s in 40? *5*
Write 5 above the 0.

Multiply. 5 × 8 = 40
Subtract.
0 is less than 5.

There are no more digits to bring down. The remainder is 0.

Barney traveled 15 meters per second.

B. Tell how to find 489 ÷ 6.

$\begin{array}{r}8\\6\overline{)489}\\-48\\\hline 0\end{array}$ $\qquad$ $\begin{array}{r}81\text{ R3}\\6\overline{)489}\\-48\downarrow\\\hline 09\\-6\\\hline 3\end{array}$

238

Check each answer. If it is wrong, give the
correct answer.

1. $8\overline{)259}$ $\overset{37}{}$ 2. $3\overline{)170}$ $\overset{56}{}$ R2   3. $5\overline{)408}$ $\overset{813}{}$ 4. $2\overline{)195}$ $\overset{42}{}$ R1

5. $6\overline{)575}$ $\overset{95}{}$ R5   6. $4\overline{)329}$ $\overset{82}{}$ R9   7. $7\overline{)200}$ $\overset{28}{}$ R4   8. $3\overline{)124}$ $\overset{48}{}$

Use the code to find the answer to the riddle.
How can Sylvester keep Barney from charging?

Code	
16 R4	K
16 R5	C
51 R4	D
51 R7	G
76 R1	B
86 R4	T
86 R5	N
87 R2	H
87 R4	Y
92 R3	A
92 R6	W
95 R2	I
95 R4	E
97 R1	R
97 R2	S

Word 1

9. $153 \div 2$

10. $526 \div 6$

Word 2

11. $778 \div 9$

12. $371 \div 4$

13. $100 \div 6$

14. $762 \div 8$

15. $521 \div 6$

16. $466 \div 9$

Word 3

17. $463 \div 5$

18. $650 \div 7$

19. $555 \div 6$

20. $439 \div 5$

Word 4

21. $350 \div 4$

22. $287 \div 3$

23. $584 \div 6$

Word 5

24. $117 \div 7$

25. $583 \div 6$

26. $764 \div 8$

27. $361 \div 7$

28. $477 \div 5$

29. $434 \div 5$

Word 6

30. $133 \div 8$

31. $647 \div 7$

32. $389 \div 4$

33. $259 \div 5$

**More practice
Set 27, page 378**

Quotients with Zeros

A. One summer, 8 people ran a pet adoption center for a total of 856 hours. Each person worked the same number of hours. How many hours did each person work?

Find 856 ÷ 8.

$$\begin{array}{r} 1 \\ 8\overline{)856} \\ -\underline{8} \\ 0 \end{array}$$

Divide. How many 8s in 8? *1*
Write 1 above the 8.

Multiply. 1 × 8 = 8
Subtract.
0 is less than 8.

$$\begin{array}{r} 10 \\ 8\overline{)856} \\ -\underline{8}\downarrow \\ 05 \\ -\underline{0} \\ 5 \end{array}$$

Bring down the 5.

Divide. How many 8s in 5? *0*
Write 0 above the 5.

Multiply. 0 × 8 = 0

Subtract.
5 is less than 8.

$$\begin{array}{r} 107 \\ 8\overline{)856} \\ -\underline{8} \\ 05 \\ -\underline{0}\downarrow \\ 56 \\ -\underline{56} \\ 0 \end{array}$$

Bring down the 6.

Divide. How many 8s in 56? 7
Write 7 above the 6.

Multiply. 7 × 8 = 56

Subtract.
0 is less than 8.

There are no more digits to bring down. The remainder is 0.

Each person worked 107 hours.

B. Tell how to find
805 ÷ 2.

$$\begin{array}{r} 4 \\ 2\overline{)805} \\ -8 \\ \hline 0 \end{array}$$

$$\begin{array}{r} 40 \\ 2\overline{)805} \\ -8\downarrow \\ \hline 00 \\ -\ 0 \\ \hline 0 \end{array}$$

$$\begin{array}{r} 402 \text{ R1} \\ 2\overline{)805} \\ -8 \\ \hline 00 \\ -\ 0\downarrow \\ \hline 05 \\ -\ 4 \\ \hline 1 \end{array}$$

Each time you bring
down a digit from the
dividend, you must write
a digit in the quotient.
Sometimes this digit
is 0.

Check each answer. If the answer is
wrong, give the correct answer.

1. $\overset{15 \text{ R25}}{5\overline{)525}}$ 2. $\overset{102 \text{ R1}}{4\overline{)409}}$ 3. $\overset{106}{6\overline{)638}}$

4. $\overset{47 \text{ R1}}{2\overline{)815}}$ 5. $\overset{190 \text{ R4}}{8\overline{)876}}$ 6. $\overset{107}{7\overline{)749}}$

Divide.

7. $2\overline{)614}$ 8. $5\overline{)545}$ 9. $4\overline{)809}$

10. $3\overline{)309}$ 11. $6\overline{)650}$ 12. $9\overline{)960}$

13. $8\overline{)823}$ 14. $7\overline{)741}$ 15. $4\overline{)830}$

16. $6\overline{)629}$ 17. $3\overline{)913}$ 18. $2\overline{)419}$

19. 520 ÷ 5   20. 867 ÷ 8   21. 620 ÷ 3

22. 408 ÷ 4   23. 965 ÷ 9   24. 731 ÷ 7

25. 806 ÷ 2   26. 605 ÷ 3   27. 935 ÷ 9

★28. 8012 ÷ 2   ★29. 5208 ÷ 4   ★30. 6158 ÷ 3

31. One month, 306 kittens were brought to the
adoption center. Ingrid put 3 kittens in
each cage. How many cages did she fill?

32. One day, 927 kilograms of pet food was
delivered to the center. Bernie stored
the food in 9-kilogram bags. How many
bags did he fill?

**More practice
Set 28, page 379**

Quotients with Zeros

A. A rancher needs 920 meters of fencing. How many 4-meter sections does the rancher need?

Find 920 ÷ 4.

$$\begin{array}{r} 2 \\ 4{\overline{\smash{\big)}\,920}} \\ -8 \\ \hline 1 \end{array}$$

Divide. How many 4s in 9? *2*
Write 2 above the 9.

Multiply. 2 × 4 = 8
Subtract.
1 is less than 4.

$$\begin{array}{r} 23 \\ 4{\overline{\smash{\big)}\,920}} \\ -8 \downarrow \\ \hline 12 \\ -12 \\ \hline 0 \end{array}$$

Bring down the 2.

Divide. How many 4s in 12? *3*
Write 3 above the 2.

Multiply. 3 × 4 = 12
Subtract.
0 is less than 4.

$$\begin{array}{r} 230 \\ 4{\overline{\smash{\big)}\,920}} \\ -8 \\ \hline 12 \\ -12 \\ \hline 00 \\ -0 \\ \hline 0 \end{array}$$

Bring down the 0.

Divide. How many 4s in 0? *0*
Write 0 above the 0.

Multiply. 0 × 4 = 0

Subtract. 0 − 0 = 0

There are no more digits to bring down. The remainder is 0.

The rancher needs 230 sections.

B. Tell how to find 602 ÷ 3. Remember, each time you bring down a digit from the dividend, you must write a digit in the quotient.

$$\begin{array}{r} 2 \\ 3{\overline{\smash{\big)}\,602}} \\ -6 \\ \hline 0 \end{array}$$

$$\begin{array}{r} 20 \\ 3{\overline{\smash{\big)}\,602}} \\ -6 \downarrow \\ \hline 00 \\ -0 \\ \hline 0 \end{array}$$

$$\begin{array}{r} 200 \text{ R2} \\ 3{\overline{\smash{\big)}\,602}} \\ -6 \\ \hline 00 \\ -0 \downarrow \\ \hline 02 \\ -0 \\ \hline 2 \end{array}$$

Check each answer. If it is wrong, give the
correct answer.

1. $\dfrac{27}{2)\overline{541}}$ R1
2. $\dfrac{105}{5)\overline{603}}$
3. $\dfrac{130}{7)\overline{913}}$ R3
4. $\dfrac{110}{6)\overline{960}}$

5. $\dfrac{204}{4)\overline{816}}$
6. $\dfrac{40}{4)\overline{802}}$ R2
7. $\dfrac{93}{8)\overline{724}}$
8. $\dfrac{240}{3)\overline{612}}$ R2

Divide.

9. $5)\overline{102}$ 10. $3)\overline{241}$ 11. $9)\overline{365}$ 12. $6)\overline{544}$ 13. $4)\overline{200}$

14. $8)\overline{480}$ 15. $7)\overline{563}$ 16. $6)\overline{422}$ 17. $8)\overline{247}$ 18. $7)\overline{425}$

19. $4)\overline{560}$ 20. $2)\overline{760}$ 21. $6)\overline{783}$ 22. $3)\overline{362}$ 23. $5)\overline{800}$

24. $2)\overline{601}$ 25. $6)\overline{605}$ 26. $2)\overline{300}$ 27. $5)\overline{544}$ 28. $3)\overline{616}$

29. $4)\overline{722}$ 30. $3)\overline{961}$ 31. $5)\overline{454}$ 32. $3)\overline{911}$ 33. $4)\overline{817}$

34. $9)\overline{908}$ 35. $4)\overline{803}$ 36. $8)\overline{406}$ ★37. $3)\overline{4802}$ ★38. $5)\overline{6500}$

39. A farmer put up 3 sections
of fence for a total cost
of $480. If each section
cost the same amount, what
was the cost of a section?

40. A roll of fencing contains
7 meters. How many rolls
are needed to make a fence
630 meters long?

More practice
Set 29, page 379

Using Division

Divide each number by 3.

1. 246   **2.** 247   **3.** 248   **4.** 249   **5.** 250   **6.** 251

7. Look at the answers in exercises 1–6. What numbers can be remainders when you divide by 3?

Divide each number by 4.

8. 120   **9.** 121   **10.** 122   **11.** 123   **12.** 124   **13.** 125   **14.** 126   **15.** 127

16. What numbers can be remainders when you divide by 4?

Divide each number by 5.

17. 720   **18.** 721   **19.** 722   **20.** 723   **21.** 724   **22.** 725   **23.** 726   **24.** 727

25. What numbers can be remainders when you divide by 5?

Divide each number by 8.

26. 800   **27.** 801   **28.** 802   **29.** 803   **30.** 804   **31.** 805

32. 806   **33.** 807   **34.** 808   **35.** 809   **36.** 810   **37.** 811

38. What numbers can be remainders when you divide by 8?

What numbers do you think can be remainders when you divide

39. by 6?   **40.** by 7?   **41.** by 9?

Divide.

42. 95 ÷ 3

43. 97 ÷ 6

44. 58 ÷ 2

45. 92 ÷ 4

46. 151 ÷ 5

47. 542 ÷ 9

48. 576 ÷ 8

49. 168 ÷ 2

50. 750 ÷ 7

51. 522 ÷ 5

52. 647 ÷ 3

53. 923 ÷ 7

54. 379 ÷ 9

55. 460 ÷ 8

56. 801 ÷ 2

57. 963 ÷ 8

58. 862 ÷ 5

59. 403 ÷ 4

60. 189 ÷ 4

61. 525 ÷ 5

62. 618 ÷ 3

63. 199 ÷ 2

Harry, Larry, and Terry were stranded on an island. They made a boat to take them to shore, but they found that the boat would only hold 80 kilograms. Harry weighed 80 kilograms, Larry weighed 50 kilograms, and Terry weighed 30 kilograms. How could the boys use the boat to get to shore?

Division: Money

A. Five tickets to Skyview Planetarium cost $5.75. How much does one ticket cost?

Find $5.75 ÷ 5.

Think of $5.75 as 575 cents. Divide as you would with whole numbers.

$$
\begin{array}{r}
115 \\
5\overline{)575} \\
-5 \\
\hline
07 \\
-5 \\
\hline
25 \\
-25 \\
\hline
0
\end{array}
$$

115 cents can be written as $1.15.

Each ticket costs $1.15.

B. Tell how to find $9.72 ÷ 3.

$$
\begin{array}{r}
324 \rightarrow \mathbf{\$3.24} \\
3\overline{)972} \\
-9 \\
\hline
07 \\
-6 \\
\hline
12 \\
-12 \\
\hline
0
\end{array}
$$

C. Tell how to find $0.84 ÷ 7.

$$
\begin{array}{r}
12 \rightarrow \mathbf{\$0.12} \\
7\overline{)84} \\
-7 \\
\hline
14 \\
-14 \\
\hline
0
\end{array}
$$

Divide. Write each answer as dollars and cents.

1. $1.75 ÷ 5
2. $1.88 ÷ 4
3. $2.36 ÷ 2
4. $3.87 ÷ 3
5. $1.65 ÷ 3
6. $4.92 ÷ 6
7. $2.34 ÷ 9
8. $4.41 ÷ 7
9. $8.40 ÷ 2
10. $6.15 ÷ 3
11. $0.76 ÷ 4
12. $0.86 ÷ 2
13. $0.65 ÷ 5
14. $0.98 ÷ 7
15. $8.16 ÷ 2
16. $9.60 ÷ 3

In each exercise, the items cost the same amount. Find the cost of one item.

17. 9 sky charts: $3.15
18. 7 post cards: $1.33
19. 4 tickets: $0.60
20. 5 lunches: $9.90
21. 8 postage stamps: $2.00
22. 2 wall posters: $5.98
23. 3 pennants: $2.52
24. 3 books: $6.57
*25. 4 books: $23.80

**More practice
Set 30, page 379**

Keeping Skillful

Add.

1. 37
 + 25

2. 82
 + 97

3. 148
 + 83

4. 273
 + 427

5. 559
 + 316

6. 1286
 + 513

7. 1493
 + 2681

8. 6514
 + 2183

9. 8920
 + 5336

Subtract.

10. 85
 − 23

11. 42
 − 17

12. 180
 − 69

13. 279
 − 149

14. 625
 − 372

15. 3417
 − 502

16. 2651
 − 1358

17. 4500
 − 1234

18. 9822
 − 8915

Add or subtract.

19. 287 + 944
20. 1375 + 624
21. 882 − 691
22. 3870 + 1445
23. 1336 − 829
24. 2615 − 1387
25. 9146 + 837
26. 6051 − 3129
27. 5003 − 3163
28. 7009 + 3624

Problem Solving: Interpreting Remainders

READ   **A.** Most of the 74 students on the school patrol work in teams of 3. What is the greatest number of teams they can make?

DECIDE   Divide 74 by 3.

SOLVE

$$\begin{array}{r} 24 \text{ R}2 \\ 3\overline{)74} \\ -6 \\ \hline 14 \\ -12 \\ \hline 2 \end{array}$$

Only the quotient is used in the answer.

ANSWER   24 teams

B. The 74 patrol members split up into teams of 3. How many members were left over?

$$\begin{array}{r} 24 \text{ R}2 \\ 3\overline{)74} \end{array}$$

Only the remainder is used in the answer.

2 members left over

C. The school patrol needs 74 patrol belts. If belts are sold in packages of 3, how many packages should the patrol buy?

$$\begin{array}{r} 24 \text{ R}2 \\ 3\overline{)74} \end{array}$$

24 packages would have fewer than 74 belts. Another package would be needed.

25 packages

The PTA will have a picnic for the school patrol. Find each answer.

1. Rita has 35 rolls of crepe paper. She needs 2 rolls for each table. How many tables can she decorate?

2. The PTA has $40 for trophies. How many $3 trophies can be bought?

3. One can of lemonade mix makes 8 cups. How many cans will be needed to make 450 cups?

4. For the picnic, 230 hot dogs will be needed. How many packages of 8 should the PTA buy?

5. 230 hot dog buns will be needed. How many packages of 6 should the PTA buy?

6. Mr. Lawler donated 320 apples. How many people can have 3 apples each?

7. There will be 107 students at the picnic. If they separate into teams of 7 for the games, how many students will be left over?

8. 125 people will come to the picnic in cars that each hold 6 people. What is the least number of cars that will be needed?

9. Gil blew up 145 balloons. How many groups of 6 balloons can he make?

10. Sabrina baked 200 pumpkin squares for the picnic. She put them on plates of 9 each. How many squares did she have left over?

Write down your age today.

Add to it your age next year at this time.

Add 9 to that sum.

Divide by 2.

Subtract your age today.

I bet your answer is 5

Problem Solving: Averages

	Kris	Mikio	Andy	Sarah	Jeff
Game 1	28	21	10	13	10
Game 2	26	19	18	14	8
Game 3	18	14	26	21	15
Game 4	25	17	19	19	23
Game 5	0	12	13	15	21
Game 6	19	14	0	11	16
Game 7	17	22	5	5	19
Total minutes	133	119	91	98	112

READ   This table shows that Kris played
a total of 133 minutes in 7 basketball
games. Suppose she had played the same
number of minutes in each game. That
number is the **_average_** number of minutes
that she played in each game.
Find the average.

DECIDE   To find the average, divide
the total number of minutes
played by the number of games.

SOLVE

$$\begin{array}{r} 19 \leftarrow \text{Average} \\ 7\overline{)133} \\ -\underline{7} \\ 63 \\ -\underline{63} \\ 0 \end{array}$$

ANSWER   19 minutes in each game

Use the table on page 250. Find the average number of minutes each of these people played per game.

1. Mikio

2. Andy

3. Sarah

4. Jeff

5. Andy's team scored 246 points in 6 games. What is the average number of points that the team scored per game?

6. Jeff practiced 250 minutes in 5 days. What is the average number of minutes he practiced each day?

7. One day, 4 players on the traveling team paid $7.16 for lunches. What was the average price of each lunch?

8. Five other players paid $9.35 for lunch. What was the average price of each lunch?

9. The traveling team spent 3 hours on a bus. They traveled 210 kilometers. This is an average of how many kilometers per hour?

10. Kris's team sold 735 tickets for 3 home games. What is the average number of tickets sold for each game?

*11. Here are scores for 6 games.

45, 36, 37, 51, 40, 25

What is the average score per game? How did you find the average?

*12. Here are scores for 4 games.

43, 43, 43, 43

What is the average score per game? How did you find the average?

Problem Solving: Choosing the Operation

READ   The Explorers Club took
372 people to Alaska. They
flew in 3 airplanes. What is
the average number of
people who flew in each
plane?

DECIDE   Divide the total number of
people by the number of
airplanes. Use this equation.

$372 \div 3 = n$

SOLVE

$$
\begin{array}{r}
124 \\
3{\overline{\smash{)}\,372}} \\
-\underline{3} \\
07 \\
-\ \underline{6} \\
12 \\
-\underline{12} \\
0
\end{array}
$$

ANSWER $n = 124$

124 people

Write an equation for each problem.
Give the answer.

1. Each of the 372 people on the tour had 2 suitcases. How many suitcases were there in all?
$(2 \times 372 = n)$

2. 236 of the 372 people were students. How many were not students?
$(372 - 236 = n)$

3. The 236 students stayed in groups of 4. How many groups were there?
$(236 \div 4 = n)$

4. Each student paid $625. Each adult paid $135 more. How much did an adult pay?
$(625 + 135 = n)$

5. An airplane flew 225 kilometers an hour for 3 hours. How far did the airplane fly?

6. An airplane has 333 seats in rows of 9 each. How many rows of seats are there?

7. Chapa's ticket cost $189. His father's ticket cost $53 more. How much did Chapa's father's ticket cost?

8. An airplane is 56 meters long. 8 of these planes are lined up end to end. How long is this line of planes?

9. In 2 hours, an airplane flew 960 kilometers. This is an average of how many kilometers per hour?

10. A large jet holds 340 people. A small jet holds 125 people. How many more people does the large jet hold?

11. A guide took 198 people on a tour in the morning and 205 people on the tour in the afternoon. How many people did he take on tour that day?

12. An airplane ticket costs $127. How much do 6 of these tickets cost?

13. A helicopter ride between airports costs $18.75. A cab ride costs $9.35. How much more does the helicopter ride cost?

14. In 7 days, 756 airplanes arrived at an airport. This is an average of how many airplanes each day?

Even Numbers, Odd Numbers, and Divisibility

One number is divisible by another number if the remainder is 0 when you divide.

When a remainder is 0, the calculator shows the quotient as a whole number. When the remainder is not 0, the calculator shows the quotient as a decimal.

$615 \div 3 = 205$
615 is divisible by 3.

$83 \div 2 = 41.5$
83 is not divisible by 2.

$737 \div 8 = 92.125$
737 is not divisible by 8.

An **even number** is divisible by 2. Some even numbers are 0, 2, 4, 6, 8, 10, 12, and 14.

An **odd number** is not divisible by 2. If a number is not an even number, it is an odd number.

Is the number divisible by 7?
Write yes or no.

1. 338   2. 4424

3. 71,999   4. 15,925

Is the number divisible by 4?
Write yes or no.

5. 2770   6. 14,775

7. 105,956 8. 256,075

Is the number divisible by 9?
Write yes or no.

9. 9407   10. 19,374

11. 691,272 12. 1,327,185

Is the number even or odd?
Write even or odd.

13. 379   14. 522

15. 1268   16. 2381

17. 4005   18. 9774

19. 16,537 20. 57,626

21. 283,400 22. 741,463

23. If a number ends in 0, 2, 4, 6, or 8, is the number even or odd?

24. If a number ends in 1, 3, 5, 7, or 9, is the number even or odd?

Supermarket Manager

Ms. Sharpe manages a supermarket. Part of her job is to list the unit prices of the items in the store.

For example, a 6-ounce can of tomato juice costs $0.72. To find the cost per ounce, Ms. Sharpe divides $0.72 by 6.

$$6\overline{)72}^{\;12} \quad \text{\$0.12 per ounce}$$

An 8-ounce can of the same tomato juice costs $0.88.

$$8\overline{)88}^{\;11} \quad \text{\$0.11 per ounce}$$

From these unit prices, a shopper can see that each ounce of tomato juice in the small can costs 1¢ more than each ounce in the large can.

Find the unit price for each item.

Toothpaste

1. 6 oz. for $0.48
2. 8 oz. for $0.56

Milk

3. 2 qts. for $0.94
4. 4 qts. for $1.76

Potatoes

5. 2 lbs. for $1.54
6. 5 lbs. for $3.85

Bananas

7. 3 lbs. for $0.54
8. 5 lbs. for $0.85

Shampoo

9. 6 oz. for $1.08
10. 8 oz. for $1.44

Which is the better buy for

11. toothpaste?
12. milk?
13. potatoes?
14. bananas?
15. shampoo?

255

Chapter 12 Test
Division: One-Digit Divisors, pages 234-255

Divide.

1. $5\overline{)80}$ 2. $7\overline{)97}$

3. $5\overline{)67}$ 4. $3\overline{)78}$

5. $6\overline{)74}$ 6. $3\overline{)56}$

7. $2\overline{)29}$ 8. $8\overline{)96}$

9. $4\overline{)383}$ 10. $7\overline{)498}$

11. $9\overline{)853}$ 12. $2\overline{)146}$

13. $3\overline{)695}$ 14. $5\overline{)756}$

15. $5\overline{)637}$ 16. $6\overline{)881}$

17. $3\overline{)347}$ 18. $2\overline{)429}$

19. $4\overline{)537}$ 20. $3\overline{)675}$

21. $7\overline{)931}$ 22. $5\overline{)972}$

23. $6\overline{)623}$ 24. $4\overline{)401}$

25. $8\overline{)873}$ 26. $3\overline{)331}$

27. $\$8.75 \div 5$

28. $\$1.35 \div 3$

29. $\$0.48 \div 2$

Find each answer.

30. A parking lot charges $3 to park all day. How many days can Ms. Komper park for $50?

31. A truck can carry 8 cars. How many trucks are needed to carry 175 cars?

32. A school bus traveled 620 kilometers in 5 days. This is an average of how many kilometers per day?

33. In 9 months, Harry spent $162 for bus tickets. What is the average amount he spent each month?

34. A storage tank holds 225 liters of gasoline. How many 7-liter gas cans can be filled? How many liters will be left in the storage tank?

35. Toni bought 4 new tires for each of 183 taxicabs. How many tires did she buy?

Problems Around Us

1. The tusks of an African elephant can weigh as much as 132 kilograms each. How much would 2 tusks of this size weigh?

2. A whistling swan can fly 88.5 kilometers per hour. A seagull can fly 57.9 kilometers per hour. How much faster can the whistling swan fly than the seagull?

3. A moving sidewalk can carry 7200 people in one hour. How many people can it carry in 8 hours?

4. A walrus swam 48 kilometers in 3 hours. This is an average of how many kilometers per hour?

5. An American bullfrog is about 30.5 centimeters long. A goliath frog is about 76.2 centimeters long. About how many centimeters longer is the goliath frog than the bullfrog?

6. An elephant can eat 318 kilograms of food a day. How many kilograms of food could an elephant eat in one week? (1 week = 7 days)

7. A homing pigeon flew 603 kilometers in 9 hours. This is an average of how many kilometers per hour?

8. Dolores Pullard's height is about 226 centimeters. Robert P. Wadlow was about 46 centimeters taller than Ms. Pullard. About how tall was Mr. Wadlow?

9. A baby guinea pig is about 12 centimeters long. An adult guinea pig is twice as long as a baby. About how many centimeters long is an adult?

10. 3 giant clams of the South Pacific can be used to make 750 bowls of clam chowder. How many bowls of chowder could be made from one giant clam?

11. One of the tallest giraffes was 5.87 meters tall. One of the tallest elephants was 3.89 meters tall. The giraffe was how many meters taller than the elephant?

Individualized Skills Maintenance

Diagnose

A *pages 130–141*

7×9

8×6

7×8

B *pages 148–159*

8×431

3×168

9×274

C *pages 174–179*

25×38

64×279

58×304

Practice

A

1. $\begin{array}{r} 9 \\ \times 7 \\ \hline \end{array}$
2. $\begin{array}{r} 6 \\ \times 3 \\ \hline \end{array}$
3. $\begin{array}{r} 4 \\ \times 8 \\ \hline \end{array}$
4. $\begin{array}{r} 3 \\ \times 1 \\ \hline \end{array}$
5. $\begin{array}{r} 1 \\ \times 4 \\ \hline \end{array}$
6. $\begin{array}{r} 5 \\ \times 2 \\ \hline \end{array}$
7. $\begin{array}{r} 9 \\ \times 3 \\ \hline \end{array}$
8. $\begin{array}{r} 7 \\ \times 5 \\ \hline \end{array}$

9. $\begin{array}{r} 8 \\ \times 5 \\ \hline \end{array}$
10. $\begin{array}{r} 2 \\ \times 7 \\ \hline \end{array}$
11. $\begin{array}{r} 6 \\ \times 4 \\ \hline \end{array}$
12. $\begin{array}{r} 8 \\ \times 6 \\ \hline \end{array}$
13. $\begin{array}{r} 5 \\ \times 0 \\ \hline \end{array}$
14. $\begin{array}{r} 5 \\ \times 4 \\ \hline \end{array}$
15. $\begin{array}{r} 3 \\ \times 4 \\ \hline \end{array}$
16. $\begin{array}{r} 6 \\ \times 2 \\ \hline \end{array}$

B

17. $\begin{array}{r} 52 \\ \times 5 \\ \hline \end{array}$
18. $\begin{array}{r} 321 \\ \times 4 \\ \hline \end{array}$
19. $\begin{array}{r} 633 \\ \times 3 \\ \hline \end{array}$
20. $\begin{array}{r} 825 \\ \times 4 \\ \hline \end{array}$
21. $\begin{array}{r} 509 \\ \times 6 \\ \hline \end{array}$
22. $\begin{array}{r} 1492 \\ \times 2 \\ \hline \end{array}$

23. $\begin{array}{r} 96 \\ \times 3 \\ \hline \end{array}$
24. $\begin{array}{r} 122 \\ \times 8 \\ \hline \end{array}$
25. $\begin{array}{r} 276 \\ \times 2 \\ \hline \end{array}$
26. $\begin{array}{r} 392 \\ \times 7 \\ \hline \end{array}$
27. $\begin{array}{r} 465 \\ \times 5 \\ \hline \end{array}$
28. $\begin{array}{r} 1383 \\ \times 3 \\ \hline \end{array}$

C

29. $\begin{array}{r} 56 \\ \times 31 \\ \hline \end{array}$
30. $\begin{array}{r} 96 \\ \times 24 \\ \hline \end{array}$
31. $\begin{array}{r} 162 \\ \times 17 \\ \hline \end{array}$
32. $\begin{array}{r} 306 \\ \times 16 \\ \hline \end{array}$
33. $\begin{array}{r} 731 \\ \times 24 \\ \hline \end{array}$
34. $\begin{array}{r} 825 \\ \times 21 \\ \hline \end{array}$

35. $\begin{array}{r} 87 \\ \times 19 \\ \hline \end{array}$
36. $\begin{array}{r} 32 \\ \times 24 \\ \hline \end{array}$
37. $\begin{array}{r} 227 \\ \times 33 \\ \hline \end{array}$
38. $\begin{array}{r} 165 \\ \times 26 \\ \hline \end{array}$
39. $\begin{array}{r} 319 \\ \times 75 \\ \hline \end{array}$
40. $\begin{array}{r} 724 \\ \times 34 \\ \hline \end{array}$

Unit 4 Review

Chapter 10, pages 194–210
Choose the more sensible measure.

1. Width of a finger:
   1 cm or 1 m

2. Length of a van:
   5 cm or 5 m

3. Weight of a dog:
   15 g or 15 kg

4. Capacity of a pitcher:
   1 mL or 1 L

5. Temperature of boiling water:
   100°C or 212°C

6. Height of a horse:
   6 in. or 6 ft.

7. Width of a desk:
   18 in. or 18 yd.

8. Weight of a book:
   2 oz. or 2 lb.

9. Capacity of a bucket:
   15 c. or 15 gal.

Chapter 11, pages 212–232
Divide.

10. $8\overline{)24}$ 11. $2\overline{)0}$ 12. $1\overline{)6}$

13. $4\overline{)4}$ 14. $2\overline{)8}$ 15. $4\overline{)20}$

16. $5\overline{)10}$ 17. $7\overline{)35}$ 18. $6\overline{)18}$

19. $9\overline{)54}$ 20. $7\overline{)28}$ 21. $3\overline{)21}$

22. $4\overline{)36}$ 23. $3\overline{)17}$ 24. $9\overline{)68}$

Copy and complete each fact.
Circle the one that does not belong
to the family of facts.

25. $7 \times 6 =$ ▦
     $42 \div 7 =$ ▦
     $48 \div 6 =$ ▦
     $42 \div 6 =$ ▦
     $6 \times 7 =$ ▦

26. $9 \times 6 =$ ▦
     $56 \div 7 =$ ▦
     $54 \div 9 =$ ▦
     $6 \times 9 =$ ▦
     $54 \div 6 =$ ▦

Chapter 12, pages 234–255
Divide.

27. $2\overline{)28}$ 28. $4\overline{)96}$ 29. $5\overline{)615}$

30. $6\overline{)828}$ 31. $3\overline{)185}$ 32. $5\overline{)426}$

33. $\$4.74 \div 6$ 34. $\$0.91 \div 7$

Find each answer.

35. Three mobiles cost $7.05.
    Each costs the same amount.
    How much did each cost?

36. Adam has $45. How many
    four-dollar records can
    he buy?

37. In 5 days, Alice read for
    450 minutes. What is the
    average number of minutes
    she read each day?

Unit 4 Test
Chapters 10–12, pages 194–256

Choose the more sensible answer.

1. Length of a baseball bat:
   1 m or 1 km

2. Height of a spool of thread:
   3 cm or 3 km

3. Distance around a track:
   2 dm or 2 km

4. Length of a whale:
   22 cm or 22 m

5. Height of a coffee can:
   16 cm or 16 m

6. Weight of a nickel:
   5 g or 5 kg

7. Weight of an automobile tire:
   18 g or 18 kg

8. Capacity of a cup:
   200 mL or 200 L

9. Room temperature:
   0°C or 20°C

10. Length of a dollar bill:
    6 in. or 6 ft.

11. Weight of a pair of shoes:
    26 oz. or 26 lb.

12. Capacity of the gas tank of
    an automobile:
    25 c. or 25 gal.

Divide.

13. $2\overline{)10}$

14. $3\overline{)27}$

15. $4\overline{)28}$

16. $5\overline{)15}$

17. $6\overline{)42}$

18. $7\overline{)56}$

19. $8\overline{)48}$

20. $9\overline{)36}$

21. $8\overline{)0}$

22. $9\overline{)9}$

23. $3\overline{)25}$

24. $8\overline{)75}$

25. $5\overline{)78}$

26. $3\overline{)129}$

27. $3\overline{)836}$

28. $2\overline{)645}$

29. $7\overline{)718}$

30. $3\overline{)750}$

31. $\$7.20 \div 4$

32. $\$0.45 \div 3$

Find each answer.

33. Three baseballs cost $8.25.
    Each cost the same amount.
    How much did each cost?

34. 139 students went on a field
    trip. Each car held 6 students.
    How many cars were
    needed?

35. Three students paid $6.75
    for lunch. What was the
    average price of each lunch?

Unit 5

Chapter 13 Ratio

Introduction to Ratio

A. There are 3 boys and 2 girls walking to the store. You can use the number pair "3 to 2" to compare the number of boys with the number of girls.

3 to 2

B. 4 records cost $5. You can use "4 to 5" to give this price.

4 to 5

C. The speed limit is 40 kilometers per hour. You can use "40 to 1" to give this speed.

40 to 1

For each exercise, write a number pair.

1. 9 to ▦

2. ▦ to 25

3. ▦ to 2

4. ▦ to 1

5. To make lemonade, use 3 scoops of mix for every 2 cups of water.

6. Chuck's heart beats 5 times every 4 seconds.

7. A jet airplane travels 750 kilometers per hour.

8. 4 students for every 7 adults attended the movie.

9. 4 quarters are worth 1 dollar.

10. 12 circus rides cost $5.

11. The speed limit on the highway is 88 kilometers per hour.

12. 3 cans of soup cost 59¢.

13. Lucy can walk 6 blocks in 10 minutes.

14. Burt's heart pumps 5 liters of blood every 30 seconds.

15. 2 kilograms of beef cost $6.50.

16. There are 24 hours in 1 day.

17. There are 5 boys and 6 girls on each team.

18. The team got 5 hits for every 8 times at bat.

Ratio Tables

A. 4 records cost $5. The number pair "4 to 5" is a **ratio** for the price. You can write a ratio like this.

Records ⟶ $\dfrac{4}{5}$
Dollars ⟶

B. 8 records cost $10. "8 to 10" is another ratio for the price.

Records ⟶ $\dfrac{8}{10}$
Dollars ⟶

C. The ratios "4 for $5" and "8 for $10" show the same price per record. Other ratios for this price are shown in the table.

Records	4	8	12	16
Dollars	5	10	15	20

For each exercise, copy and complete the table of ratios.

1. 1 out of every 6 horses in the rodeo is white.

White horses	1	2	3		
Horses	6			24	30

2. To make punch, use 3 oranges with
2 cups of grapefruit juice.

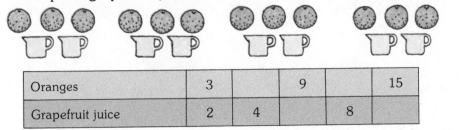

Oranges	3		9		15
Grapefruit juice	2	4		8	

3. 3 tickets cost 25¢.

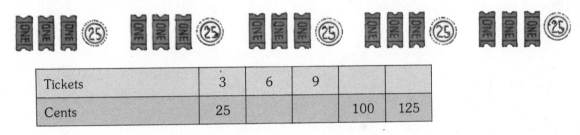

Tickets	3	6	9		
Cents	25			100	125

4. Raquel can ride her bicycle 4 kilometers
in 10 minutes.

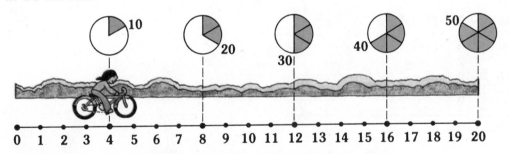

Kilometers	4		12		20
Minutes	10	20		40	

5. Joyce works 5 out of every 7 days.

SMTWTFS SMTWTFS SMTWTFS SMTWTFS SMTWTFS

Days worked	5	10			25
Days	7		21	28	

265

Equal Ratios

It takes 2 drops of red food coloring
and 3 drops of yellow to make orange.

$\dfrac{2}{3}$ ← Drops of red
        ← Drops of yellow

You can use the ratio "2 to 3" to
find other ratios to tell how many
drops of red and yellow make
orange.

		2 × 2	3 × 2	4 × 2	5 × 2	6 × 2	7 × 2
Drops of red	2	4	6	8	10	12	14
Drops of yellow	3	6	9	12	15	18	21
		2 × 3	3 × 3	4 × 3	5 × 3	6 × 3	7 × 3

Multiply both 2 and 3 by 2.⌐
Multiply both 2 and 3 by 3.⌐
Multiply both 2 and 3 by 4.⌐

The ratios "2 to 3," "4 to 6," "6 to 9"
are **equal ratios.**

Copy and complete each table to give a list
of equal ratios.

1. 3 jars of poster paint cost 50¢.

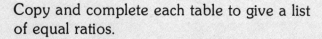

		2 × 3	3 × 3	4 × 3	5 × 3	6 × 3
Jars	3					
Cents	50					
		2 × 50	3 × 50	4 × 50	5 × 50	6 × 50

2. 4 pretzel sticks cost 15¢.

Pretzel sticks	4	8				
Cents	15	30				

3. 1 meter = 100 centimeters.

Meters	1	2				
Centimeters	100	200				

4. Manuel can jog 4 blocks in 5 minutes.

Blocks	4					
Minutes	5	10				

5. 2 out of every 9 band members play the drums.

Drum players	2					
Band members	9					

6. Mr. Papini uses 2 kilograms of meat to make 17 hamburgers.

Kilograms meat	2					
Hamburgers	17					

7. 1 day = 24 hours.

Days	1					
Hours	24					

*8. 3 out of every 40 students has patrol duty. Make a table that shows six equal ratios.

Keeping Skillful

Add or subtract.

1. $\begin{array}{r} 1.7 \\ +2.8 \\ \hline \end{array}$ **2.** $\begin{array}{r} 1.15 \\ +2.79 \\ \hline \end{array}$

3. $\begin{array}{r} 8.5 \\ -4.6 \\ \hline \end{array}$ **4.** $\begin{array}{r} 23.7 \\ -16.2 \\ \hline \end{array}$

5. $\begin{array}{r} 3.90 \\ -0.75 \\ \hline \end{array}$ **6.** $\begin{array}{r} 4.09 \\ +0.56 \\ \hline \end{array}$

7. $\begin{array}{r} 3.47 \\ +2.95 \\ \hline \end{array}$ **8.** $\begin{array}{r} 5.62 \\ -3.80 \\ \hline \end{array}$

9. 42.8 + 3.7

10. 73.2 − 8

11. 3.29 − 1.75

12. 7.92 + 1.08

13. 6.45 + 8.97

14. 24 − 15.6

15. 1.85 − 1.79

16. 15.32 + 69.74

17. 13.70 + 3.84

18. 8.43 − 7.49

19. 28.21 + 97

20. 42.53 − 12.73

21. 237.4 + 142.9

22. 342.8 − 215.7

Problem Solving: Tables of Equal Ratios

READ   Dawn Niatum works in a restaurant.
To make scrambled eggs, she uses
5 eggs for every 3 people. How many
eggs does she need for 12 people?

DECIDE   Make a table of equal ratios.
Stop at 12 people.

SOLVE

Eggs	5	10	15	20
People	3	6	9	12

ANSWER   20 eggs

For each problem, make a table of equal ratios to find the answer. The first two tables are started for you.

1. Dawn uses 3 cups of mix to make 16 pancakes. How many cups of mix does she need for 48 pancakes?
(Stop at 48 pancakes.)

Cups of mix	3
Pancakes	16

2. The restaurant can buy 15 sausages for $2. How many sausages can be bought for $8?
(Stop at $8.)

Sausages	15
Dollars	2

3. Larry works in the restaurant 4 out of every 7 days. How many days does he work in 28 days?

4. Eleanor works 5 days in 1 week. How many days does she work in 6 weeks?

5. One day there were 8 students for every 8 adults in the restaurant. If there were 16 students, how many adults were there?

6. 3 cans of orange syrup make 4 liters of orange drink. How many cans are needed to make 20 liters of orange drink?

7. On Tuesday, Larry served 5 beef dinners for every 6 chicken dinners he served. If he served 20 beef dinners, how many chicken dinners did he serve?

8. Kim earns $7 in tips for every 2 hours she works. How much would she earn in tips if she worked 6 hours?

9. The cost of 2 breakfast rolls is 55¢. How much would 6 rolls cost?

10. Submarine sandwiches are sold by the centimeter. A sandwich that is 3 centimeters long costs 40¢. How much would a 9-centimeter sandwich cost?

*11. There are 10 millimeters in 1 centimeter. How many millimeters are there in a 7-centimeter sandwich?

*12. To make salad dressing, use 3 cups of vinegar, 8 cups of salad oil, and 1 cup of water. How many cups of vinegar and oil should be used with 3 cups of water?

Multiplying to Find Equal Ratios

A. 3 baseball cards cost 10¢. The ratios in the table are equal.

	2×3	3×3	4×3	5×3
Cards	3	6	9	12	15
Cents	10	20	30	40	50
	2×10	3×10	4×10	5×10

You can find equal ratios by multiplying.

$$\frac{3}{10} = \frac{9}{30}$$ Multiply both 3 and 10 by 3 to get "9 to 30."

$$\frac{3}{10} = \frac{15}{50}$$ Multiply both 3 and 10 by 5 to get "15 to 50."

You can multiply to find a missing number in equal ratios.

B. $\dfrac{3}{10} = \dfrac{n}{80}$ You multiply 10 by 8 to get 80.

$\dfrac{3}{10} = \dfrac{24}{80}$ So, multiply 3 by 8 to find n. $8 \times 3 = 24$

C. $\dfrac{3}{10} = \dfrac{18}{n}$ You multiply 3 by 6 to get 18.

$\dfrac{3}{10} = \dfrac{18}{60}$ So, multiply 10 by 6 to find n. $6 \times 10 = 60$

Tell what you multiply each number of the first ratio by to find the second ratio.

Here's how
$$\frac{2}{3} = \frac{6}{9} \quad 3$$

1. $\dfrac{1}{4} = \dfrac{5}{20}$ 2. $\dfrac{7}{10} = \dfrac{28}{40}$ 3. $\dfrac{3}{5} = \dfrac{6}{10}$ 4. $\dfrac{4}{3} = \dfrac{12}{9}$ 5. $\dfrac{8}{10} = \dfrac{32}{40}$

6. $\dfrac{5}{2} = \dfrac{30}{12}$ 7. $\dfrac{7}{8} = \dfrac{42}{48}$ 8. $\dfrac{2}{9} = \dfrac{18}{81}$ 9. $\dfrac{3}{7} = \dfrac{24}{56}$ 10. $\dfrac{2}{3} = \dfrac{18}{27}$

11. $\dfrac{9}{5} = \dfrac{45}{25}$ 12. $\dfrac{4}{7} = \dfrac{12}{21}$ 13. $\dfrac{6}{7} = \dfrac{36}{42}$ 14. $\dfrac{3}{8} = \dfrac{15}{40}$ 15. $\dfrac{1}{10} = \dfrac{9}{90}$

Find *n*.

16. $\frac{1}{3} = \frac{n}{9}$ **17.** $\frac{1}{2} = \frac{n}{8}$

18. $\frac{3}{4} = \frac{6}{n}$ **19.** $\frac{2}{5} = \frac{6}{n}$

20. $\frac{1}{6} = \frac{4}{n}$ **21.** $\frac{2}{7} = \frac{n}{21}$

22. $\frac{4}{5} = \frac{n}{25}$ **23.** $\frac{1}{8} = \frac{2}{n}$

24. $\frac{5}{6} = \frac{n}{18}$ **25.** $\frac{9}{10} = \frac{n}{20}$

26. $\frac{2}{3} = \frac{20}{n}$ **27.** $\frac{4}{9} = \frac{16}{n}$

28. $\frac{5}{1} = \frac{n}{12}$ **29.** $\frac{3}{1} = \frac{n}{15}$

30. $\frac{4}{7} = \frac{28}{n}$ **31.** $\frac{5}{8} = \frac{35}{n}$

32. $\frac{3}{10} = \frac{24}{n}$ **33.** $\frac{5}{6} = \frac{25}{n}$

34. $\frac{9}{4} = \frac{n}{12}$ **35.** $\frac{8}{3} = \frac{n}{15}$

36. $\frac{8}{9} = \frac{56}{n}$ **37.** $\frac{7}{8} = \frac{42}{n}$

★38. $\frac{19}{25} = \frac{n}{100}$ **★39.** $\frac{3}{8} = \frac{36}{n}$

Side Trip

Cross-Products

A. $\frac{14}{76}$ and $\frac{35}{190}$ are equal ratios. The products shown below are the cross-products. The cross-products of equal ratios are equal.

$$76 \times 35 = 2660$$

$$\frac{14}{76} \diagdown \frac{35}{190}$$

$$14 \times 190 = 2660$$

B. $\frac{7}{38}$ and $\frac{28}{150}$ are not equal ratios. The cross-products for these ratios are not equal.

$$38 \times 28 = 1064$$

$$\frac{7}{38} \diagdown \frac{28}{150}$$

$$7 \times 150 = 1050$$

For each pair of ratios, use your calculator to find the cross-products. Are the ratios equal? Write yes or no.

1. $\frac{12}{23}$ and $\frac{36}{69}$ **2.** $\frac{42}{55}$ and $\frac{84}{105}$

3. $\frac{18}{37}$ and $\frac{72}{148}$ **4.** $\frac{8}{124}$ and $\frac{32}{496}$

5. $\frac{26}{31}$ and $\frac{234}{275}$ **6.** $\frac{33}{67}$ and $\frac{195}{402}$

Problem Solving: Equal Ratios

READ   2 out of every 3 fish Gayle caught were trout. If Gayle caught 24 fish, how many were trout?

DECIDE   Write equal ratios. Use n for the number of trout out of 24 fish.

Trout $\longrightarrow$
Fish $\longrightarrow$ $\dfrac{2}{3} = \dfrac{n}{24}$

SOLVE

$$\dfrac{2}{3} = \dfrac{n}{24}$$ Multiply 3 by 8 to get 24.

$$\dfrac{2}{3} = \dfrac{16}{24}$$ So, multiply 2 by 8 to find n.

ANSWER $n = 16$
16 trout

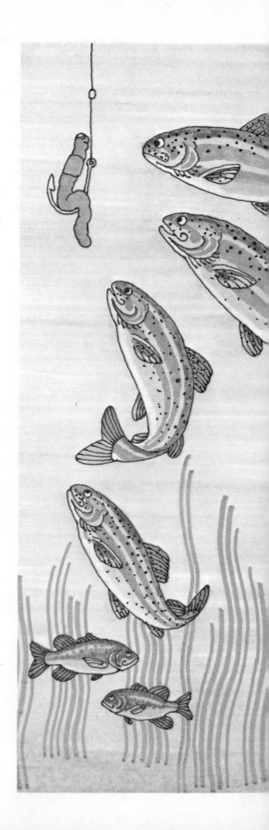

Write equal ratios. Give each answer.

1. Nick prepares 5 fish for every 3 people. How many fish does he prepare for 12 people?

Fish $\longrightarrow$
People $\longrightarrow$ $\dfrac{5}{3} = \dfrac{n}{12}$

2. Aldo's boat drifted 9 meters in 2 minutes. At this speed, how long would it take to drift 45 meters?

Meters $\longrightarrow$
Minutes $\longrightarrow$ $\dfrac{9}{2} = \dfrac{45}{n}$

3. On a camping trip, Irene spent 3 hours each day fishing. How many hours did she fish in 7 days?

4. There are 24 hours in 1 day. How many hours are there in 7 days?

5. It costs $3 to rent a rowboat for 4 hours. How long could you rent the boat for $9?

6. On a fish farm you can buy the fish you catch. 3 kilograms of catfish cost $8. How much do 6 kilograms of catfish cost?

7. 12 worms are in 1 can of bait. How many worms are there in 4 cans?

8. It costs $7 to rent a motor boat for 2 hours. How much does it cost for 6 hours?

9. A stream was stocked with 5 bass for every 8 trout. If 30 bass were put in the stream, how many trout were put in?

10. A motor boat travels at a speed of 32 kilometers per hour. How far can the boat go in 3 hours?

11. 2 fishing bobbers cost 35¢. How much do 8 bobbers cost?

12. 2 centimeters on the map of Lake Winnemack represent 25 kilometers. 10 centimeters on this map represent how many kilometers?

★13. A dozen worms for bait cost 79¢. How much do 36 worms cost?

Time Out

495 or 0

Pick any three-digit number.	Rearrange the digits to name the greatest and least numbers.	Subtract.	Repeat with 297.	Repeat with 693.	Repeat with 594.
Example 1 758	875 and 578	875 − 578 297	972 − 279 693	963 − 369 594	954 − 459 495
Example 2 777	777 and 777	777 − 777 0			

Choose any three-digit number. What answers do you get?

Paleontologist

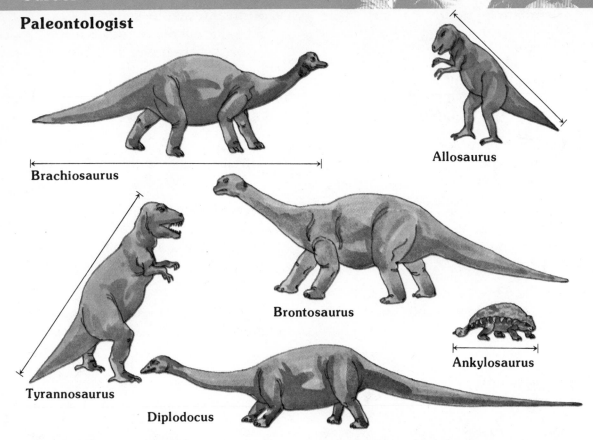

Brachiosaurus

Allosaurus

Tyrannosaurus

Brontosaurus

Ankylosaurus

Diplodocus

Ginny Lopez studies dinosaur fossils and makes sketches of the dinosaurs. In all her drawings, 2 centimeters represents 5 meters in actual length.

Ginny Lopez's sketch of Allosaurus is 4 centimeters long. Use these ratios to find the actual length.

$$\frac{2}{5} = \frac{4}{x}$$ ⟵ Drawing length (cm)
⟵ Actual length (m)

$$\frac{2}{5} = \frac{4}{10}$$

Allosaurus was about 10 meters long.

For each exercise, measure the length in the drawing to the nearest centimeter. Then find the actual length.

1. Ankylosaurus

2. Brachiosaurus

3. Tyrannosaurus

For each exercise, the actual length is given. Find the length of the dinosaur in Ginny's drawing.

4. Brontosaurus, 25 meters long

5. Diplodocus, 30 meters long

Chapter 13 Test
Ratio, pages 262–274

For each exercise, write a number pair.

1. Roy can jog 4 blocks in 5 minutes.

2. 2 cans of dog food cost 43¢.

3. There are 365 days in 1 year.

4. To make iced tea, use 5 scoops of mix for 2 cups of water.

Complete each table of equal ratios.

5. 4 pears cost 35¢.

4	8			20	24
35		105	140		

6. 6 paper clips weigh 3 grams.

6		18		30	
3	6		12		18

7. Joy made 7 pancakes for 2 people.

7	14		28	35	
2		6			12

8. 3 zoo tickets cost $8.

3		9	12		18
8	16			40	

Find n.

9. $\dfrac{1}{4} = \dfrac{n}{12}$ 10. $\dfrac{3}{5} = \dfrac{n}{20}$

11. $\dfrac{4}{7} = \dfrac{16}{n}$ 12. $\dfrac{3}{10} = \dfrac{15}{n}$

13. $\dfrac{8}{9} = \dfrac{n}{72}$ 14. $\dfrac{7}{3} = \dfrac{49}{n}$

15. $\dfrac{3}{1} = \dfrac{18}{n}$ 16. $\dfrac{8}{5} = \dfrac{n}{30}$

Find each answer. Use ratios.

17. Jose can buy 2 peppers for 25¢. How much will 8 cost?

18. Juanita uses 5 test tubes for every 3 experiments she does. How many does she need to do 15 experiments?

19. To make green food dye, use 2 drops of yellow color for every 3 drops of blue color. How many drops of blue are needed for 10 drops of yellow?

20. 4 out of every 7 students in fourth grade take the bus to school. If there are 42 fourth-graders, how many take the bus?

275

Chapter 14 Geometry

Points, Lines, and Segments

A. Imagine railroad tracks that go on and on and never stop. You can think of these tracks as *lines.* These lines are *parallel lines* because they will never cross.

B. Roads can also show lines. These lines are *intersecting* lines because they cross.

C. A *segment* is a part of a line. The picture shows segment AB.

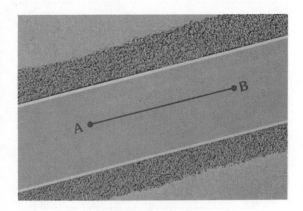

●*Discuss* Name things that make you think of lines and segments.

Name each segment.

1.

2.

3.

4.
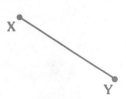

5.

6.

For each exercise, tell whether the lines are
intersecting lines or parallel lines.
Remember that lines go on and on.

Here's how

Intersecting lines

7.
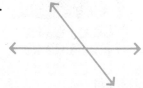

8.
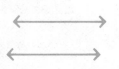

9.

10.

11.
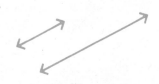

12.
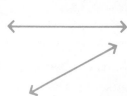

Angles

A. These pictures show **angles.**

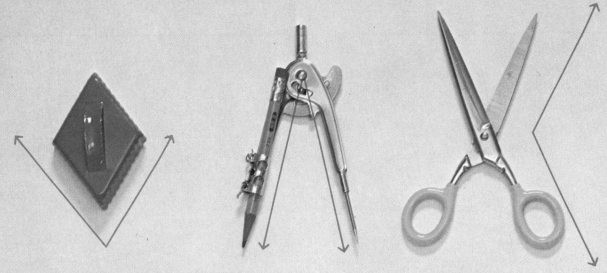

B. These pictures show **right angles.**
By using a square corner of a card,
you can test for right angles.

• *Discuss* Name things in your classroom that make you
think of angles. Tell if they are right angles.

c. This angle is called angle MNP
or angle PNM.

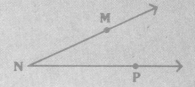

Is the angle a right angle? Write yes or no.

1.

2.

3.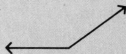

4.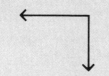

5.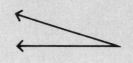

6.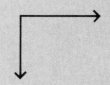

7.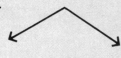

8.

9.

Give two names for each angle.

10.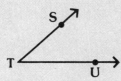

11.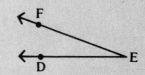

12.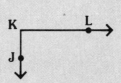

13.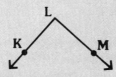

14.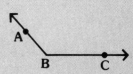

15.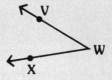

Polygons

A. These figures are polygons.

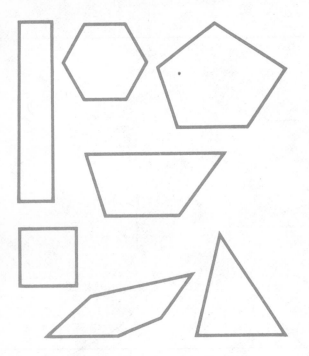

B. These figures are *not* polygons.

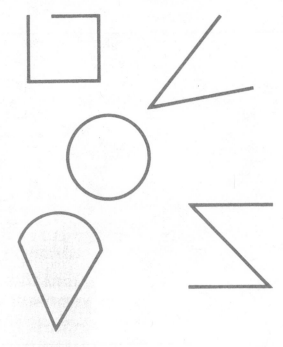

C. Each side of a polygon is a segment.

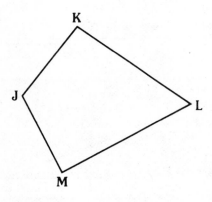

4 sides
Sides JK, KL, LM, and MJ

D. The sides of a polygon meet to form angles.

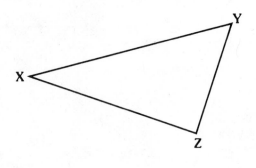

3 angles
Angles XYZ, YZX, ZXY

For each polygon, name the sides and the angles.

1.

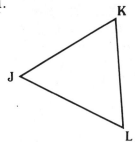

2.

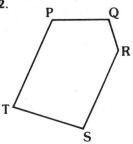

3.

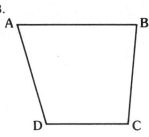

Complete the table.

Polygon	Number of sides	Number of angles
Triangle	4.	5.
Quadrilateral	6.	7.
Pentagon	8.	9.
Hexagon	10.	11.
Octagon	12.	13.

*14. How many angles are there in a nine-sided polygon?

*15. How many sides are there in a polygon with 15 angles?

Congruence

A. Segments that are the same length are **congruent segments.** Are segments AB and CD congruent?

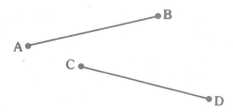

Use tracing paper. Trace segment AB.

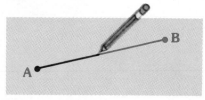

Place the tracing of AB over CD. AB is the same length as CD.

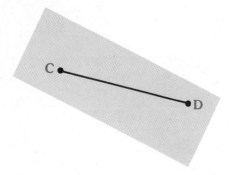

Segments AB and CD are congruent.

B. Polygons that are the same size and shape are **congruent polygons.** Are these polygons congruent?

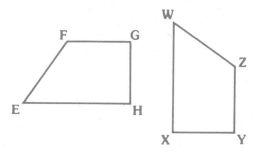

Trace the first polygon.

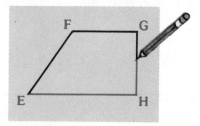

Place the tracing over the second polygon. They are the same size and shape.

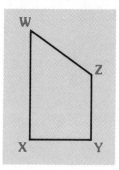

The two polygons are congruent.

Tell whether the segments or polygons are congruent.
Write yes or no.

1.    2.

3.    4.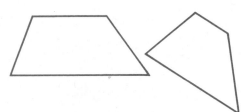

5. 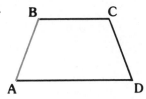   6.

For each polygon, name the side that is congruent
to the side shown in red.

7. R   U   8. B   C   9.   M
                                                N
                                                         L
   S   T   A   D   J
                                                    K

10.   F   11.   Z   12. Q   R
                         Y
                                   V   P   S
   E   G   X   W   U   T

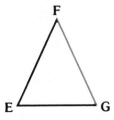 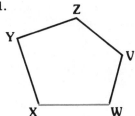 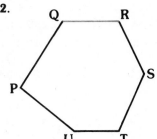  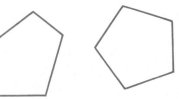 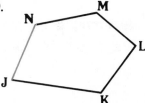

Parallelograms

A. A ***parallelogram*** is a four-sided polygon.

The opposite sides of a parallelogram are parallel.

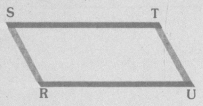 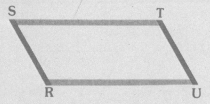

Sides ST and RU are parallel.   Sides RS and UT are parallel.

The opposite sides of a parallelogram are the same length. They are congruent.

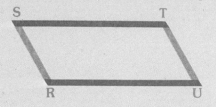 

Sides ST and RU are congruent.   Sides RS and UT are congruent.

B. A ***rectangle*** is a parallelogram with four right angles. These figures are rectangles.

C. A ***square*** is a rectangle with four congruent sides. These figures are squares.

Is the figure a parallelogram? Write yes or no.

1.

2.

3.

4.

5.

6.

Is the figure a rectangle? Write yes or no.

7.

8.

9.

10.

11.

12.

Is the figure a square? Write yes or no.

13.

14.

15.

16.

17.

18.

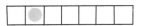

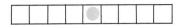

Circles

A. The dog is walking in a **circle.** The stake is at the center of the circle. The points that form the circle are all the same distance from the center.

The center of the circle is labeled point S, so the circle is called circle S.

B. The leash forms a segment from the center of the circle to a point on the circle. This segment is a **radius** of the circle.

Look at circle S. Segment SD is a radius of the circle.

C. A **diameter** of a circle is a segment through the center that connects two points on the circle. Segment QR is a diameter of circle S.

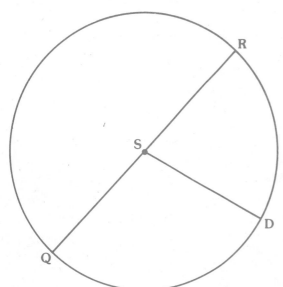

•**Discuss** Can a circle have more than one radius? Can a circle have more than one diameter?

Name a radius of each circle.

1.

2.

3.

Name a diameter of each circle.

4.

5.

6.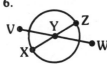

Name the center, one radius, and one diameter of each circle.

7. Center

8. Radius

9. Diameter

10. Center

11. Radius

12. Diameter

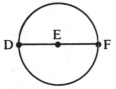

13. Center

14. Radius

15. Diameter

Is is possible to draw two different circles with

★**16.** the same center?

★**17.** the same radius?

Keeping Skillful

1. $6\overline{)73}$

2. $3\overline{)64}$

3. $4\overline{)97}$

4. $8\overline{)93}$

5. $3\overline{)459}$

6. $6\overline{)615}$

7. $2\overline{)846}$

8. $4\overline{)107}$

9. $7\overline{)526}$

10. $6\overline{)427}$

11. $2\overline{)126}$

12. $614 \div 8$

13. $97 \div 3$

14. $88 \div 8$

15. $493 \div 4$

16. $972 \div 9$

17. $819 \div 6$

18. $714 \div 5$

19. $172 \div 3$

20. $537 \div 6$

21. $365 \div 7$

22. $346 \div 5$

One Line of Symmetry

A. Loretta folded a piece of paper like this.

She cut a figure by starting and ending on the fold.

Then she unfolded the cut-out. It is a **symmetric** figure.

A figure is symmetric if you can fold it and make the two parts match. The fold is a **line of symmetry**.

B. Is the red line a line of symmetry?

When the figure is folded on the red line the two parts do not match. The red line is not a line of symmetry.

C. Is the blue line a line of symmetry?

When the figure is folded on the blue line, the two parts match. The blue line is a line of symmetry.

Trace each figure and cut it out. Is the red
line a line of symmetry? Write yes or no.

1.

2.

3.

4.

The black line is a line of symmetry. Copy and
complete each figure.

5.

6.

7.

8. Fold a piece of paper once. Use the fold as a
line of symmetry and cut out a symmetric figure.

Lines of Symmetry

Some figures have more than one line of symmetry.
A square has four lines of symmetry.

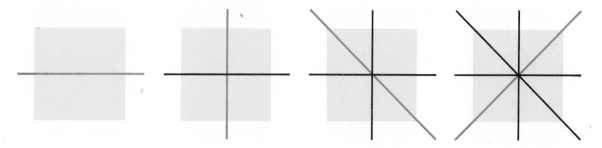

Trace each figure and cut it out. Fold to find
each line of symmetry.

1. Find two lines of symmetry.

2. Find one line of symmetry.

3. Find three lines of symmetry.

4. Find six lines of symmetry.

Trace each figure and cut it out. Fold
to find as many lines of symmetry as you
can. Tell how many you found.

5.

6.

7.

8.

Trace each letter. Show as many lines of
symmetry as you can for each letter. Some
letters have no lines of symmetry.

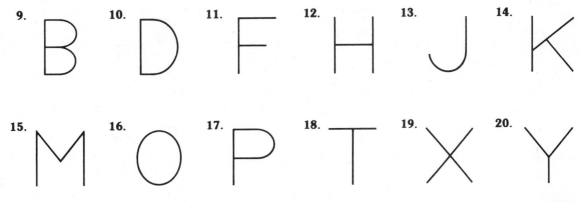

9. B **10.** D **11.** F **12.** H **13.** J **14.** K

15. M **16.** O **17.** P **18.** T **19.** X **20.** Y

Making Polygons with Congruent Sides

Fold a sheet of paper in half lengthwise.

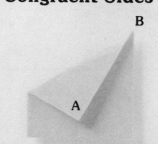

Open the paper. Make a fold through point B so that point A is on the first crease, as shown.

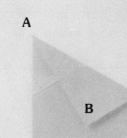

Open the paper. Make a fold through point A so that point B is on the first crease, as shown.

Open the paper. Cut along the red line. You have cut out a triangle with three congruent sides.

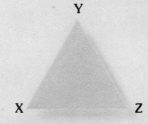

To form a hexagon with six congruent sides, start with the triangle you just made.

Fold the triangle as shown.

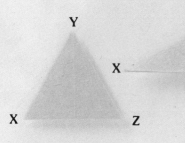

Open the triangle. and fold again as shown.

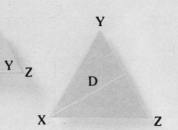

Label the point where the two creases cross point D.

Fold points X, Y, and Z to meet point D. You have made a hexagon with six congruent sides.

Chapter 14 Test
Geometry, pages 276–292

Tell whether the lines are parallel or intersecting.

1.

2.

3.

4.

5. Name the segment.

 C •————————• D

6. Name the angle.

7. Which side is congruent to side EF?

For exercises 8–25, answer the question by writing yes or no.

Is the angle a right angle?

8. 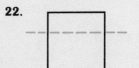   **9.**

Is the figure a polygon?

10. 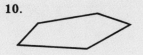   **11.**

Is the figure a parallelogram?

12. **13.** **14.**

15. Are the two polygons congruent?

Is the segment a radius of circle M?

16. **17.** **18.**

Is the segment a diameter of circle M?

19. **20.** **21.**

  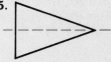

Is the blue line a line of symmetry?

22. **23.**

24. **25.**

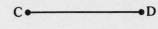  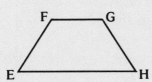

Meaning of Fractions

Italy

Colombia

Mauritius

A. The Italian flag is divided into 3 equal parts, or thirds.

One of the thirds is red. You can use the *fraction* one third to tell how much of the flag is red.

Number of equal parts → $\dfrac{1}{3}$ ← Number of red parts

one third

B. The Colombian flag is divided into 3 parts. The parts are not equal.

The flag is not divided into thirds.

C. The flag of the island of Mauritius is divided into 4 equal parts, or fourths.

$\frac{1}{4}$ of the flag is blue.

$\frac{1}{4}$

one fourth

Give the number of equal parts suggested by each word.

Here's how

fourths 4

1. thirds
2. eighths
3. ninths
4. halves
5. tenths
6. twelfths
7. sixths
8. fifths
9. sevenths

Each figure is divided into equal parts. Give the number of equal parts and tell what they are called.

Here's how

 *10 equal parts tenths*

10. **11.** **12.**

13. **14.** **15.**

Tell which figure shows

16. thirds.

   a. **b.**

17. fourths.

   a. **b.**

18. halves.

   a. **b.**

19. fifths.

   a. **b.**

20. eighths.

   a. **b.**

21. tenths.

   a. **b.**

22. Design a flag that shows halves.

23. Design a flag that shows fifths.

Fractions in Flags

Use an encyclopedia.

Try to find flags that show halves, thirds, and fourths.

Draw each flag and color it. Give the name of the country.

Try to find flags that show two, three, and four parts that are not equal.

Draw each flag and color it. Give the name of the country.

Fraction of a Whole

A. The circle is divided into 8 equal parts. Three eighths of the circle is green.

$$\text{Number of equal parts} \rightarrow \frac{3}{8} \leftarrow \text{Number of green parts}$$

Five eighths of the circle is not green.

$$\text{Number of equal parts} \rightarrow \frac{5}{8} \leftarrow \text{Number of parts not green}$$

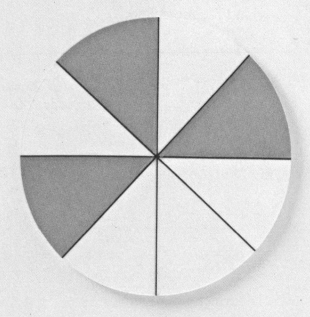

B. The triangle is divided into 3 equal parts.

$\frac{3}{3}$ of the triangle is yellow.

$\frac{3}{3}$ is the same as 1.

$\frac{0}{3}$ of the triangle is brown.

$\frac{0}{3}$ is the same as 0.

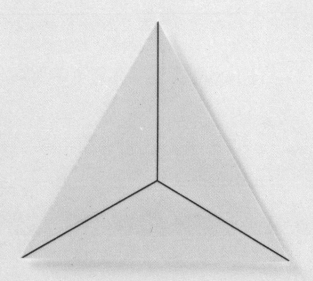

For each exercise, give a fraction to tell
how much of the figure is shaded.

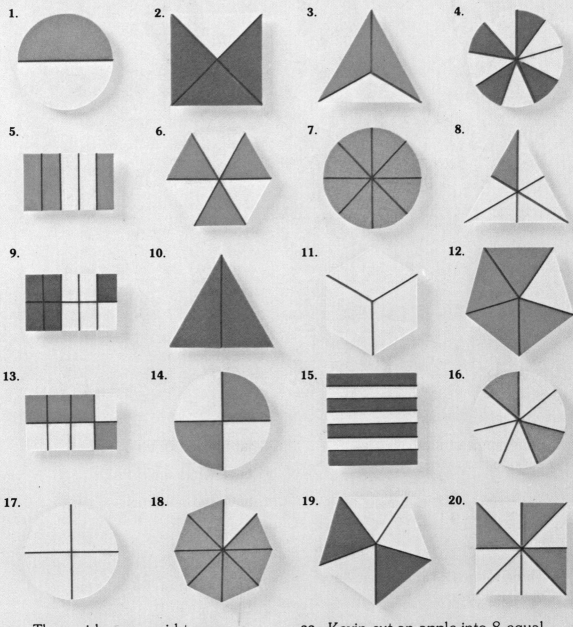

1.
2.
3.
4.
5.
6.
7.
8.
9.
10.
11.
12.
13.
14.
15.
16.
17.
18.
19.
20.

21. Three girls were paid to mow a
lawn. They divided the money
equally. What fraction of the
money did each girl receive?

22. Kevin cut an apple into 8 equal
pieces. He ate three of them.
What fraction of the apple was
left?

Fraction of a Set

A. Four ninths of the balls are basketballs.

$$\text{Number of} \rightarrow \frac{4}{9} \leftarrow \text{Number of basketballs}$$

balls

B. Three fourths of the players have blue uniforms.

$$\text{Number of} \rightarrow \frac{3}{4} \leftarrow \text{Number of players in blue uniforms}$$

players

What fraction of the players

1. have white uniforms?

2. have red uniforms?

3. are boys?

What fraction of the balls are

4. footballs?

5. golf balls?

6. tennis balls?

7. What fraction of the jars are open?

8. What fraction of the balloons are red?

9. What fraction of the animals are cats?

10. What fraction of the coins are nickels?

11. What fraction of the books are open?

12. What fraction of the girls are sitting?

The letters A, E, I, O, and U are vowels.

13. What fraction of the letters in the word MATH are vowels?

14. What fraction of the letters in the word FRACTION are vowels?

15. What fraction of the letters in the word FRACTION are *not* vowels?

16. What fraction of the letters in the word NUMERATOR are vowels?

17. What fraction of the letters in the word DENOMINATOR are vowels?

18. What fraction of the letters in the word DENOMINATOR are *not* vowels?

Writing Fractions

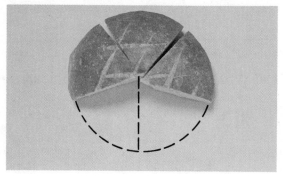

A. One sixth of the muffins have been eaten.

B. Three fifths of the loaf of bread is left.

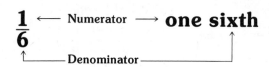

$\dfrac{1}{6}$ ←— Numerator —→ **one sixth**

The **denominator** gives the number of muffins there were altogether. The **numerator** tells how many have been eaten.

$\dfrac{3}{5}$ **three fifths**

• Discuss What does the numerator of $\frac{3}{5}$ tell? What does the denominator tell?

Give each numerator.

1. $\frac{7}{8}$ 2. $\frac{1}{10}$ 3. $\frac{0}{4}$ 4. $\frac{5}{6}$ 5. $\frac{2}{3}$ 6. $\frac{3}{5}$

7. two fifths 8. four ninths 9. three sevenths

Give each denominator.

10. $\frac{3}{4}$ 11. $\frac{1}{2}$ 12. $\frac{1}{6}$ 13. $\frac{4}{5}$ 14. $\frac{0}{9}$ 15. $\frac{7}{8}$

16. eight tenths 17. one third 18. eleven twelfths

300

Write each fraction

Here's how

four fifths $\frac{4}{5}$

19. two thirds

20. four sevenths

21. five fifths

22. eight ninths

23. six tenths

24. one half

25. zero sixths

26. eleven sixteenths

Here's how

$\frac{2}{3}$ *two thirds*

27. $\frac{1}{4}$ 28. $\frac{3}{8}$ 29. $\frac{0}{10}$

30. $\frac{5}{6}$ 31. $\frac{1}{3}$ 32. $\frac{2}{2}$

There are 7 days in one week. What fraction of a week is

33. 3 days?

34. 0 days?

There are 12 months in one year. What fraction of a year is

35. 7 months?

36. 12 months?

Writing Fractions as Decimals

To write a fraction as a decimal, divide the numerator of the fraction by the denominator.

A. Write $\frac{1}{4}$ as a decimal.

$$1 \div 4 = 0.25 \qquad \frac{1}{4} = 0.25$$

25 hundredths

B. Write $\frac{7}{8}$ as a decimal.

$$7 \div 8 = 0.875 \qquad \frac{7}{8} = 0.875$$

875 thousandths

Use your calculator. Write each fraction as a decimal.

1. $\frac{3}{4}$ 2. $\frac{1}{5}$ 3. $\frac{7}{10}$ 4. $\frac{19}{100}$ 5. $\frac{11}{25}$

6. $\frac{5}{8}$ 7. $\frac{6}{25}$ 8. $\frac{3}{10}$ 9. $\frac{1}{8}$ 10. $\frac{26}{50}$

11. $\frac{2}{4}$ 12. $\frac{1}{2}$ 13. $\frac{3}{6}$ 14. $\frac{8}{16}$ 15. $\frac{28}{56}$

16. $\frac{1}{4}$ 17. $\frac{3}{12}$ 18. $\frac{5}{20}$ 19. $\frac{8}{32}$ 20. $\frac{25}{100}$

21. What do you notice in exercises 11–15?

22. What do you notice in exercises 16–20?

The decimals for these fractions have more places than your calculator can show. Write each fraction as a decimal with as many places as your calculator shows.

23. $\frac{1}{3}$ 24. $\frac{5}{6}$ 25. $\frac{1}{7}$ 26. $\frac{2}{9}$ 27. $\frac{8}{11}$

Fraction of an Inch

A. When an inch is marked off into two equal parts, you can measure in half inches.

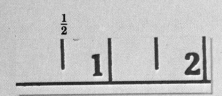

B. When an inch is marked off into four equal parts, you can measure in fourth inches.

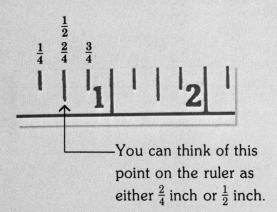

You can think of this point on the ruler as either $\frac{2}{4}$ inch or $\frac{1}{2}$ inch.

C. How long is the peanut shell? How long is the peanut?

The peanut shell is about $\frac{3}{4}$ inch long. The length of the peanut is about $\frac{2}{4}$ inch, or $\frac{1}{2}$ inch.

Give the length of each object.

1.

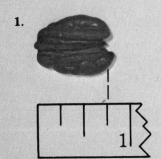

2.

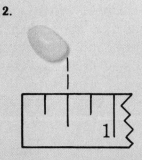

3.

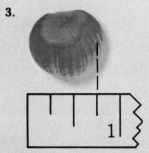

4.

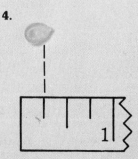

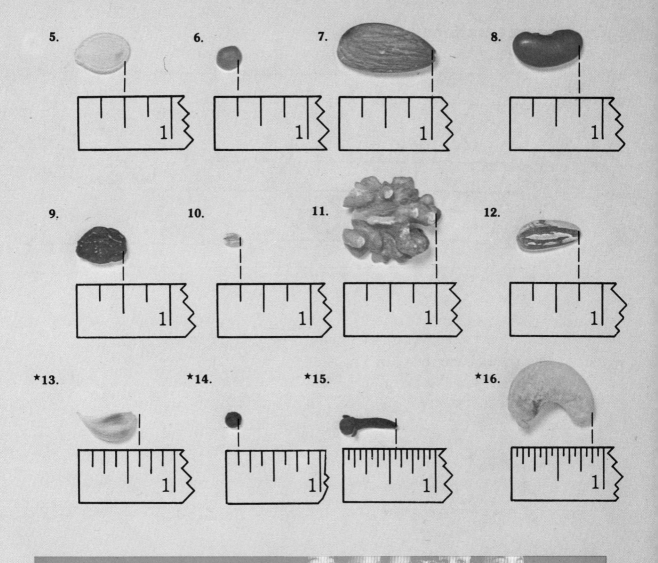

5.

6.

7.

8.

9.

10.

11.

12.

★13.

★14.

★15.

★16.

Draw 16 dots so that there are
10 rows of 4 dots each.

Comparing Fractions

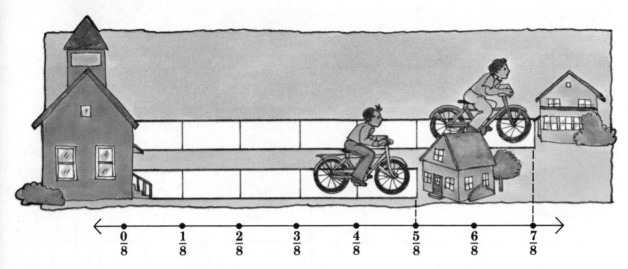

$$\frac{0}{8} \quad \frac{1}{8} \quad \frac{2}{8} \quad \frac{3}{8} \quad \frac{4}{8} \quad \frac{5}{8} \quad \frac{6}{8} \quad \frac{7}{8}$$

Roberto and Miguel rode their bicycles home from school. Miguel rode $\frac{5}{8}$ of a mile. Roberto rode $\frac{7}{8}$ of a mile.

A. Roberto rode the greater distance.

$\frac{7}{8}$ is greater than $\frac{5}{8}$.

$$\frac{7}{8} > \frac{5}{8}$$ The denominators are the same. Compare the numerators. 7 > 5.

B. Miguel rode the shorter distance.

$\frac{5}{8}$ is less than $\frac{7}{8}$.

$$\frac{5}{8} < \frac{7}{8}$$ Compare the numerators. 5 < 7.

Compare the fractions.

C. $\frac{5}{6} \; \bullet \; \frac{4}{6}$ 5 > 4

$$\frac{5}{6} > \frac{4}{6}$$

D. $\frac{7}{12} \; \bullet \; \frac{10}{12}$ 7 < 10

$$\frac{7}{12} < \frac{10}{12}$$

• Discuss When two fractions have the same denominator, how do you compare the fractions?

E. You can compare the numerator and denominator of a fraction to see if the fraction is greater than, less than, or equal to 1.

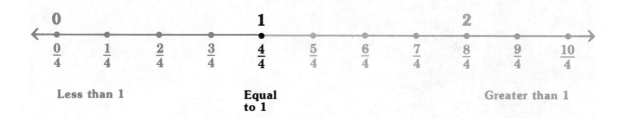

Less than 1   Equal to 1   Greater than 1

• **Discuss** How can you tell if a fraction is less than 1? Equal to 1? Greater than 1?

Compare the fractions. Use > or <.

1. $\frac{3}{4}$ ● $\frac{2}{4}$ {3 > 2} 2. $\frac{4}{6}$ ● $\frac{5}{6}$ {4 < 5}

3. $\frac{0}{2}$ ● $\frac{2}{2}$ {0 < 2} 4. $\frac{8}{7}$ ● $\frac{5}{7}$ {8 > 5}

5. $\frac{2}{3}$ ● $\frac{1}{3}$ 6. $\frac{2}{4}$ ● $\frac{1}{4}$ 7. $\frac{1}{6}$ ● $\frac{2}{6}$

8. $\frac{3}{10}$ ● $\frac{1}{10}$ 9. $\frac{3}{5}$ ● $\frac{4}{5}$ 10. $\frac{1}{3}$ ● $\frac{3}{3}$

11. $\frac{1}{4}$ ● $\frac{0}{4}$ 12. $\frac{7}{8}$ ● $\frac{3}{8}$ 13. $\frac{3}{4}$ ● $\frac{4}{4}$

14. $\frac{0}{8}$ ● $\frac{5}{8}$ 15. $\frac{7}{12}$ ● $\frac{9}{12}$ 16. $\frac{7}{10}$ ● $\frac{3}{10}$

17. $\frac{2}{6}$ ● $\frac{4}{6}$ 18. $\frac{6}{7}$ ● $\frac{4}{7}$ 19. $\frac{7}{8}$ ● $\frac{12}{8}$

20. $\frac{2}{2}$ ● $\frac{5}{2}$ 21. $\frac{5}{4}$ ● $\frac{4}{4}$ 22. $\frac{16}{6}$ ● $\frac{9}{6}$

Write yes or no.
Is the fraction greater than 1?

23. $\frac{5}{4}$ 24. $\frac{3}{2}$ 25. $\frac{1}{6}$

26. $\frac{10}{7}$ 27. $\frac{7}{8}$ 28. $\frac{3}{3}$

Is the fraction less than 1?

29. $\frac{5}{3}$ 30. $\frac{3}{8}$ 31. $\frac{2}{5}$

32. $\frac{9}{9}$ 33. $\frac{13}{4}$ 34. $\frac{0}{10}$

Is the fraction equal to 1?

35. $\frac{6}{6}$ 36. $\frac{5}{9}$ 37. $\frac{7}{7}$

38. $\frac{7}{2}$ 39. $\frac{0}{12}$ 40. $\frac{5}{5}$

More practice
Set 31, page 380

305

Meaning of Mixed Numbers

A. During practice, the team drank $3\frac{2}{3}$ pitchers of juice.

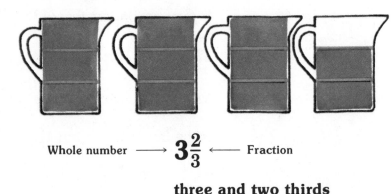

Whole number ⟶ $3\frac{2}{3}$ ⟵ Fraction

three and two thirds

Numbers like $3\frac{2}{3}$ are *mixed numbers.*

A mixed number is made up of a whole number and a fraction.

B. Maria ran around the track $1\frac{3}{4}$ times.

$1\frac{3}{4}$

one and three fourths

C. It took Maria $2\frac{1}{2}$ minutes to run around the track.

$2\frac{1}{2}$

two and one half

Tell if the number is a mixed number.
Write yes or no.

1. $4\frac{2}{3}$ 2. $\frac{6}{10}$ 3. $2\frac{4}{7}$ 4. $2\frac{1}{4}$ 5. $\frac{1}{8}$ 6. $15\frac{1}{2}$

Give each mixed number.

Here's how

four and one third $4\frac{1}{3}$

7. two and one half   8. five and one eighth
9. four and three fifths   10. six and one fourth
11. seven and five sixths   12. three and seven ninths
13. two and three fourths   14. eighteen and one tenth
15. eleven and thirteen sixteenths   16. eight and five twelfths
17. two and one third   18. four and five eighths
19. nine and one half   20. three and four fifths
21. six and three fourths   22. seven and nine tenths

Give the mixed number for each picture.

23.    24.

25. 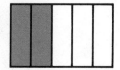   26.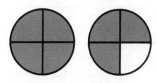

27.   28.

Mixed Numbers in Measurement

A. The carrot is about $2\frac{3}{4}$ inches long.

B. The bean is about 2 inches long.

C. The pickle is about $1\frac{2}{4}$, or $1\frac{1}{2}$, inches long.

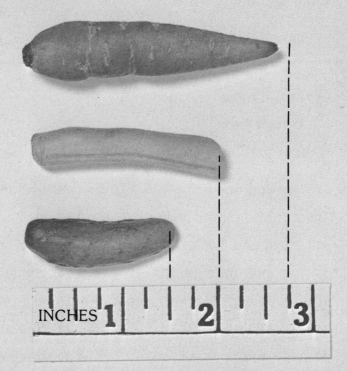

Give the length of each vegetable. Use a mixed number or a whole number.

1.

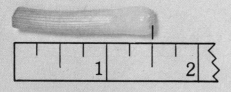

2.

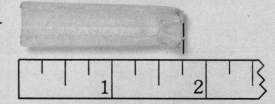

3.

4.

Measure each length.

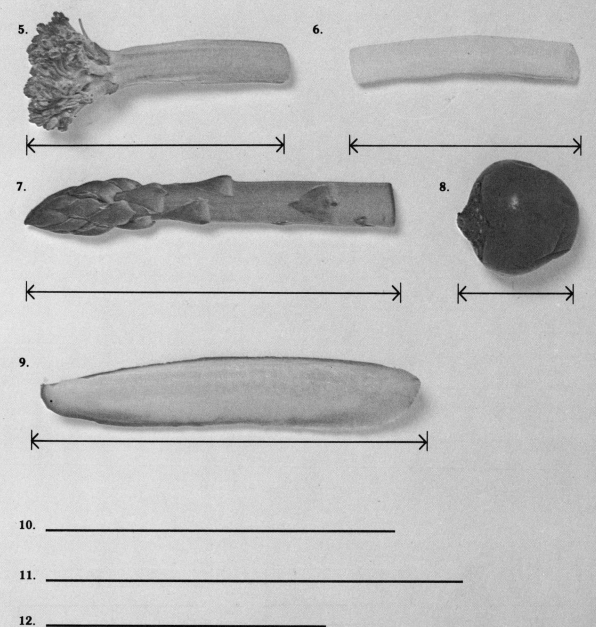

5.

6.

7.

8.

9.

10. _____

11. _____

12. _____

13. _____

14. Draw a segment that is $3\frac{1}{2}$ inches long.

Relating Mixed Numbers and Fractions

A. Jeff saved 11 quarters.
A quarter is $\frac{1}{4}$ of a dollar.

$\frac{11}{4}$ dollars

$2\frac{3}{4}$ dollars

1 **1** $\frac{3}{4}$

$\frac{11}{4} = 2\frac{3}{4}$ ←——— Mixed number

↑ ————— Fraction

B.

$\frac{10}{3} = 3\frac{1}{3}$

C.

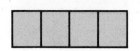

$\frac{8}{4} = 2$

D.

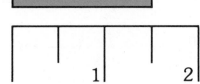

1   2

$\frac{3}{2} = 1\frac{1}{2}$

How much is shaded? Give a mixed number
and a fraction.

Here's how

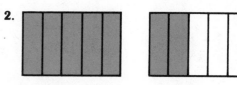

$2\frac{1}{2} = \frac{5}{2}$

1. 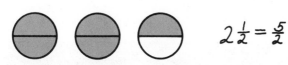   2.

3. 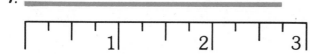   4.

Give the length of each segment as a fraction
and as a mixed number.

5.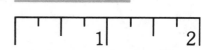

6.

7.

8.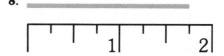

Draw a picture. Then write the
fraction as a mixed number.

9. $\frac{4}{3}$ 10. $\frac{5}{2}$ 11. $\frac{8}{5}$ 12. $\frac{15}{4}$ 13. $\frac{7}{6}$ 14. $\frac{9}{2}$

Draw a picture. Then write the mixed
number as a fraction.

15. $2\frac{1}{2}$ 16. $1\frac{3}{4}$ 17. $1\frac{4}{5}$ 18. $3\frac{5}{6}$ 19. $4\frac{1}{3}$ 20. $4\frac{1}{2}$

★21. Without drawing a picture, give the fraction for $9\frac{7}{8}$.

Roman Numerals

The Romans of long ago used numerals very
different from ours. They used the symbols
I, V, and X to write some of their numerals.

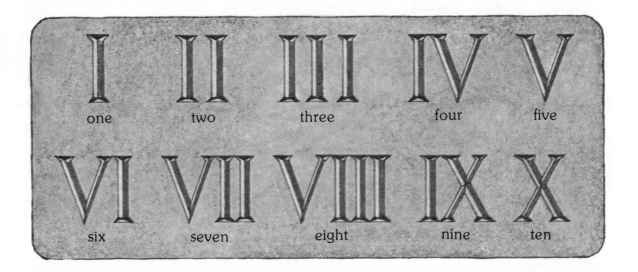

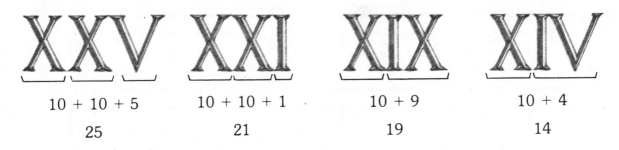

10 + 10 + 5	10 + 10 + 1	10 + 9	10 + 4
25	21	19	14

Give the standard form.

1. V 2. VIII 3. IV 4. I 5. X 6. XIX

7. XXIII 8. XXV 9. XXXI 10. XXIV 11. XXVI 12. XXXVII

Give the Roman numeral.

13. 2 14. 7 15. 9 16. 6 17. 3 18. 14 19. 18 20. 11

21. 28 22. 29 23. 34 24. 38 25. 21 26. 15 27. 35 28. 30

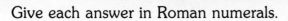

Give each answer in Roman numerals.

29. How old are you?

30. How many teachers do you have in all?

31. What grade are you in at school?

32. How many chapters are in your mathematics book?

33. How many school books do you have?

34. How many students are in your class?

35. Copy this clock. Use Roman numerals to put the numbers on the clock.

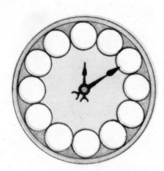

36. This is how you write 1976 in Roman numerals.

M C M L X X V I
1000 + 900 + 70 + 6
1976

Write the current year in Roman numerals.

Keeping Skillful

Multiply.

1. 7 ×3	**2.** 4 ×9	**3.** 6 ×5	**4.** 8 ×6
5. 2 ×6	**6.** 9 ×7	**7.** 4 ×8	**8.** 6 ×9
9. 7 ×2	**10.** 5 ×4	**11.** 8 ×7	**12.** 3 ×6
13. 3 ×4	**14.** 5 ×9	**15.** 9 ×8	**16.** 8 ×2
17. 2 ×7	**18.** 6 ×6	**19.** 7 ×4	**20.** 9 ×9
21. 3 ×5	**22.** 8 ×8	**23.** 2 ×5	**24.** 9 ×3

Divide.

25. $8\overline{)48}$ **26.** $4\overline{)36}$ **27.** $2\overline{)14}$

28. $7\overline{)35}$ **29.** $8\overline{)64}$ **30.** $7\overline{)63}$

31. $6\overline{)42}$ **32.** $9\overline{)81}$ **33.** $5\overline{)20}$

34. $8\overline{)72}$ **35.** $7\overline{)14}$ **36.** $4\overline{)24}$

37. $2\overline{)18}$ **38.** $6\overline{)24}$ **39.** $7\overline{)56}$

40. $6\overline{)54}$ **41.** $8\overline{)56}$ **42.** $9\overline{)45}$

Chapter 15 Test
Meaning of Fractions, pages 294–313

Does the picture show sixths?
Write yes or no.

1.   **2.**

How much is shaded? Give a fraction.

3.  **4.**

5.   **6.**

7. Give the denominator of $\frac{5}{6}$.

8. Write the mixed number for three and two sevenths.

9. Write the mixed number for two and three fourths.

For exercises 10–15, answer each question by writing yes or no.

Is the fraction less than 1?

10. $\frac{3}{2}$ **11.** $\frac{4}{5}$ **12.** $\frac{7}{7}$

Is the fraction greater than 1?

13. $\frac{8}{5}$ **14.** $\frac{4}{3}$ **15.** $\frac{1}{4}$

Compare the fractions. Use > or <.

16. $\frac{1}{5}$ ● $\frac{3}{5}$ **17.** $\frac{5}{6}$ ● $\frac{4}{6}$

18. $\frac{2}{3}$ ● $\frac{3}{3}$ **19.** $\frac{7}{8}$ ● $\frac{5}{8}$

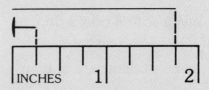

20. Give a fraction for the length of the tack.

21. Give a mixed number for the length of the wire.

How much is shaded?

22. Give a fraction.

23. Give a mixed number.

How much is shaded?

24. Give a fraction.

25. Give a mixed number.

Problems Around Us

1. The first Ferris wheel had 36 cars on it. Each car could hold 60 people. How many people could this Ferris wheel carry?

2. A trolley car, built in 1889, was used for 73 years in the District of Columbia. In what year was this trolley car taken out of service?

3. The body of an eleven-year-old contains about 2.83 liters of blood. The body of an adult contains about 4.72 liters of blood. An adult's body contains about how much more blood?

4. Scientists believe that a day on Venus is about 25 earth days. An earth day is 24 hours. A day on Venus would be about how many hours?

5. A very large turkey grown in California weighed 31.75 kilograms. An average turkey weighs about 6.80 kilograms. How much more did the large turkey weigh?

6. An ostrich egg is so large that it could hold 24 chicken eggs inside. How many chicken eggs could 12 ostrich eggs hold?

7. A duck hawk can fly about 867 kilometers in 3 hours. At this rate, what is the average speed a duck hawk can fly in one hour?

8. A human body has 68 bones in the hands and face. There are 138 bones in the rest of the body. What is the total number of bones in a human body?

This graph shows how many blocks Judy ran each day for a week.

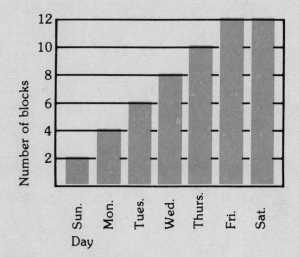

How many blocks did Judy run on

9. Monday?   10. Friday?

On which day did Judy run

11. 6 blocks?   12. 10 blocks?

Individualized Skills Maintenance

Diagnose

A *pages 214–225*

$64 \div 8$

$72 \div 9$

$56 \div 7$

B *pages 234–244*

$473 \div 8$

$905 \div 3$

$354 \div 5$

Practice

A

1. $2\overline{)6}$
2. $8\overline{)16}$
3. $3\overline{)24}$
4. $5\overline{)35}$
5. $7\overline{)49}$

6. $2\overline{)18}$
7. $4\overline{)24}$
8. $8\overline{)56}$
9. $9\overline{)72}$
10. $3\overline{)0}$

11. $7\overline{)7}$
12. $1\overline{)8}$
13. $5\overline{)20}$
14. $4\overline{)36}$
15. $6\overline{)42}$

16. $2\overline{)14}$
17. $3\overline{)27}$
18. $4\overline{)32}$
19. $7\overline{)63}$
20. $9\overline{)45}$

21. $6\overline{)54}$
22. $8\overline{)48}$
23. $5\overline{)40}$
24. $7\overline{)28}$
25. $8\overline{)64}$

26. $8\overline{)40}$
27. $9\overline{)18}$
28. $8\overline{)32}$
29. $6\overline{)30}$
30. $9\overline{)54}$

31. $4\overline{)12}$
32. $7\overline{)56}$
33. $9\overline{)63}$
34. $7\overline{)35}$
35. $6\overline{)24}$

B

36. $2\overline{)38}$
37. $4\overline{)50}$
38. $6\overline{)78}$
39. $7\overline{)91}$
40. $5\overline{)62}$

41. $4\overline{)526}$
42. $5\overline{)659}$
43. $3\overline{)387}$
44. $6\overline{)728}$
45. $7\overline{)879}$

46. $9\overline{)327}$
47. $4\overline{)156}$
48. $8\overline{)261}$
49. $7\overline{)546}$
50. $3\overline{)288}$

51. $6\overline{)614}$
52. $2\overline{)441}$
53. $5\overline{)903}$
54. $4\overline{)123}$
55. $8\overline{)862}$

56. $9\overline{)76}$
57. $7\overline{)861}$
58. $5\overline{)472}$
59. $6\overline{)483}$
60. $8\overline{)804}$

Unit 5 Review

Chapter 13, pages 262–274

Find *n*.

1. $\dfrac{2}{5} = \dfrac{n}{15}$ 2. $\dfrac{1}{6} = \dfrac{4}{n}$

3. Rita can buy 3 folders for 40¢. How much will 6 folders cost?

Chapter 14, pages 276–292

Are the polygons congruent? Write yes or no.

4. 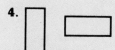 5.

Is the line a line of symmetry? Write yes or no.

6.   7.

Give the name for each segment. Use radius or diameter.

8.   9.

Give a name for each shape. Use square, rectangle, or parallelogram.

10.   11.

Chapter 15, pages 294–313

Give a fraction to tell how much is shaded.

12.   13.

Compare the fractions. Use > or <.

14. $\dfrac{3}{4}$ $\dfrac{1}{4}$ 15. $\dfrac{1}{3}$ ● $\dfrac{2}{3}$

Is the fraction greater than 1? Write yes or no.

16. $\dfrac{5}{3}$ 17. $\dfrac{0}{4}$ 18. $\dfrac{2}{3}$

How much is shaded?

19. Give a fraction.

20. Give a mixed number.

21. Give a mixed number for the length of the pin.

Unit 5 Test

Chapters 13–15, pages 262–314

Find *n*.

1. $\frac{1}{3} = \frac{8}{n}$ **2.** $\frac{4}{7} = \frac{n}{21}$

For exercises 3–11, answer the question by writing yes or no.

Are the polygons congruent?

3.

Is the polygon a parallelogram?

4.   **5.**

Is the polygon a square?

6.   **7.**

Is the line a line of symmetry?

8.    **9.**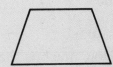

Is the segment a diameter?

10.   **11.**

How much is shaded? Give a fraction.

12.    **13.**

Compare the fractions. Use > or <.

14. $\frac{3}{4}$ ⬤ $\frac{1}{4}$ **15.** $\frac{1}{3}$ ⬤ $\frac{2}{3}$

Is the fraction less than 1?
Write yes or no.

16. $\frac{5}{3}$ **17.** $\frac{2}{5}$

18. Give a mixed number for the length of the ribbon.

How much is shaded?

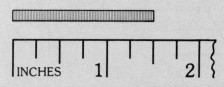

19. Give a fraction.

20. Give a mixed number.

Unit 6

Addition: Same Denominator

A. On Saturday, $\frac{3}{10}$ of an inch of rain fell during
the morning. $\frac{6}{10}$ of an inch fell during
the afternoon. How much rain fell in all?

Find $\frac{3}{10} + \frac{6}{10}$.

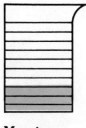
Morning

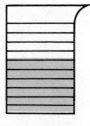
Afternoon

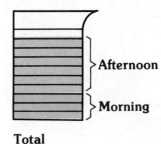
Total

Add the numerators.

$$\frac{3}{10} + \frac{6}{10} = \frac{3 + 6}{10} = \frac{9}{10}$$

$3 + 6 = 9$

Use the same denominator.

$\frac{9}{10}$ of an inch of rain fell in all.

B. Find $\frac{1}{4} + \frac{2}{4}$.

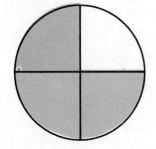

$$\begin{array}{r} \frac{1}{4} \\ + \frac{2}{4} \\ \hline \frac{3}{4} \end{array}$$

Add the numerators.

$1 + 2 = 3$

Use the same denominator.

● **Discuss** When two fractions have the same
denominator, how can you find the sum?

Add.

1. $\frac{1}{5} + \frac{1}{5} = \frac{⫶}{5}$ (1 + 1)   2. $\frac{2}{10} + \frac{7}{10} = \frac{⫶}{10}$ (2 + 7)   3. $\frac{4}{8} + \frac{3}{8} = \frac{⫶}{8}$ (4 + 3)

4. $\frac{0}{3} + \frac{2}{3} = \frac{⫶}{3}$ (0 + 2)   5. $\frac{1}{4} + \frac{3}{4} = \frac{⫶}{4}$ (1 + 3)   6. $\frac{5}{2} + \frac{4}{2} = \frac{⫶}{2}$ (5 + 4)

7. $\frac{2}{4} + \frac{1}{4}$ 8. $\frac{1}{5} + \frac{3}{5}$ 9. $\frac{2}{6} + \frac{2}{6}$ 10. $\frac{1}{8} + \frac{5}{8}$ 11. $\frac{3}{12} + \frac{7}{12}$

12. $\frac{4}{10} + \frac{4}{10}$ 13. $\frac{1}{9} + \frac{2}{9}$ 14. $\frac{3}{12} + \frac{5}{12}$ 15. $\frac{1}{4} + \frac{1}{4}$ 16. $\frac{3}{6} + \frac{2}{6}$

17. $\begin{array}{r} \frac{1}{3} \\ +\frac{1}{3} \\ \hline \end{array}$ 18. $\begin{array}{r} \frac{2}{8} \\ +\frac{3}{8} \\ \hline \end{array}$ 19. $\begin{array}{r} \frac{1}{2} \\ +\frac{0}{2} \\ \hline \end{array}$ 20. $\begin{array}{r} \frac{5}{10} \\ +\frac{3}{10} \\ \hline \end{array}$ 21. $\begin{array}{r} \frac{0}{4} \\ +\frac{3}{4} \\ \hline \end{array}$ 22. $\begin{array}{r} \frac{2}{8} \\ +\frac{1}{8} \\ \hline \end{array}$ 23. $\begin{array}{r} \frac{1}{5} \\ +\frac{2}{5} \\ \hline \end{array}$

24. $\begin{array}{r} \frac{1}{2} \\ +\frac{1}{2} \\ \hline \end{array}$ 25. $\begin{array}{r} \frac{1}{6} \\ +\frac{5}{6} \\ \hline \end{array}$ 26. $\begin{array}{r} \frac{3}{7} \\ +\frac{2}{7} \\ \hline \end{array}$ 27. $\begin{array}{r} \frac{4}{3} \\ +\frac{2}{3} \\ \hline \end{array}$ 28. $\begin{array}{r} \frac{6}{4} \\ +\frac{4}{4} \\ \hline \end{array}$ 29. $\begin{array}{r} \frac{4}{5} \\ +\frac{3}{5} \\ \hline \end{array}$ 30. $\begin{array}{r} \frac{7}{8} \\ +\frac{3}{8} \\ \hline \end{array}$

31. Angela shoveled snow for $\frac{1}{3}$ of an hour in the morning. She shoveled for $\frac{2}{3}$ of an hour in the afternoon. How long did Angela shovel in all?

*32. On Monday, $\frac{3}{10}$ of an inch of rain fell. On Tuesday, $\frac{1}{10}$ of an inch fell, and on Wednesday, $\frac{5}{10}$ of an inch fell. How much rain fell in all during the three days?

**More practice
Set 32, page 380**

Subtraction: Same Denominator

A. Yana had $\frac{7}{8}$ of a yard of fabric. He used $\frac{5}{8}$ of a yard for a vest. How much fabric was left?

Find $\frac{7}{8} - \frac{5}{8}$.

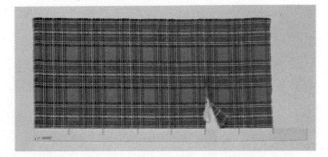

Subtract the numerators.

$$\frac{7}{8} - \frac{5}{8} = \frac{7-5}{8} = \frac{2}{8}$$

$7 - 5 = 2$

Use the same denominator.

$\frac{2}{8}$ of a yard of fabric was left.

B. Find $\frac{5}{6} - \frac{3}{6}$.

$$\begin{array}{r} \frac{5}{6} \\ -\,\frac{3}{6} \\ \hline \frac{2}{6} \end{array}$$

Subtract the numerators.

$5 - 3 = 2$

Use the same denominator.

Subtract.

1. $\frac{3}{4} - \frac{1}{4} = \frac{}{4}$ $3 - 1$

2. $\frac{2}{3} - \frac{1}{3} = \frac{}{3}$ $2 - 1$

3. $\frac{7}{8} - \frac{4}{8} = \frac{}{8}$ $7 - 4$

4. $\frac{5}{3} - \frac{2}{3} = \frac{}{3}$ $5 - 2$

5. $\frac{4}{7} - \frac{0}{7} = \frac{}{7}$ $4 - 0$

6. $\frac{8}{9} - \frac{8}{9} = \frac{}{9}$ $8 - 8$

7. $\frac{4}{5} - \frac{3}{5}$

8. $\frac{5}{6} - \frac{2}{6}$

9. $\frac{8}{10} - \frac{3}{10}$

10. $\frac{9}{12} - \frac{5}{12}$

11. $\frac{2}{4} - \frac{0}{4}$

12. $\frac{7}{6} - \frac{1}{6}$

13. $\frac{12}{8} - \frac{5}{8}$

14. $\frac{1}{2} - \frac{0}{2}$

15. $\frac{3}{2} - \frac{1}{2}$

• **Discuss** When two fractions have the same denominator, how can you find the difference?

16. $\frac{2}{4}$
$-\frac{1}{4}$

17. $\frac{5}{7}$
$-\frac{3}{7}$

18. $\frac{11}{12}$
$-\frac{3}{12}$

19. $\frac{5}{6}$
$-\frac{0}{6}$

20. $\frac{9}{10}$
$-\frac{3}{10}$

21. $\frac{3}{5}$
$-\frac{3}{5}$

22. $\frac{2}{2}$
$-\frac{1}{2}$

23. $\frac{6}{9}$
$-\frac{5}{9}$

24. $\frac{6}{8}$
$-\frac{6}{8}$

25. $\frac{6}{7}$
$-\frac{2}{7}$

26. $\frac{7}{10}$
$-\frac{4}{10}$

27. $\frac{4}{4}$
$-\frac{3}{4}$

28. $\frac{3}{3}$
$-\frac{1}{3}$

29. $\frac{2}{4}$
$-\frac{2}{4}$

30. $\frac{4}{6}$
$-\frac{1}{6}$

31. $\frac{3}{5}$
$-\frac{0}{5}$

32. It took Niabi $\frac{1}{4}$ of an hour to cut out a skirt and $\frac{3}{4}$ of an hour to sew it. How much longer did it take to sew the skirt?

33. A button is $\frac{3}{8}$ of an inch wide. The buttonhole is $\frac{5}{8}$ of an inch wide. How much wider is the buttonhole?

★34. Alice's sweater is $\frac{2}{3}$ finished. How much more does she have to knit?

**More practice
Set 33, page 380**

Time Out

See if you can draw this robot in one continuous line. Do not take your pencil point off the paper. Do not go over any part of the line twice or cross any line.

The eyes are not part of the puzzle.

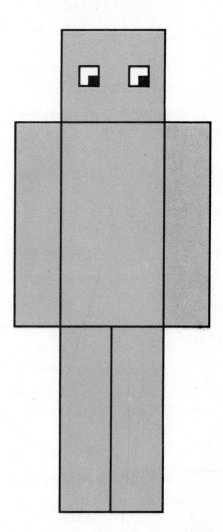

323

Equal Fractions

A. Phil folded a sheet of paper to show two equal parts. He colored one part green.

One of the two equal parts is green.

$\frac{1}{2}$ of the paper is green.

Phil folded the same paper to show four equal parts.

$\frac{2}{4}$ of the paper is green.

He folded the same paper again to show eighths.

$\frac{4}{8}$ of the paper is green.

$\frac{1}{2}$, $\frac{2}{4}$, and $\frac{4}{8}$ describe the same amount. They are **equal fractions.**

$$\frac{1}{2} = \frac{2}{4} = \frac{4}{8}$$

B. Look at the parts that are colored blue. What equal fractions do they show?

$$\frac{1}{2} = \frac{3}{6}$$

• *Discuss* Can you give other fractions equal to $\frac{1}{2}$?

How much is shaded? Give the equal fractions.

1.

$$\frac{\vdots}{3} = \frac{2}{6}$$

2.

$$\frac{1}{4} = \frac{\vdots}{8}$$

3.

$$\frac{\vdots}{5} = \frac{\vdots}{10}$$

4.

$$\frac{\vdots}{\vdots} = \frac{\vdots}{\vdots}$$

5.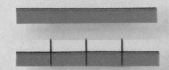

$$\frac{\vdots}{\vdots} = \frac{\vdots}{\vdots}$$

6.

$$\frac{\vdots}{\vdots} = \frac{\vdots}{\vdots}$$

7.

$$\frac{\vdots}{\vdots} = \frac{\vdots}{\vdots}$$

8.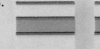

$$\frac{\vdots}{\vdots} = \frac{\vdots}{\vdots}$$

9.

$$\frac{\vdots}{\vdots} = \frac{\vdots}{\vdots}$$

10.

$$\frac{\vdots}{\vdots} = \frac{\vdots}{\vdots}$$

Keeping Skillful

1. $2\overline{)84}$

2. $5\overline{)165}$

3. $4\overline{)75}$

4. $8\overline{)122}$

5. $7\overline{)238}$

6. $3\overline{)676}$

7. $9\overline{)308}$

8. $5\overline{)749}$

9. $2\overline{)980}$

10. $9\overline{)96}$

11. $4\overline{)966}$

12. $6\overline{)735}$

13. $795 \div 7$

14. $108 \div 9$

15. $869 \div 4$

16. $735 \div 2$

17. $964 \div 8$

18. $497 \div 5$

19. $573 \div 8$

20. $112 \div 2$

325

Equal Fractions on the Number Line

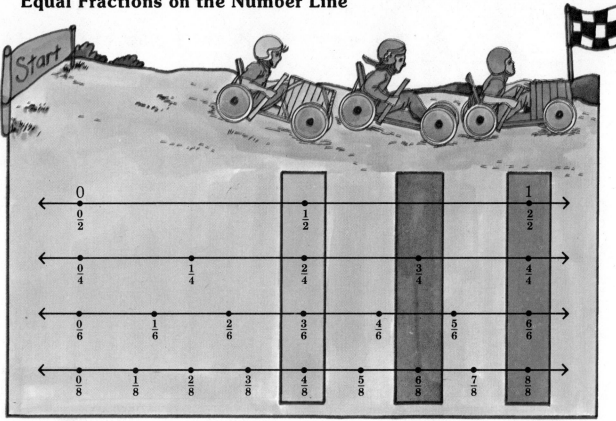

These cars are in a soapbox derby.

A. The yellow car has gone $\frac{1}{2}$ of the distance. The yellow stripe shows fractions equal to $\frac{1}{2}$.

$$\frac{1}{2} = \frac{2}{4} = \frac{3}{6} = \frac{4}{8}$$

B. The green car has gone $\frac{3}{4}$ of the distance. The green stripe shows a fraction equal to $\frac{3}{4}$.

$$\frac{3}{4} = \frac{6}{8}$$

C. The blue car has finished the race. The blue stripe shows fractions equal to 1.

$$1 = \frac{2}{2} = \frac{4}{4} = \frac{6}{6} = \frac{8}{8}$$

•*Discuss* What other equal fractions do the number lines show? How can you tell if a fraction is equal to 1? How can you tell if a fraction is equal to 0? Name five fractions equal to 0.

Copy and complete each pair of equal fractions. You can use the number lines to help you.

1. $\frac{1}{2} = \frac{\square}{6}$ **2.** $\frac{1}{3} = \frac{\square}{6}$

3. $\frac{4}{6} = \frac{\square}{3}$ **4.** $\frac{2}{2} = \frac{\square}{3}$

5. $\frac{0}{3} = \frac{\square}{6}$ **6.** $\frac{6}{6} = \frac{\square}{2}$

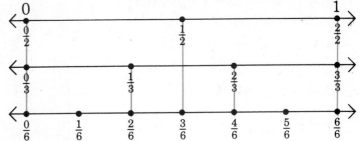

7. $\frac{1}{5} = \frac{\square}{10}$ **8.** $\frac{1}{2} = \frac{\square}{10}$

9. $\frac{8}{10} = \frac{\square}{5}$ **10.** $\frac{5}{5} = \frac{\square}{2}$

11. $\frac{0}{2} = \frac{\square}{10}$ **12.** $\frac{4}{10} = \frac{\square}{5}$

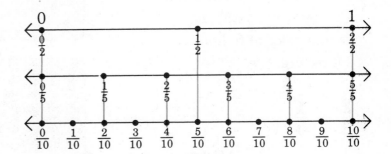

13. $\frac{2}{4} = \frac{\square}{8}$ **14.** $\frac{1}{4} = \frac{\square}{12}$

15. $\frac{6}{12} = \frac{\square}{8}$ **16.** $\frac{3}{12} = \frac{\square}{8}$

17. $\frac{6}{8} = \frac{\square}{4}$ **18.** $\frac{3}{4} = \frac{\square}{12}$

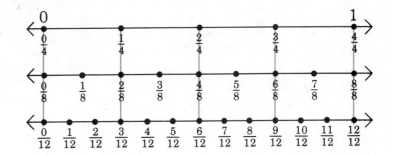

19. $\frac{3}{4} = \frac{\square}{8}$ **20.** $\frac{3}{2} = \frac{\square}{4}$

21. $\frac{8}{4} = \frac{\square}{8}$ **22.** $\frac{5}{4} = \frac{\square}{8}$

23. $\frac{14}{8} = \frac{\square}{4}$ **24.** $\frac{4}{2} = \frac{\square}{4}$

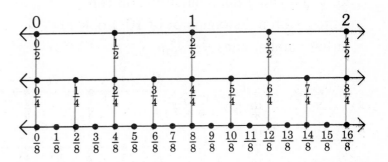

Addition: Different Denominators

A. Mrs. Williams planted $\frac{2}{3}$ of her garden in vegetables. She planted $\frac{1}{6}$ of her garden in flowers. What fraction of the garden is planted?

Find $\frac{2}{3} + \frac{1}{6}$.

6 is the larger denominator. You can write $\frac{2}{3}$ with a denominator of 6. Look at the picture. $\frac{2}{3} = \frac{4}{6}$.

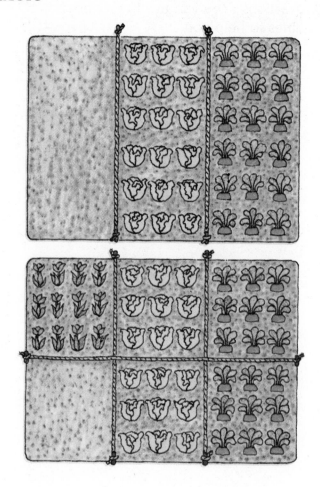

$$\frac{2}{3} + \frac{1}{6}$$

$$\frac{4}{6} + \frac{1}{6} = \frac{5}{6}$$

Add the numerators.

$4 + 1 = 5$

Use the same denominator.

$\frac{5}{6}$ of the garden is planted.

B. Find $\frac{2}{5} + \frac{3}{10}$.

10 is the larger denominator. You can write $\frac{2}{5}$ with a denominator of 10. Look at the number lines. $\frac{2}{5} = \frac{4}{10}$.

$$\begin{array}{r} \frac{2}{5} = \frac{4}{10} \\ + \frac{3}{10} = + \frac{3}{10} \\ \hline \frac{7}{10} \end{array}$$

$4 + 3 = 7$

Add. You can use the number lines
to find equal fractions.

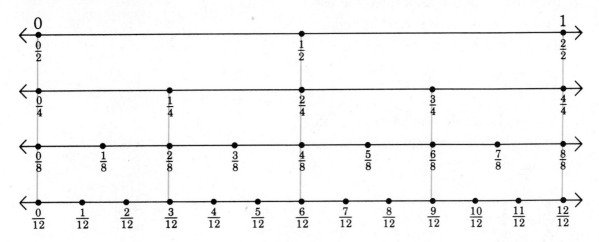

1. $\frac{1}{2} + \frac{1}{4}$ 2. $\frac{1}{4} + \frac{3}{8}$ 3. $\frac{3}{8} + \frac{1}{2}$ 4. $\frac{1}{4} + \frac{1}{8}$ 5. $\frac{1}{12} + \frac{1}{2}$

6. $\frac{5}{12} + \frac{1}{4}$ 7. $\frac{0}{2} + \frac{1}{4}$ 8. $\frac{3}{4} + \frac{1}{12}$ 9. $\frac{1}{2} + \frac{1}{8}$ 10. $\frac{0}{8} + \frac{3}{4}$

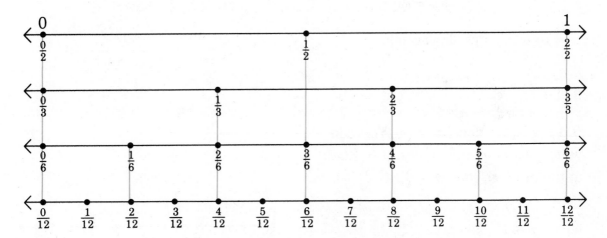

11. $\frac{1}{2} + \frac{1}{6}$ 12. $\frac{7}{12} + \frac{1}{3}$ 13. $\frac{1}{2} + \frac{4}{12}$ 14. $\frac{0}{3} + \frac{1}{6}$ 15. $\frac{1}{2} + \frac{2}{6}$

16. $\frac{2}{2}$ $+ \frac{5}{6}$ 17. $\frac{5}{12}$ $+ \frac{6}{6}$ 18. $\frac{5}{6}$ $+ \frac{11}{12}$ 19. $\frac{2}{3}$ $+ \frac{2}{6}$ 20. $\frac{5}{6}$ $+ \frac{2}{12}$ 21. $\frac{0}{6}$ $+ \frac{1}{3}$ ★22. $\frac{1}{2}$ $+ \frac{1}{3}$

Subtraction: Different Denominators

A. Kent had $\frac{1}{2}$ of a cup of milk. He used $\frac{1}{4}$ of a cup to make scrambled eggs. How much milk did he have left?

Find $\frac{1}{2} - \frac{1}{4}$.

4 is the larger denominator. You can write $\frac{1}{2}$ with a denominator of 4. Look at the picture. $\frac{1}{2} = \frac{2}{4}$.

Milk used

$$\frac{1}{2} - \frac{1}{4}$$

Subtract the numerators.

$$\frac{2}{4} - \frac{1}{4} = \frac{1}{4} \qquad \{2 - 1 = 1\}$$

Use the same denominator.

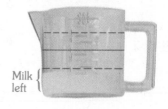

Milk left

$\frac{1}{4}$ of a cup of milk was left.

B. Find $\frac{5}{6} - \frac{2}{3}$.

6 is the larger denominator. You can write $\frac{2}{3}$ with a denominator of 6. Look at the number lines. $\frac{2}{3} = \frac{4}{6}$.

$$\begin{array}{r} \frac{5}{6} = \frac{5}{6} \\ -\frac{2}{3} = -\frac{4}{6} \\ \hline \frac{1}{6} \end{array} \qquad \{5 - 4 = 1\}$$

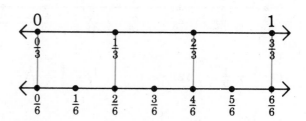

Subtract. You can use the number
lines to find equal fractions.

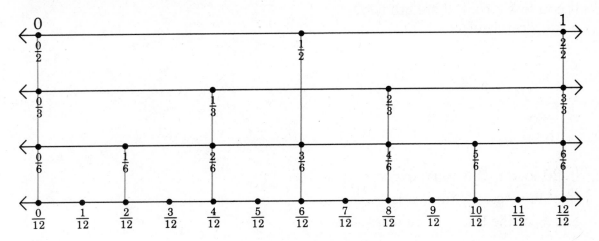

1. $\frac{1}{2} - \frac{1}{6}$ 2. $\frac{2}{3} - \frac{1}{6}$ 3. $\frac{5}{12} - \frac{1}{6}$ 4. $\frac{2}{3} - \frac{0}{6}$ 5. $\frac{1}{6} - \frac{1}{12}$

6. $\frac{11}{12} - \frac{1}{3}$ 7. $\frac{2}{3} - \frac{5}{12}$ 8. $\frac{1}{6} - \frac{0}{3}$ 9. $\frac{11}{12} - \frac{1}{6}$ 10. $\frac{5}{6} - \frac{2}{3}$

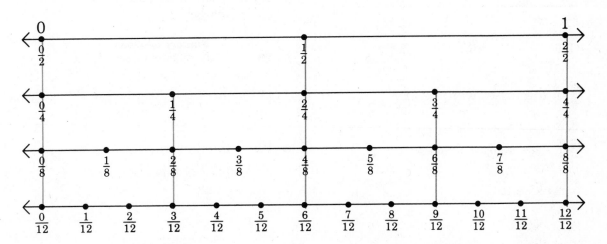

11. $\frac{1}{2} - \frac{1}{4}$ 12. $\frac{5}{8} - \frac{1}{4}$ 13. $\frac{7}{8} - \frac{1}{2}$ 14. $\frac{10}{12} - \frac{4}{8}$ 15. $\frac{5}{8} - \frac{1}{4}$

16. $\frac{11}{12}$ 17. $\frac{1}{2}$ 18. $\frac{3}{4}$ 19. $\frac{8}{8}$ 20. $\frac{4}{4}$ 21. $\frac{3}{8}$ ★22. $\frac{2}{3}$

   $-\frac{1}{2}$ $-\frac{5}{12}$ $-\frac{5}{12}$ $-\frac{3}{4}$ $-\frac{7}{8}$ $-\frac{0}{2}$ $-\frac{1}{2}$
   ___   ___   ___   ___   ___   ___   ___

Lab Activity

Fractions in Experiments

If you toss a coin, there are two ways it can land.

Heads

Tails

In 20 tosses, you could expect $\frac{10}{20}$ of the tosses to be heads, and $\frac{10}{20}$ of the tosses to be tails.

Joy tossed a coin 20 times. Here are her results.

	Tally	Total
Heads	/NĬ ///	8
Tails	/NĬ /NĬ //	12

$\frac{8}{20}$ of the tosses were heads.

$$\frac{8}{20} \quad \longleftarrow \text{ Number of heads} \\ \longleftarrow \text{ Number of tosses}$$

$\frac{8}{20}$ is close to $\frac{10}{20}$.

$\frac{12}{20}$ of the tosses were tails.

$\frac{12}{20}$ is close to $\frac{10}{20}$.

1. Toss a coin 20 times. Record your results in a table.

2. What fraction of your tosses were heads?

$$\frac{\text{⠿}}{20} \quad \begin{array}{l} \longleftarrow \text{ Number of heads} \\ \longleftarrow \text{ Number of tosses} \end{array}$$

Is this fraction close to $\frac{10}{20}$?

3. What fraction of your tosses were tails? Is this fraction close to $\frac{10}{20}$?

• **Discuss** If you toss a coin 50 times, what fraction of the tosses would you expect to be heads? If you toss a coin 100 times, what fraction of the tosses would you expect to be heads?

332

Chapter 16 Test
Addition and Subtraction of Fractions, pages 320–332

Add.

1. $\frac{3}{5} + \frac{1}{5}$ **2.** $\frac{2}{7} + \frac{0}{7}$ **3.** $\frac{2}{6} + \frac{3}{6}$

4. $\frac{1}{3} + \frac{1}{3}$ **5.** $\frac{3}{4} + \frac{3}{4}$ **6.** $\frac{5}{6} + \frac{0}{6}$

Subtract.

7. $\frac{4}{7} - \frac{3}{7}$ **8.** $\frac{4}{5} - \frac{2}{5}$ **9.** $\frac{8}{8} - \frac{5}{8}$

10. $\frac{7}{3} - \frac{5}{3}$ **11.** $\frac{3}{6} - \frac{1}{6}$ **12.** $\frac{1}{4} - \frac{0}{4}$

Copy and complete each pair of equal fractions.

13.

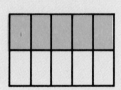

$$\frac{5}{10} = \frac{\text{\tiny III}}{2}$$

14.

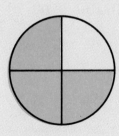

$$\frac{3}{4} = \frac{\text{\tiny III}}{8}$$

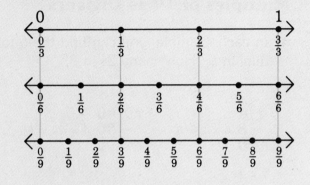

Copy and complete each pair of equal fractions. You can use the number lines to help you.

15. $\frac{1}{3} = \frac{\text{\tiny III}}{6}$ **16.** $\frac{6}{9} = \frac{\text{\tiny III}}{3}$ **17.** $\frac{0}{6} = \frac{\text{\tiny III}}{9}$

Add. You can use the number lines to help you.

18. $\frac{1}{6} + \frac{2}{3}$ **19.** $\frac{5}{9} + \frac{1}{3}$

20. $\begin{array}{r} \frac{1}{3} \\ + \frac{1}{9} \\ \hline \end{array}$ **21.** $\begin{array}{r} \frac{5}{6} \\ + \frac{2}{3} \\ \hline \end{array}$

Subtract. You can use the number lines to help you.

22. $\frac{3}{6} - \frac{1}{3}$ **23.** $\frac{8}{9} - \frac{2}{3}$

24. $\begin{array}{r} \frac{7}{9} \\ - \frac{1}{3} \\ \hline \end{array}$ **25.** $\begin{array}{r} \frac{6}{6} \\ - \frac{2}{3} \\ \hline \end{array}$

Chapter 17   Division: Two-Digit Divisors

Multiples of 10 as Divisors

A. In each example, you can find the quotient by thinking, "How many 2s in 8?"

$$\begin{array}{r} 4 \\ 2\overline{)8} \\ -8 \\ \hline 0 \end{array} \quad 4 \times 2 = 8$$

$$\begin{array}{r} 4 \\ 20\overline{)80} \\ -80 \\ \hline 0 \end{array} \quad 4 \times 20 = 80$$

$$\begin{array}{r} 4 \text{ R7} \\ 20\overline{)87} \\ -80 \\ \hline 7 \end{array} \quad 4 \times 20 = 80$$

B. In each example, you can find the quotient by thinking, "How many 3s in 16?"

$$\begin{array}{r} 5 \text{ R1} \\ 3\overline{)16} \\ -15 \\ \hline 1 \end{array} \quad 5 \times 3 = 15$$

$$\begin{array}{r} 5 \text{ R10} \\ 30\overline{)160} \\ -150 \\ \hline 10 \end{array} \quad 5 \times 30 = 150$$

$$\begin{array}{r} 5 \text{ R19} \\ 30\overline{)169} \\ -150 \\ \hline 19 \end{array} \quad 5 \times 30 = 150$$

Divide. Look for a pattern.

1. $3\overline{)24}$ 2. $30\overline{)240}$ 3. $30\overline{)247}$ 4. $8\overline{)40}$ 5. $80\overline{)400}$ 6. $80\overline{)409}$

7. $4\overline{)8}$ 8. $40\overline{)80}$ 9. $40\overline{)85}$ 10. $5\overline{)27}$ 11. $50\overline{)270}$ 12. $50\overline{)273}$

13. $2\overline{)19}$ 14. $20\overline{)190}$ 15. $20\overline{)191}$ 16. $7\overline{)13}$ 17. $70\overline{)130}$ 18. $70\overline{)134}$

Divide.

19. $70\overline{)630}$ 20. $80\overline{)560}$ 21. $50\overline{)100}$

22. $40\overline{)200}$ 23. $60\overline{)365}$ 24. $40\overline{)283}$

25. $30\overline{)97}$ 26. $20\overline{)44}$ 27. $50\overline{)222}$

28. $70\overline{)359}$ 29. $30\overline{)120}$ 30. $60\overline{)360}$

31. $90\overline{)486}$ 32. $50\overline{)128}$ 33. $20\overline{)154}$

34. $80\overline{)791}$ 35. $20\overline{)74}$ 36. $30\overline{)88}$

37. $90\overline{)400}$ 38. $70\overline{)500}$ 39. $80\overline{)140}$

★40. $500\overline{)2214}$ ★41. $900\overline{)7540}$ ★42. $600\overline{)3907}$

43. How many hours and minutes are 450 minutes?

Hours $\rightarrow$ ▦ R▦ $\leftarrow$ Minutes
$60\overline{)450}$

44. How many minutes and seconds are 290 seconds?

Minutes $\rightarrow$ ▦ R▦ $\leftarrow$ Seconds
$60\overline{)290}$

45. How many hours and minutes are 500 minutes?

46. How many minutes and seconds are 400 seconds?

Keeping Skillful

Add.

1. $54 + 35$

2. $278 + 691$

3. $384 + 806$

4. $8320 + 459$

5. $5006 + 2008$

Subtract.

6. $90 - 65$

7. $173 - 105$

8. $987 - 93$

9. $5235 - 3172$

10. $6091 - 5625$

Multiply.

11. 83×9

12. 4×672

13. 20×36

14. 45×73

15. 183×27

Divide.

16. $384 \div 6$

17. $613 \div 3$

18. $353 \div 6$

19. $186 \div 5$

20. $957 \div 7$

One-Digit Quotients

A. Linda picked 450 apples. She put them in boxes of 72. How many boxes did she fill? How many apples were left over?

Find 450 ÷ 72.

$$72\overline{)450}$$

Divide.
How many 72s in 4? *None*

$$72\overline{)450}$$

Divide.
How many 72s in 45? *None*

$$\begin{array}{r} 6 \\ 72\overline{)450} \\ -432 \\ \hline 18 \end{array}$$

Divide.
How many 72s in 450?
Think: How many 7s in 45? 6
Write 6 above the 0.

Multiply. 6 × 72 = 432
Subtract. The remainder must be less than the divisor. 18 is less than 72.

$$\begin{array}{r} 6 \ \text{R18} \\ 72\overline{)450} \\ -432 \\ \hline 18 \end{array}$$

There are no digits to bring down. The remainder is 18. Write R18 in the answer.

She filled 6 boxes.
There were 18 apples left over.

Check
$$\begin{array}{r} 72 \\ \times\ 6 \\ \hline 432 \\ +\ 18 \\ \hline 450 \end{array}$$
Multiply the quotient and the divisor.

Add the remainder.
The result should be the dividend.

B. Tell how to find and check the answer for 97 ÷ 23.

$$\begin{array}{r} 4 \ \text{R5} \\ 23\overline{)97} \\ -92 \\ \hline 5 \end{array} \qquad \begin{array}{r} 23 \\ \times\ 4 \\ \hline 92 \\ +\ 5 \\ \hline 97 \end{array}$$

C. Tell how to find and check the answer for 357 ÷ 51.

$$\begin{array}{r} 7 \\ 51\overline{)357} \\ -357 \\ \hline 0 \end{array} \qquad \begin{array}{r} 51 \\ \times\ 7 \\ \hline 357 \end{array}$$

Divide.

1. $21\overline{)85}$ 2. $42\overline{)89}$ 3. $36\overline{)72}$ 4. $25\overline{)75}$ 5. $68\overline{)94}$

6. $38\overline{)88}$ 7. $22\overline{)70}$ 8. $75\overline{)90}$ 9. $22\overline{)74}$ 10. $31\overline{)95}$

11. $23\overline{)138}$ 12. $43\overline{)230}$ 13. $34\overline{)115}$ 14. $21\overline{)193}$ 15. $52\overline{)422}$

16. $49\overline{)199}$ 17. $62\overline{)387}$ 18. $32\overline{)269}$ 19. $45\overline{)225}$ 20. $37\overline{)148}$

21. $46\overline{)99}$ 22. $37\overline{)57}$ 23. $92\overline{)205}$ 24. $83\overline{)590}$ 25. $78\overline{)482}$

26. $67\overline{)340}$ 27. $57\overline{)399}$ 28. $63\overline{)90}$ 29. $33\overline{)73}$ 30. $74\overline{)666}$

31. $139 \div 44$ 32. $59 \div 28$ 33. $69 \div 58$ 34. $185 \div 56$

35. $623 \div 81$ 36. $318 \div 53$ 37. $549 \div 61$ 38. $119 \div 39$

39. Rod planted 256 apple trees in rows of 32 each. How many rows did he plant?

40. Brenda paid $3.78 for a bag of 42 apples. How much did each apple cost? Remember to think of $3.78 as 378 cents.

More practice
Set 34, page 381

337

Adjusting the Quotient in Division

It took Ferdinand Magellan's ships about
154 weeks to travel around the world.
154 weeks is how many years and weeks?
Use 52 weeks for 1 year.

Find 154 ÷ 52.

$$
\begin{array}{r}
3 \\
52{\overline{\smash{\big)}\,154}} \\
-156 \\
\hline
\end{array}
$$

Divide.
How many 52s in 154?
Think: How many 5s in 15? *3*
Write 3 above the 4.

Multiply. 3 × 52 = 156
156 is greater than 154, so 3 is too big.

$$
\begin{array}{r}
2 \\
52{\overline{\smash{\big)}\,154}} \\
-104 \\
\hline
50
\end{array}
$$

Try 2.

Multiply. 2 × 52 = 104.
Subtract. 50 is less than 52.
The remainder is 50.

$$
\begin{array}{r}
2 \; R50 \\
52{\overline{\smash{\big)}\,154}} \\
-104 \\
\hline
50
\end{array}
$$

Write R50 in the answer.

There are 2 years and 50 weeks
in 154 weeks.

Check

$$
\begin{array}{r}
52 \\
\times\ 2 \\
\hline
104 \\
+\ 50 \\
\hline
154
\end{array}
$$

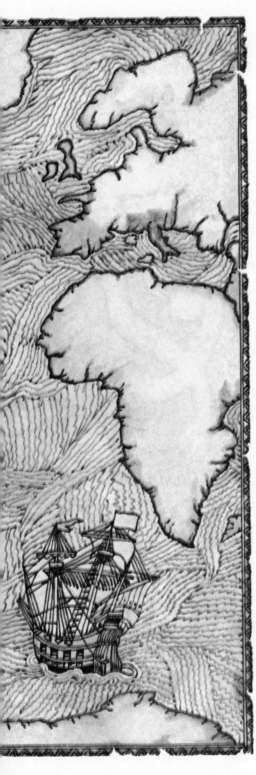

If the exercise has been started correctly, complete it. If it has been started incorrectly, rework the exercise correctly.

1. $\overset{6}{46\overline{)265}}$ -276 2. $\overset{3}{79\overline{)255}}$ -237 3. $\overset{3}{33\overline{)96}}$ -99 4. $\overset{9}{24\overline{)198}}$ -216

Divide.

5. $37\overline{)259}$ 6. $25\overline{)125}$ 7. $44\overline{)172}$ 8. $45\overline{)389}$

9. $51\overline{)408}$ 10. $78\overline{)415}$ 11. $23\overline{)173}$ 12. $36\overline{)216}$

13. $48\overline{)89}$ 14. $27\overline{)94}$ 15. $35\overline{)110}$ 16. $63\overline{)260}$

17. $39\overline{)174}$ 18. $73\overline{)282}$ 19. $12\overline{)89}$ 20. $14\overline{)58}$

21. $84\overline{)465}$ 22. $67\overline{)549}$ 23. $56\overline{)214}$ 24. $96\overline{)258}$

25. $89\overline{)390}$ 26. $74\overline{)286}$ 27. $65\overline{)455}$ 28. $94\overline{)850}$

29. $46\overline{)279}$ 30. $77\overline{)579}$ ★31. $15\overline{)105}$ ★32. $19\overline{)120}$

33. The Strait of Magellan at the southern tip of South America is about 360 miles long. If it took Magellan's ships 40 days to travel through this strait, how many miles did they average each day?

34. At a speed of 45 miles per day, how many days would it take a ship to travel 360 miles?

**More practice
Set 35, page 381**

Two-Digit Quotients

A. The Sheriff of Nottingham locked Robin Hood in a dungeon for 519 hours. For how many days and hours was Robin Hood locked up? (1 day = 24 hours)

Find 519 ÷ 24.

$$\begin{array}{r} 2 \\ 24\overline{)519} \\ -48 \\ \hline 3 \end{array}$$

Divide.
How many 24s in 5? *None.*
How many 24s in 51?
Think: How many 2s in 5? *2*
Write 2 above the 1.

Multiply. 2 × 24 = 48

Subtract. 3 is less than 24.

$$\begin{array}{r} 21 \\ 24\overline{)519} \\ -48\downarrow \\ \hline 39 \\ -24 \\ \hline 15 \end{array}$$

Bring down the 9.

Divide.
How many 24s in 39?
Think: How many 2s in 3? *1*
Write 1 above the 9.

Multiply. 1 × 24 = 24.

Subtract. 15 is less than 24.
There are no more digits to bring down.
The remainder is 15.

$$\begin{array}{r} 21 \quad R15 \\ 24\overline{)519} \\ -48\downarrow \\ \hline 39 \\ -24 \\ \hline 15 \end{array}$$

Write R15 in the answer.

Check

$$\begin{array}{r} 24 \\ \times 21 \\ \hline 24 \\ 480 \\ \hline 504 \\ +\ 15 \\ \hline 519 \end{array}$$

Robin Hood was locked up for 21 days and 15 hours.

B. Tell how to find and check the answer for 779 ÷ 42.

$$42\overline{)779} \\ \underline{-42}^{\displaystyle 1} \\ 35$$

$$42\overline{)779} \\ \underline{-42}^{\displaystyle 18\ R\,23} \\ 359 \\ \underline{-336} \\ 23$$

Check
$$\begin{array}{r} 42 \\ \times 18 \\ \hline 336 \\ 420 \\ \hline 756 \\ +\ 23 \\ \hline 779 \end{array}$$

Divide.

1. $31\overline{)673}$
2. $51\overline{)689}$
3. $64\overline{)896}$
4. $37\overline{)827}$

5. $23\overline{)743}$
6. $24\overline{)992}$
7. $50\overline{)834}$
8. $40\overline{)917}$

9. $52\overline{)867}$
10. $65\overline{)999}$
11. $56\overline{)952}$
12. $36\overline{)468}$

13. $34\overline{)791}$
14. $25\overline{)789}$
15. $12\overline{)398}$
16. $13\overline{)275}$

17. $30\overline{)988}$
18. $20\overline{)976}$
19. $34\overline{)887}$
20. $47\overline{)987}$

21. $26\overline{)598}$
22. $38\overline{)463}$
★23. $24\overline{)817}$
★24. $58\overline{)925}$

25. Robin escaped from the dungeon by digging a tunnel 585 centimeters long. If he dug 45 centimeters per hour, how many hours did it take to dig the tunnel?

26. Robin had 945 pieces of silver when he escaped. He divided the silver equally among 63 of his followers. How many pieces did he give each of his followers?

More practice
Set 36, page 381

Time Out

I was a three-digit number
with digits all the same.
When multiplied by one of my digits,
3996 I became.

What number was I?

Problem Solving: Choosing the Operation

READ   One July, Old Faithful Geyser erupted
713 times. This is an average of how
many times per day? July has 31 days.

DECIDE   Divide the total number of eruptions by
the number of days. Use this equation.
$713 \div 31 = n$

SOLVE

$$
\begin{array}{r}
23 \\
31{\overline{\smash{\big)}\,713}} \\
\underline{-62} \\
93 \\
\underline{-93} \\
0
\end{array}
$$

ANSWER $n = 23$
23 times per day

Write an equation. You can use addition,
subtraction, multiplication, or division.
Then give the answer.

1. The height of the water from Old Faithful
   varies from 3200 centimeters to
   5500 centimeters. What is the difference
   in these heights? $(5500 - 3200 = n)$

2. A tram ride to the top of Snow Queen
   Mountain costs $1.75. How much do 12 rides
   cost? $(12 \times 1.75 = n)$

3. Laura hiked 1629 meters from camp to
   Jenny Lake. Then she hiked 795 meters to
   Hidden Falls. How many meters did she
   hike in all? $(1629 + 795 = n)$

4. Grand Teton Mountain is 4131 meters high. Mt. Moran is 3605 meters high. How much higher is Grand Teton than Mt. Moran?

5. Lone Star Geyser erupts about 56 times a week. About how many times does it erupt in one year? Use 52 weeks for one year.

6. A grizzly bear charged 325 meters in 25 seconds. This bear ran an average of how many meters per second?

7. A float ride down the Snake River costs $13.75 for adults and $8.50 for children. How much does it cost for one adult and one child?

8. In 95 days, Teton Resort got 760 centimeters of snow. Find the average number of centimeters per day.

9. One day, 275 ski-lift tickets were sold. Each ticket cost $6. What was the total cost of these tickets?

10. A glacier moved 525 centimeters in 75 years. This is an average of how many centimeters per year?

11. Land was set aside for Yellowstone Park in 1872. How old will the park be in the year 1990?

*12. When Old Faithful erupts, as much as 24,000 liters of water may be thrown into the air in 60 seconds. This is an average of how many liters per second?

Get Rich Quick

Rhonda Snowbird wants to save one million pennies. She plans to begin saving next Monday. Each day, she will save twice as much as the day before. She will start with 1 cent on Monday (Day 1), 2 cents on Tuesday (Day 2), 4 cents on Wednesday (Day 3), and so on. How many days will it take her to save one million pennies?

Use your calculator. Make a chart that starts like this. Stop when the "Total saved" reaches or goes over 1,000,000 cents.

Day	Amount put away	Total saved
1 (Monday)	1¢	1¢
2 (Tuesday)	2¢	3¢
3 (Wednesday)	4¢	7¢
4 (Thursday)	8¢	15¢
5 (Friday)	16¢	
6 (Saturday)		
7 (Sunday)		
8 (Monday)		

•**Discuss**   How much did Rhonda save in dollars and cents?

344

Chapter 17 Test
Division: Two-Digit Divisors, pages 334-344

Divide.

1. $40\overline{)320}$ 2. $80\overline{)723}$

3. $30\overline{)83}$ 4. $60\overline{)471}$

5. $23\overline{)138}$ 6. $91\overline{)394}$

7. $34\overline{)179}$ 8. $65\overline{)535}$

9. $48\overline{)183}$ 10. $59\overline{)472}$

11. $25\overline{)157}$ 12. $89\overline{)689}$

13. $21\overline{)714}$ 14. $53\overline{)862}$

15. $32\overline{)879}$ 16. $79\overline{)958}$

Find each answer.

17. In 24 days, Glenda worked in a dress shop a total of 144 hours. She worked an average of how many hours a day?

18. Gary has 590 cans of soup to pack in cartons of 48 cans each. How many cartons will he fill? How many cans will be left over?

19. Pikes Peak is 4305 meters high. Mt. McKinley is 6194 meters high. Mt. McKinley is how much higher than Pikes Peak?

20. Miss O'Brien drives 123 kilometers every day. How many kilometers does she drive in 25 days?

Perimeter

Sharda is furnishing a miniature house.
She wants to put metal stripping around
the edge of the hallway floor. She
needs to find the distance around, or
the **perimeter,** of the floor. How many
centimeters of stripping does she need?

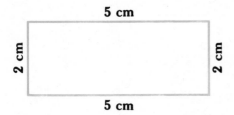

$$2 + 5 + 2 + 5 = 14$$

The perimeter is 14 centimeters.

Find the perimeter of each figure.

1.

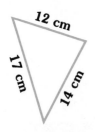

12 cm
17 cm
14 cm

2.

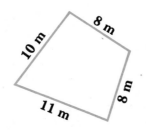

8 m
10 m
8 m
11 m

3.

30 km
30 km
17 km
25 km
21 km

4.

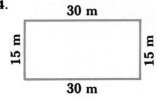

30 m
15 m
15 m
30 m

5.

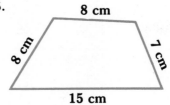

8 cm
8 cm
7 cm
15 cm

6.

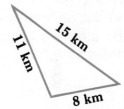

15 km
11 km
8 km

7.

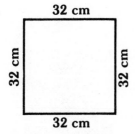

32 cm
32 cm
32 cm
32 cm

8.

86 km
86 km
86 km

9.

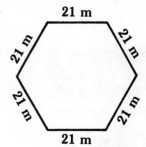

21 m
21 m
21 m
21 m
21 m
21 m

10. Find the amount of fencing used to enclose this yard.

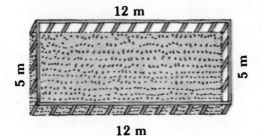

12 m
5 m
5 m
12 m

11. Find the amount of fringe used to trim the edges of this shawl.

60 cm
60 cm
60 cm

Meaning of Area

The **square centimeter** is a unit of **area**.

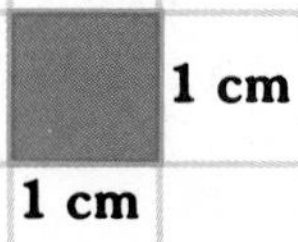

1 cm

1 cm

To tile the hallway floor in the miniature house, Sharda uses tiles that are each 1 square centimeter. It takes 10 of these tiles to cover the hallway floor. The area of the floor is 10 square centimeters.

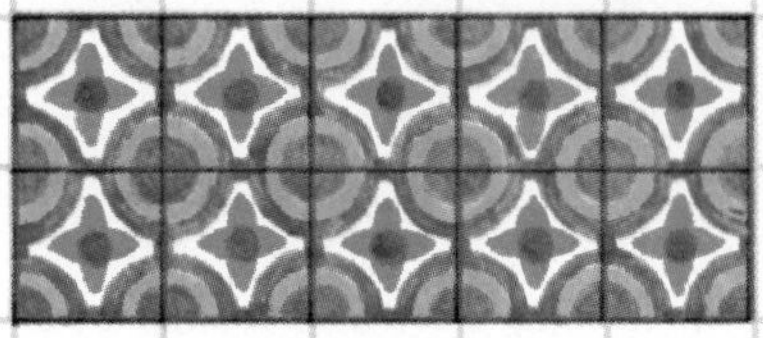

Give the area of each shape in square centimeters.

1.

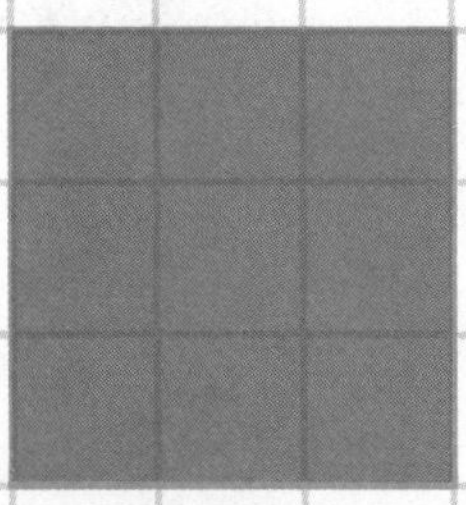

2.

3.

4.

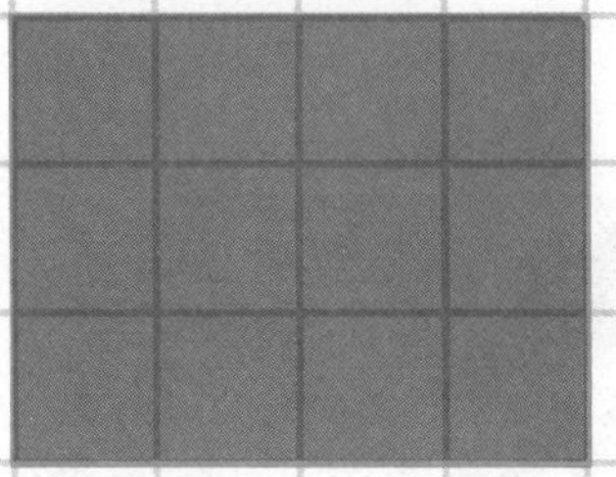

5.

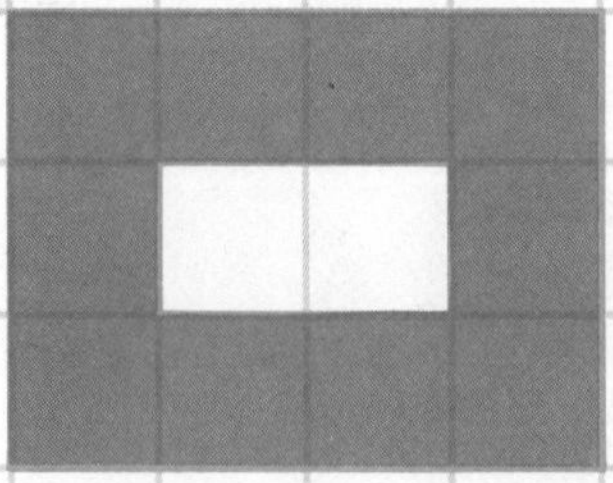

6.

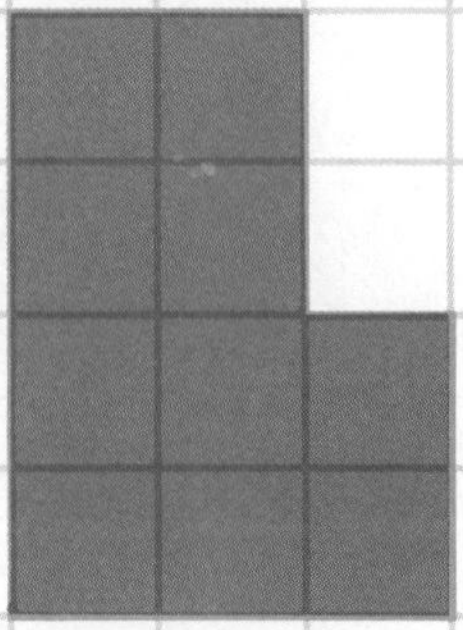

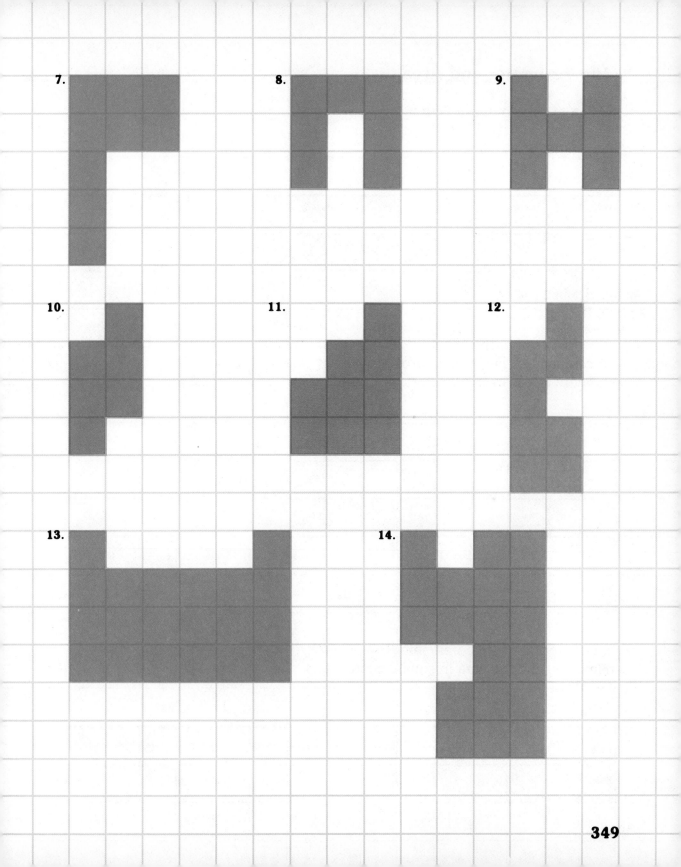

349

Using Perimeter and Area

The area of each of these figures is
9 square centimeters. Find the perimeter
of each figure in centimeters.

1.

2.

3.

The perimeter of each of these figures
is 16 centimeters. Find the area of
each figure in square centimeters.

4.

5.

6.

For each figure, find the perimeter in
centimeters, and the area in square centimeters.

7.

8.

9.

10.

11.

12.

13.

14. On square centimeter paper, draw 6 figures each with an area of 12 square centimeters.

15. On square centimeter paper, draw 6 figures each with a perimeter of 18 centimeters.

*16. Is it possible to draw a figure with an area of 16 square centimeters and a perimeter of 16 centimeters?

Keeping Skillful

1. $\begin{array}{r} 48 \\ \times 51 \end{array}$	2. $\begin{array}{r} 52 \\ \times 63 \end{array}$
3. $\begin{array}{r} 89 \\ \times 73 \end{array}$	4. $\begin{array}{r} 46 \\ \times 26 \end{array}$
5. $\begin{array}{r} 58 \\ \times 27 \end{array}$	6. $\begin{array}{r} 42 \\ \times 29 \end{array}$
7. $\begin{array}{r} 59 \\ \times 15 \end{array}$	8. $\begin{array}{r} 19 \\ \times 16 \end{array}$
9. $\begin{array}{r} 369 \\ \times\ 85 \end{array}$	10. $\begin{array}{r} 350 \\ \times\ 62 \end{array}$
11. $\begin{array}{r} 584 \\ \times\ 94 \end{array}$	12. $\begin{array}{r} 406 \\ \times\ 17 \end{array}$
13. $\begin{array}{r} 271 \\ \times\ 87 \end{array}$	14. $\begin{array}{r} 946 \\ \times\ 84 \end{array}$
15. $\begin{array}{r} 712 \\ \times\ 26 \end{array}$	16. $\begin{array}{r} 637 \\ \times\ 19 \end{array}$
17. $\begin{array}{r} 209 \\ \times\ 59 \end{array}$	18. $\begin{array}{r} 627 \\ \times\ 93 \end{array}$
19. $\begin{array}{r} 158 \\ \times\ 38 \end{array}$	20. $\begin{array}{r} 274 \\ \times\ 14 \end{array}$

351

Half of a Square Centimeter

Two halves of a square centimeter
make one square centimeter.

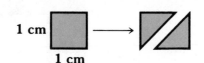

Count square centimeters to find
the area of this shape.

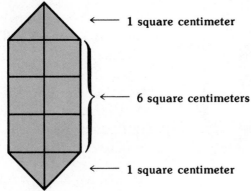

← 1 square centimeter

← 6 square centimeters

← 1 square centimeter

The area of this shape is
8 square centimeters.

Give the area of each shape in square centimeters.

1.

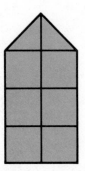

2.

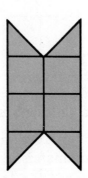

3.

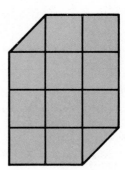

4.

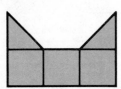

5.

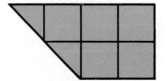

6.

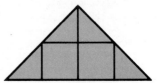

7.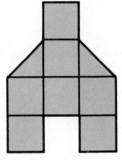

8.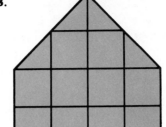

9.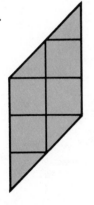

10.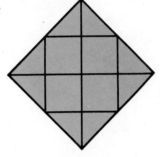

11.

12.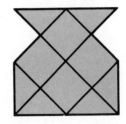

★13.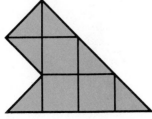

★14.

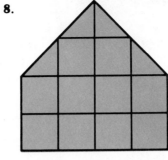

Time Out

Copy the puzzle. See how many true number sentences you can find in the square.

Use 3 numbers. You may also use one symbol (+, −, ×, or ÷) and one equal sign (=). The number sentences may be vertical, horizontal, or diagonal. You may not change the order of the numbers. You may use a number more than once.

The first one is done for you.

3	9	12	2	10	35
6	8	12	20	4	5
18	0	24	4	6	7
12	9	3	6	24	4
4	2	8	9	4	36
3	48	6	8	14	22

(3 × 8 = 24 circled diagonally)

I found 25!

353

Area of a Triangle

A. Vijay cut this rectangle out of square-centimeter paper.

He drew segment AB and cut along it.

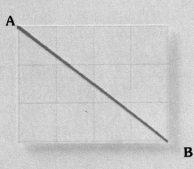

The two triangles formed have equal area.

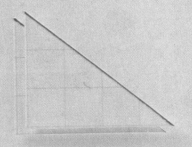

B. To find the area of the blue triangle, first find the area of the rectangle.

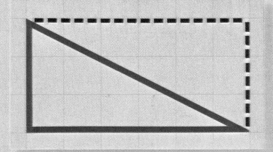

The area of the rectangle is 18 square centimeters. The area of the blue triangle is half the area of the rectangle. Divide 18 by 2.

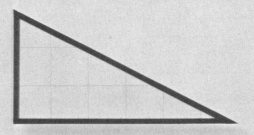

The area of the blue triangle is 9 square centimeters.

Give the area of each triangle in square centimeters.

1.

2.

3.

4.

5.

6.

7.

8.

9.

Three-Dimensional Shapes

These are some other geometric figures.

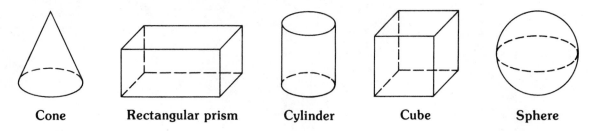

| Cone | Rectangular prism | Cylinder | Cube | Sphere |

Some objects around you have these shapes.

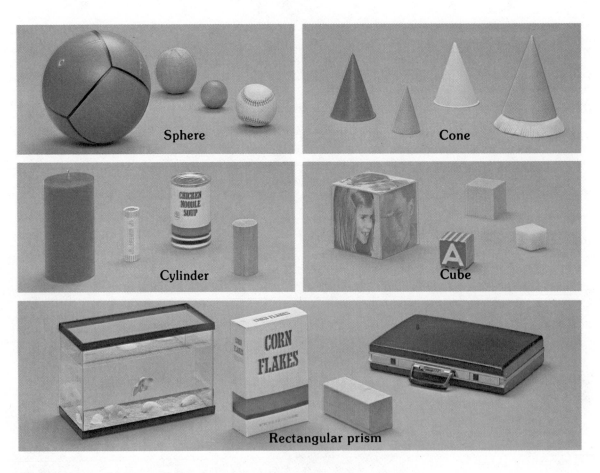

Sphere

Cone

Cylinder

Cube

Rectangular prism

● **Discuss** Name other objects in your classroom
that are shaped like these geometric figures.

Give the name for each shape.
Use sphere, cone, rectangular prism, cylinder, or cube.

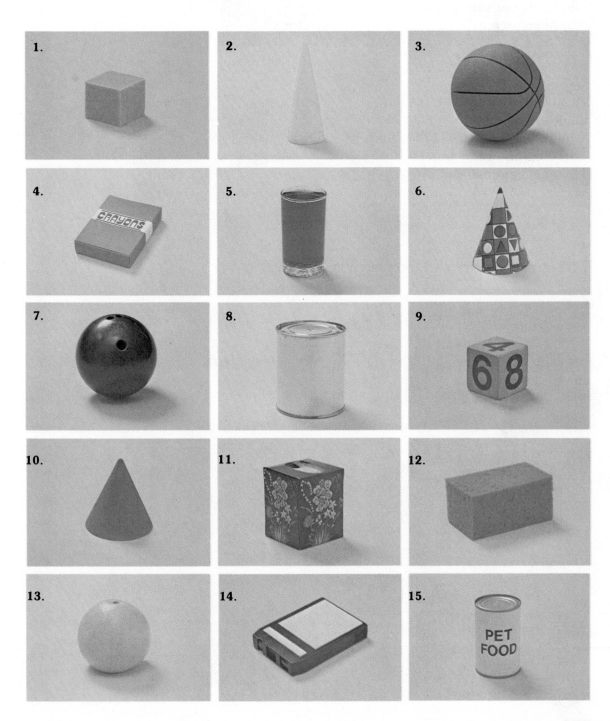

1.

2.

3.

4.

5.

6.

7.

8.

9.

10.

11.

12.

13.

14.

15.

Volume

The **cubic centimeter** is a
unit of **volume**.

1 cm
1 cm
1 cm

To find the volume of this box,
think of filling the box with cubes.
It takes 12 cubes to fill this box.
The volume of this box is
12 cubic centimeters.

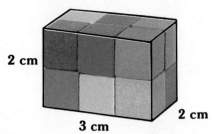

2 cm

3 cm

2 cm

Give the volume of each box in cubic centimeters.

1.

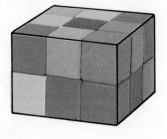

2.

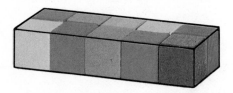

3.

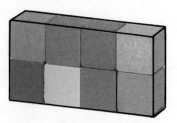

4.

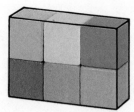

5.

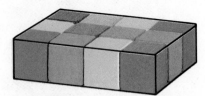

6.

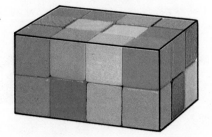

7.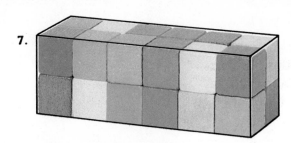

8.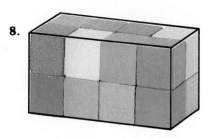

9.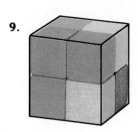

★10. How many cubes will fit in this box?

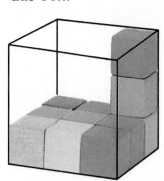

Build three straight fences across each corral. Each horse must be in its own section. No section can be empty.

Number Patterns

Compute the answers with your calculator. Use the calculator until you see a pattern, or until the numbers get too big for the display. Then use the pattern to give the remaining answers. In Sets B and C, multiply first and then add.

Set A

1. 7×15873
2. 14×15873
3. 21×15873
4. 28×15873
5. 35×15873
6. 42×15873
7. 49×15873
8. 56×15873
9. 63×15873

Set B

10. $(1 \times 8) + 1$
11. $(12 \times 8) + 2$
12. $(123 \times 8) + 3$
13. $(1234 \times 8) + 4$
14. $(12345 \times 8) + 5$
15. $(123456 \times 8) + 6$
16. $(1234567 \times 8) + 7$
17. $(12345678 \times 8) + 8$
18. $(123456789 \times 8) + 9$

Set C

19. $(1 \times 9) + 2$
20. $(12 \times 9) + 3$
21. $(123 \times 9) + 4$
22. $(1234 \times 9) + 5$
23. $(12345 \times 9) + 6$
24. $(123456 \times 9) + 7$
25. $(1234567 \times 9) + 8$
26. $(12345678 \times 9) + 9$
27. $(123456789 \times 9) + 10$

Set D

28. 1×1
29. 11×11
30. 111×111
31. 1111×1111
32. 11111×11111
33. 111111×111111
34. 1111111×1111111
35. 11111111×11111111
36. $111111111 \times 111111111$

Interior Designer

Teresa Valdez is an interior designer. She is figuring the amount and the cost of tiles and metal stripping for a living room and hall. This is a scale drawing she made. Each square represents one floor tile.

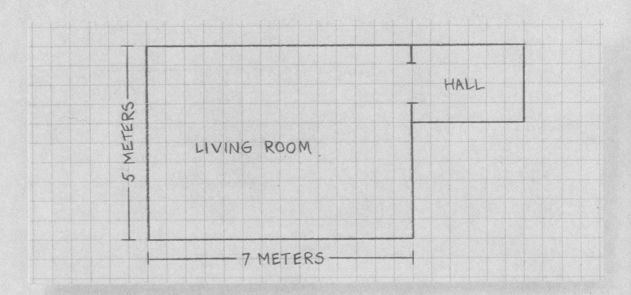

1. Teresa plans to use ceramic tiles in the hall. How many tiles does she need?

2. The ceramic tiles come in packages of 5. How many packages does she need?

3. Each package of ceramic tiles costs $7.25. How much will she spend on ceramic tiles?

4. Teresa will use carpet tiles in the living room. How many tiles does she need?

5. The carpet tiles come in packages of 8. How many packages does she need?

6. Each package of carpet tiles costs $9.50. How much will she spend on carpet tiles?

7. Teresa will put metal stripping around the perimeter of the living room. How many meters of stripping does she need?

*8. The metal stripping costs $3.35 for a package containing 7 meters. How much will the stripping cost?

Chapter 18 Test
Perimeter, Area, and Volume, pages 346–361

Give the perimeter of each shape in centimeters.

1.

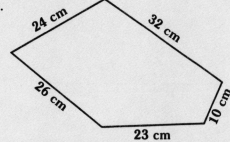

24 cm 32 cm 26 cm 23 cm 10 cm

2.

22 cm 22 cm 22 cm 22 cm 22 cm 22 cm

Give the area of each shape in square centimeters.

3.

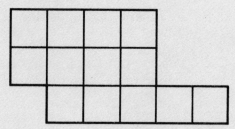

4.

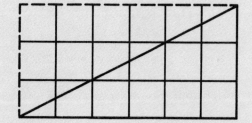

Give the volume of each shape in cubic centimeters.

5.

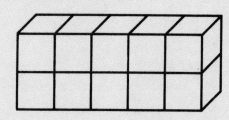

6.

Give the name of each shape. Use sphere, cone, cylinder, cube, or rectangular prism.

7.

8.

9.

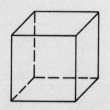

10.

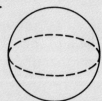

Problems Around Us

1. A bakery in Rockville, Maryland, bakes an average of 1875 loaves of bread each hour. How many loaves of bread does this bakery make in 8 hours?

2. A cat has 5 toes on each front paw and 4 toes on each hind paw. How many toes does a cat have?

3. Halley's comet was last seen in 1910. It will be seen from earth again in 1986. How many years apart are the two appearances?

4. A hen lays about 240 eggs per year. About how many eggs does a hen lay in one month? (1 year is 12 months.)

5. The base of the Washington Monument has 4 sides. Each side is about 1676 centimeters long. What is the perimeter of the base?

6. George Washington was 67 years old on February 22, 1799. In what year was he born?

7. A 20-centimeter frog can jump 15 times the length of its body in a single leap. How far can a frog of this size jump?

8. Running water was installed in the White House in 1834. A hot water system was installed in 1853. How many years did the White House have only cold running water?

9. The Pacific Ocean covers about $\frac{3}{10}$ of the earth's surface. The Atlantic Ocean covers about $\frac{2}{10}$ of the earth's surface. The Pacific Ocean covers about how much more of the earth's surface than the Atlantic Ocean?

10. From 1878 until 1929, the telephone of the President of the United States was in a booth in the hallway outside his office. How many years was the President's phone kept in the hall?

11. One winter Four Lakes ski lodge had 500 pairs of rental skis. The next season the lodge increased its rental supply by 150 pairs. How many rental pairs did the lodge then have?

Individualized Skills Maintenance

Diagnose

A *pages 174–179*

52×31

96×144

75×360

B *pages 234–244*

$428 \div 6$

$724 \div 3$

$532 \div 5$

C *pages 336–341*

$357 \div 43$

$139 \div 25$

$848 \div 32$

Practice

A

1. 83×40
2. 45×13
3. 67×21
4. 72×18
5. 56×56
6. 53×39

7. 375×30
8. 483×22
9. 142×65
10. 308×47
11. 250×93
12. 829×28

B

13. $3\overline{)97}$
14. $5\overline{)68}$
15. $2\overline{)632}$
16. $7\overline{)925}$
17. $4\overline{)896}$

18. $3\overline{)562}$
19. $8\overline{)168}$
20. $4\overline{)259}$
21. $6\overline{)500}$
22. $9\overline{)493}$

23. $5\overline{)351}$
24. $7\overline{)763}$
25. $4\overline{)773}$
26. $8\overline{)831}$
27. $6\overline{)722}$

C

28. $61\overline{)244}$
29. $32\overline{)295}$
30. $46\overline{)118}$
31. $53\overline{)338}$
32. $47\overline{)175}$

33. $84\overline{)463}$
34. $26\overline{)117}$
35. $59\overline{)413}$
36. $35\overline{)291}$
37. $21\overline{)798}$

38. $75\overline{)937}$
39. $34\overline{)858}$
40. $64\overline{)986}$
41. $23\overline{)598}$
42. $12\overline{)398}$

Unit 6 Review

Chapter 16, pages 320–332

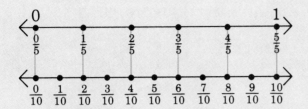

Use the number lines to help you find equal fractions.

1. $\frac{2}{5} = \frac{}{10}$ 2. $\frac{6}{10} = \frac{}{5}$

Add. Use the number lines to help you find equal fractions.

3. $\frac{1}{5} + \frac{3}{5}$ 4. $\frac{4}{10} + \frac{3}{5}$

5. $\begin{array}{r} \frac{4}{5} \\ + \frac{1}{10} \\ \hline \end{array}$ 6. $\begin{array}{r} \frac{1}{5} \\ + \frac{1}{10} \\ \hline \end{array}$ 7. $\begin{array}{r} \frac{9}{10} \\ + \frac{3}{5} \\ \hline \end{array}$

Subtract. Use the number lines to help you find equal fractions.

8. $\frac{3}{5} - \frac{2}{5}$ 9. $\frac{4}{5} - \frac{1}{10}$

10. $\begin{array}{r} \frac{1}{5} \\ - \frac{1}{10} \\ \hline \end{array}$ 11. $\begin{array}{r} \frac{3}{5} \\ - \frac{5}{10} \\ \hline \end{array}$ 12. $\begin{array}{r} \frac{10}{10} \\ - \frac{2}{5} \\ \hline \end{array}$

Chapter 17, pages 334–344

Divide.

13. $20\overline{)180}$ 14. $60\overline{)267}$

15. $81\overline{)196}$ 16. $44\overline{)308}$

17. $310 \div 54$ 18. $551 \div 32$

19. How many days and hours are there in 339 hours? (1 day is 24 hours.)

Chapter 18, pages 346–361

20. Give the perimeter in centimeters.

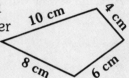

Give each area in square centimeters.

21.   22.

23. Give the volume in cubic centimeters.

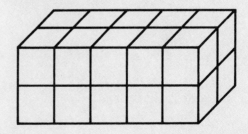

365

Unit 6 Test
Chapters 16–18, pages 320–362

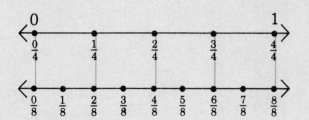

Use the number lines to help you find equal fractions.

1. $\frac{2}{8} = \frac{\text{⫶}}{4}$ 2. $\frac{3}{4} = \frac{\text{⫶}}{8}$

Add. Use the number line to help you find equal fractions.

3. $\frac{1}{8} + \frac{3}{8}$ 4. $\frac{1}{4} + \frac{1}{8}$

5. $\begin{array}{r} \frac{1}{4} \\ + \frac{5}{8} \\ \hline \end{array}$ 6. $\begin{array}{r} \frac{3}{4} \\ + \frac{3}{4} \\ \hline \end{array}$ 7. $\begin{array}{r} \frac{7}{8} \\ + \frac{1}{4} \\ \hline \end{array}$

Subtract. Use the number line to help you find equal fractions.

8. $\frac{3}{4} - \frac{2}{4}$ 9. $\frac{3}{4} - \frac{3}{8}$

10. $\begin{array}{r} \frac{7}{8} \\ - \frac{3}{8} \\ \hline \end{array}$ 11. $\begin{array}{r} \frac{8}{8} \\ - \frac{1}{4} \\ \hline \end{array}$ 12. $\begin{array}{r} \frac{3}{4} \\ - \frac{5}{8} \\ \hline \end{array}$

13. How many years and weeks are there in 166 weeks? (1 year is 52 weeks.)

Divide.

14. $40\overline{)225}$ 15. $70\overline{)437}$

16. $51\overline{)459}$ 17. $85\overline{)605}$

18. $293 \div 36$ 19. $118 \div 28$

20. $945 \div 63$ 21. $499 \div 12$

22. Give the perimeter in centimeters.

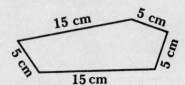

Give each area in square centimeters.

23.

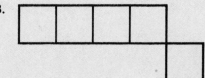

24.

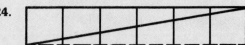

25. Give the volume in cubic centimeters.

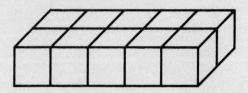

End-of-Book Test

Add.

1. 9
+7

2. 48
+25

3. 492
+369

4. 7317
+ 926

5. $16.84
+ 32.17

6. 65.4
+27.3

7. 21 + 9 + 45

Subtract.

8. 15
− 7

9. 35
−19

10. 513
−278

11. 704
−246

12. $15.42
− 13.91

13. 7.32
−2.16

Multiply.

14. 8
×3

15. 4
×9

16. 7
×8

17. 6
×7

18. 413
× 2

19. 52
× 8

20. 372
× 4

21. 340
× 6

22. 548
× 3

23. 126
× 30

24. 63
×45

25. $1.81
× 6

Divide.

26. 5)45

27. 4)28

28. 9)72

29. 7)56

30. 4)37

31. 6)83

32. 2)516

33. 41)85

34. 21)346

35. $7.38 ÷ 9

36. Would you use centimeters, meters, or kilometers to measure the length of your mathematics book?

Continued on next page

367

37. Compare these numbers.
Use > or <.

480 ● 792

38. List these numbers in order
from least to greatest.

629   518   614

Tell what each 6 means.

39. 6138

40. 72.56

41. Give a decimal for
8 and 65 hundredths.

42. Give a fraction to tell how
much of the figure is shaded.

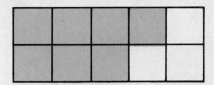

43. What fraction of these coins
have heads showing?

44. Compare these fractions.
Use > or <.

$\frac{7}{8}$ ● $\frac{3}{8}$

Add or subtract.

45. $\frac{3}{5}$ **46.** $\frac{9}{10}$
$+\frac{1}{5}$ $-\frac{6}{10}$

47. Give the area of this figure
in square centimeters.

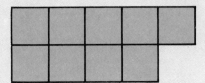

Find each answer.

48. A teller at a bank served
84 people in a 6-hour period.
This is an average of how
many people served per hour?

49. Attilio bought 3 cans of
tennis balls for $2.10 each.
How much money did he spend
in all?

50. Ellen drove 248 kilometers
in the morning and
329 kilometers in the
afternoon. She drove how
many kilometers in all?

Acknowledgments

Puzzle on 109 adaption of text and illustration of #420 "Footprints in the Snow" is reprinted by permission of Charles Scribner's Sons from 536 PUZZLES AND CURIOUS PROBLEMS by Henry Ernest Dudeney. Copyright © 1967 Charles Scribner's Sons. Data in Exercise 1 on 123 from YOUR HEART AND HOW IT WORKS by Herbert S. Zim. Copyright © 1959 by Herbert S. Zim. Reprinted by permission of William Morrow and Company, Inc. Data in Exercises 2, 5, 9 on 123 from FIRSTS FACTS AND FEATS by Bill Adler. Copyright © 1975 by Bill Adler. Reprinted by permission of Grosset & Dunlap, Inc. Data in Exercises 3, 7 on 123 and 1, 3, 4, 6, 7, 11 on 189 from the book, NATURE'S WORLD RECORDS by John R. Quinn. Copyright © 1977 by John R. Quinn. Used with permission of the publisher, Walker and Company. Riddle on 182 reprinted by permission of Grosset & Dunlap, Inc. from 1001 RIDDLES FOR CHILDREN by George L. Carlson, copyright 1949 by Platt & Munk Co., Inc. Data in Exercises 1, 6, 8, 10, 11 on 257 and 5 on 315 excerpts from GIANT ANIMALS by Howard E. Smith, Jr., illustrated by John Lane. Copyright © 1977 by Howard E. Smith, Jr. Reprinted by permission of Doubleday & Company, Inc. Riddle on 285 from THE RIDDLE AGES by Ann Bishop. Copyright © 1977 by Ann Bishop. Reprinted with permission of Albert Whitman & Company. Data in Exercise 4 on 315 from THE BIG STRAWBERRY BOOK OF QUESTIONS AND ANSWERS by Anita Malnig. Copyright © 1977 by One Strawberry Inc. Reprinted by permission. Puzzle on 323 from PERPLEXING PUZZLES AND TANTALIZING TEASERS by Martin Gardner, illustrated by Laszlo Kubinyi. Copyright © 1969 by Martin Gardner, illustration © 1969 by Laszlo Kubinyi. Reprinted by permission of Simon & Schuster, a Division of Gulf & Western Corporation.

For permission to reproduce photographs on the following pages, acknowledgment is made to:

Photos on 12 and 88, Heinz Kluetmeier/Sports Illustrated © 1979 Time, Inc. Photo on 55, Bureau of Engraving and Printing. Photo on 78, William Parker. Photos on 98 and 152, NASA. Photos on 100 and 169, H. Armstrong Roberts. Photo on 180–181, Jack Weiss. Photo on 243, H. C. Allen & Son. Photo on 246, Copyright by the California Institute of Technology and the Carnegie Institution of Washington. Reproduced by permission from the Hale Observatories. Photos on 252 and 342–343, Dan Morrill. Photo on 306, Walter S. Iooss, Jr./Sports Illustrated © 1970 Time, Inc. Photo on 363, Library of Congress.

Photo on the cover, James V. Neill.

More Practice

Set 1 *pages 8–9*

Which number is greater?

1. 45 or 41　　　　**2.** 63 or 65　　　　**3.** 244 or 247　　　　**4.** 508 or 506

5. 729 or 722　　　　**6.** 3465 or 3479　　　**7.** 2958 or 2949　　　**8.** 1367 or 1822

Which number is less?

9. 34 or 31　　　　**10.** 68 or 62　　　　**11.** 542 or 547　　　　**12.** 219 or 213

13. 663 or 629　　　**14.** 1352 or 1358　　**15.** 3542 or 3642　　**16.** 7678 or 7694

Compare the numbers. Use < or >.

17. 31 ● 21　　　　**18.** 57 ● 72　　　　**19.** 631 ● 647　　　　**20.** 297 ● 289

21. 128 ● 120　　　**22.** 3348 ● 5348　　**23.** 1213 ● 1221　　**24.** 6794 ● 6800

Set 2 *pages 10–11*

Give the numbers in order from least to greatest.

1. 22　38　19　56　　　　**2.** 44　15　97　66　　　　**3.** 31　52　28　47

4. 297　341　302　416　　**5.** 621　542　397　580　　**6.** 728　459　137　735

7. 289　62　224　88　　　**8.** 124　39　527　47　　　**9.** 632　73　654　92

10. 16　679　58　315　　**11.** 98　732　16　419　　**12.** 459　97　234　47

13. 2367　2358　2421　　**14.** 3643　3522　4117　　**15.** 5361　5378　5249

Set 3 *pages 22–23*

1. 4
 +3

2. 5
 +5

3. 0
 +1

4. 8
 +4

5. 6
 +7

6. 2
 +4

7. 6
 +9

8. 1
 +2

9. 0
 +6

10. 8
 +1

11. 6
 +5

12. 7
 +0

13. 9
 +9

14. 3
 +8

15. 7
 +6

16. 3
 +6

17. 4 + 5　　**18.** 0 + 9　　**19.** 6 + 2　　**20.** 1 + 8　　**21.** 9 + 6　　**22.** 1 + 4

23. 7 + 3　　**24.** 5 + 8　　**25.** 2 + 1　　**26.** 7 + 9　　**27.** 9 + 2　　**28.** 2 + 7

29. 3 + 3　　**30.** 5 + 1　　**31.** 4 + 1　　**32.** 8 + 7　　**33.** 4 + 9　　**34.** 8 + 8

Set 4 *pages 30–31*

1. 53
   +17

2. 29
   +44

3. 36
   +15

4. 841
   +294

5. 606
   +787

6. 323
   +684

7. 6513
   +2467

8. 9105
   +2913

9. 3471
   +2624

10. 593
   + 70

11. 3647
   + 421

12. 9528
   +6391

13. 46 + 39

14. 28 + 57

15. 86 + 15

16. 243 + 162

17. 537 + 244

18. 618 + 348

19. 6327 + 149

20. 5783 + 161

21. 6394 + 4081

22. 2685 + 7243

23. 3472 + 5723

24. 6255 + 3738

Set 5 *pages 32–33*

1. 347
   +164

2. 298
   +403

3. 156
   +575

4. 728
   +197

5. 4157
   +2924

6. 9223
   +2378

7. 918
   +2532

8. 6478
   + 731

9. 3297
   +1054

10. 504
   +5738

11. 61
   +479

12. 8324
   + 929

13. 934 + 277

14. 499 + 351

15. 536 + 295

16. 827 + 199

17. 7642 + 1675

18. 3156 + 3970

19. 2413 + 1996

20. 9724 + 4837

21. 3675 + 4036

22. 9254 + 1927

23. 8709 + 434

24. 3851 + 790

Set 6 *pages 36–37*

1. 6
    5
   +7

2. 3
    9
   +4

3. 91
    65
   +84

4. 42
    37
   +63

5. 76
    64
   +23

6. 395
    896
   +527

7. 234
    162
   +319

8. 4285
    3216
   +2457

9. 3628
    1492
   +3357

10. 3648
     524
    7204
   + 93

11. 892
     35
     79
   +624

12. 156
     29
    4378
   + 362

13. 50 + 839 + 472

14. 5679 + 849 + 7249

15. 63,428 + 3479 + 285

More Practice

Set 7   *pages 42–43*

1. 7 −3	2. 5 −4	3. 6 −2	4. 11 − 4	5. 10 − 3	6. 15 − 8	7. 10 − 7	8. 12 − 6

9. 9 −0	10. 12 − 4	11. 17 − 9	12. 16 − 8	13. 18 − 9	14. 13 − 5	15. 11 − 6	16. 10 − 9

17. 14 − 7	18. 7 −5	19. 3 −3	20. 14 − 9	21. 11 − 7	22. 15 − 7	23. 8 −6	24. 13 − 6

25. 14 − 6   **26.** 15 − 6   **27.** 17 − 8   **28.** 13 − 8   **29.** 12 − 9   **30.** 12 − 7

Set 8   *pages 50–51*

1. 42 −15	2. 63 −28	3. 50 −35	4. 86 −57	5. 247 −195	6. 618 −423

7. 685 −149	8. 235 −217	9. 7396 −5483	10. 3674 −1921	11. 3785 −2607	12. 4577 −2385

13. 628 − 345   **14.** 2957 − 165   **15.** 420 − 311   **16.** 989 − 97
17. 2850 − 1306   **18.** 4516 − 2704   **19.** 3674 − 713   **20.** 6528 − 2319

Set 9   *pages 52–53*

1. 432 − 65	2. 915 − 48	3. 820 − 37	4. 245 −147	5. 727 −539	6. 643 −566

7. 2478 − 539	8. 4629 − 742	9. 3275 − 188	10. 9421 −6715	11. 6326 −5473	12. 8306 −4652

13. 743 − 96   **14.** 225 − 167   **15.** 4238 − 1629   **16.** 5704 − 258
17. 970 − 399   **18.** 827 − 58   **19.** 2634 − 1576   **20.** 2497 − 1398

Set 10 *pages 56–57*

1. 508
  − 329
	2. 600
	  − 247
		3. 200
		  − 136
			4. 702
			  − 158
				5. 630
				  − 98
					6. 208
					  − 29

7. 4501
  − 621
	8. 6004
	  − 532
		9. 2406
		  − 1258
			10. 3040
			  − 1270
				11. 1042
				  − 631
					12. 5200
					  − 3260

13. 807
  − 98
	14. 300
	  − 256
		15. 6208
		  − 3467
			16. 1024
			  − 933
				17. 4200
				  − 1730
					18. 6059
					  − 792

19. 4007 − 2436   **20.** 3060 − 590   **21.** 5208 − 2637   **22.** 9200 − 175

23. 1005 − 423   **24.** 5309 − 2657   **25.** 4900 − 657   **26.** 7020 − 3517

Set 11 *pages 72–73*

1. $64.59
  + 8.32
	2. $42.88
	  − 7.93
		3. $9.60
		  − 3.47
			4. $0.75
			  + 0.93
				5. $12.86
				  − 3.47
					6. $15.78
					  + 0.52

7. $48.06
  − 27.15
	8. $63.95
	  + 12.37
		9. $43.87
		  − 24.97
			10. $12.54
			  + 9.15
				11. $62.59
				  − 57.99
					12. $8.75
					  + 6.49

13. $75.37
  − 28.43
	14. $29.54
	  − 6.47
		15. $13.08
		  + 17.66
			16. $98.43
			  − 56.87
				17. $54.16
				  − 18.31
					18. $3.27
					  + 9.42

19. $17.93
  + 42.64
	20. $29.25
	  − 13.67
		21. $0.98
		  + 0.64
			22. $37.68
			  + 9.36
				23. $7.08
				  − 0.56
					24. $8.23
					  + 0.54

Set 12 *pages 90–91*

Compare these decimals. Use <, >, or =.

1. 0.9 ● 0.6   **2.** 5.1 ● 5.7   **3.** 8.5 ● 8.4   **4.** 0.3 ● 0.30

5. 0.21 ● 0.15   **6.** 32.8 ● 32.5   **7.** 18.11 ● 18.01   **8.** 0.35 ● 0.35

9. 14.26 ● 14.20   **10.** 2.37 ● 2.07   **11.** 27.84 ● 27.48   **12.** 7.6 ● 7.60

13. 0.06 ● 0.60   **14.** 8.98 ● 8.80   **15.** 7.2 ● 7.20   **16.** 14.10 ● 14.01

More Practice

Set 13 *pages 94–95*

1. 8.4 +6.2	**2.** 4.3 +1.7	**3.** 2.4 +9.5	**4.** 6.6 +5.5	**5.** 17.4 + 6.9	**6.** 13.07 + 9.88
7. 14.26 + 9.35	**8.** 6.62 +8.84	**9.** 15.45 +12.96	**10.** 34.92 +15.67	**11.** 48.71 +32.15	**12.** 67.90 +14.66

13. 83.47 + 22.15   **14.** 67.02 + 19.85   **15.** 15 + 8.07

16. 0.9 + 1.5 + 6.7   **17.** 0.3 + 7.9 + 1.7   **18.** 3.4 + 8 + 6.2

Set 14 *pages 98–99*

1. 8.4 −3.7	**2.** 2.5 − 0.9	**3.** 8.7 − 1.3	**4.** 24.3 − 5.6	**5.** 56.5 −22.8	**6.** 19.7 − 9.4
7. 8.94 −6.32	**8.** 15.72 − 8.37	**9.** 32.95 −16.82	**10.** 58.71 −36.94	**11.** 29.63 −22.47	**12.** 16.75 −12.86

13. 29.52 − 18.35   **14.** 7 − 3.4   **15.** 68.45 − 38   **16.** 66.65 − 54.82

17. 8.07 − 4.32   **18.** 42 − 17.35   **19.** 16 − 0.7   **20.** 90 − 40.38

Set 15 *pages 132–133*

1. 2 ×2	**2.** 4 ×2	**3.** 5 ×3	**4.** 6 ×3	**5.** 2 ×4	**6.** 4 ×3	**7.** 5 ×7	**8.** 4 ×7
9. 5 ×4	**10.** 7 ×3	**11.** 2 ×3	**12.** 5 ×6	**13.** 8 ×2	**14.** 5 ×9	**15.** 3 ×9	**16.** 2 ×5
17. 3 ×5	**18.** 4 ×5	**19.** 3 ×8	**20.** 6 ×2	**21.** 4 ×4	**22.** 3 ×4	**23.** 4 ×8	**24.** 3 ×2

Set 16 *pages 138–139*

| 1. 9 ×2 | 2. 0 ×9 | 3. 8 ×3 | 4. 9 ×4 | 5. 8 ×8 | 6. 4 ×7 | 7. 9 ×8 | 8. 5 ×6 |

| 9. 8 ×2 | 10. 8 ×9 | 11. 9 ×3 | 12. 4 ×8 | 13. 5 ×4 | 14. 9 ×1 | 15. 4 ×4 | 16. 7 ×9 |

| 17. 3 ×7 | 18. 9 ×6 | 19. 6 ×8 | 20. 5 ×3 | 21. 8 ×0 | 22. 8 ×5 | 23. 0 ×6 | 24. 6 ×6 |

Set 17 *pages 150–151*

| 1. 35 × 2 | 2. 24 × 3 | 3. 42 × 6 | 4. 63 × 5 | 5. 46 × 4 | 6. 86 × 3 | 7. 17 × 8 | 8. 18 × 6 |

| 9. 22 × 7 | 10. 54 × 9 | 11. 97 × 2 | 12. 78 × 4 | 13. 56 × 5 | 14. 49 × 3 | 15. 33 × 8 | 16. 52 × 7 |

| 17. 27 × 9 | 18. 74 × 4 | 19. 67 × 5 | 20. 45 × 8 | 21. 39 × 7 | 22. 62 × 6 | 23. 99 × 2 | 24. 58 × 9 |

25. 89 × 3   **26.** 28 × 6   **27.** 77 × 4   **28.** 83 × 8   **29.** 72 × 7   **30.** 93 × 5

Set 18 *pages 152–153*

| 1. 116 × 6 | 2. 239 × 2 | 3. 312 × 8 | 4. 451 × 3 | 5. 215 × 4 | 6. 413 × 5 | 7. 551 × 3 |

| 8. 121 × 7 | 9. 613 × 6 | 10. 132 × 4 | 11. 181 × 9 | 12. 712 × 7 | 13. 816 × 5 | 14. 193 × 2 |

| 15. 3314 × 3 | 16. 2116 × 4 | 17. 4372 × 2 | 18. 1327 × 3 | 19. 1422 × 4 | 20. 3311 × 5 | 21. 2151 × 6 |

22. 114 × 7   **23.** 231 × 6   **24.** 1281 × 3   **25.** 3 × 719   **26.** 4253 × 2

More Practice

pages 156–157

1. 105 × 3	2. 120 × 5	3. 502 × 6	4. 630 × 4	5. 204 × 7	6. 740 × 8
7. 190 × 2	8. 406 × 7	9. 108 × 9	10. 603 × 6	11. 260 × 3	12. 450 × 9
13. 4270 × 2	14. 3107 × 3	15. 1150 × 5	16. 9103 × 8	17. 2009 × 7	18. 6300 × 5

Set 20 *pages 158–159*

1. 139 × 7	2. 418 × 6	3. 243 × 5	4. 669 × 2	5. 375 × 4	6. 736 × 3
7. 835 × 6	8. 284 × 8	9. 983 × 4	10. 617 × 7	11. 878 × 2	12. 593 × 4
13. 754 × 6	14. 957 × 3	15. 299 × 7	16. 1085 × 7	17. 4093 × 5	18. 2246 × 4
19. 3917 × 2	20. 1372 × 3	21. 2770 × 8	22. 5906 × 5	23. 1994 × 2	24. 9306 × 7

Set 21 *pages 172–173*

1. 19 ×60	2. 51 ×40	3. 27 ×80	4. 36 ×70	5. 48 ×20	6. 94 ×90	7. 42 ×30
8. 37 ×60	9. 59 ×40	10. 86 ×50	11. 67 ×70	12. 14 ×60	13. 29 ×40	14. 132 × 90
15. 215 × 30	16. 273 × 50	17. 517 × 80	18. 166 × 90	19. 631 × 50	20. 390 × 60	21. 726 × 20

Set 22 *pages 176–177*

1. $\begin{array}{r}15\\\times94\end{array}$	2. $\begin{array}{r}85\\\times12\end{array}$	3. $\begin{array}{r}14\\\times89\end{array}$	4. $\begin{array}{r}92\\\times16\end{array}$	5. $\begin{array}{r}37\\\times29\end{array}$	6. $\begin{array}{r}53\\\times34\end{array}$	7. $\begin{array}{r}48\\\times62\end{array}$	8. $\begin{array}{r}71\\\times67\end{array}$

9. $\begin{array}{r}54\\\times54\end{array}$	10. $\begin{array}{r}26\\\times85\end{array}$	11. $\begin{array}{r}36\\\times27\end{array}$	12. $\begin{array}{r}63\\\times38\end{array}$	13. $\begin{array}{r}49\\\times86\end{array}$	14. $\begin{array}{r}84\\\times23\end{array}$	15. $\begin{array}{r}75\\\times24\end{array}$	16. $\begin{array}{r}13\\\times99\end{array}$

17. $\begin{array}{r}46\\\times73\end{array}$	18. $\begin{array}{r}28\\\times65\end{array}$	19. $\begin{array}{r}44\\\times59\end{array}$	20. $\begin{array}{r}76\\\times52\end{array}$	21. $\begin{array}{r}83\\\times83\end{array}$	22. $\begin{array}{r}58\\\times19\end{array}$	23. $\begin{array}{r}72\\\times47\end{array}$	24. $\begin{array}{r}69\\\times42\end{array}$

25. 33×87 26. 39×93 27. 79×57 28. 94×18 29. 56×37 30. 78×25

31. 42×64 32. 17×99 33. 38×73 34. 22×88 35. 43×52 36. 39×86

Set 23 *pages 178–179*

1. $\begin{array}{r}122\\\times\ 58\end{array}$	2. $\begin{array}{r}314\\\times\ 62\end{array}$	3. $\begin{array}{r}227\\\times\ 53\end{array}$	4. $\begin{array}{r}139\\\times\ 73\end{array}$	5. $\begin{array}{r}450\\\times\ 34\end{array}$	6. $\begin{array}{r}678\\\times\ 28\end{array}$	7. $\begin{array}{r}225\\\times\ 83\end{array}$

8. $\begin{array}{r}196\\\times\ 97\end{array}$	9. $\begin{array}{r}244\\\times\ 65\end{array}$	10. $\begin{array}{r}318\\\times\ 93\end{array}$	11. $\begin{array}{r}207\\\times\ 86\end{array}$	12. $\begin{array}{r}454\\\times\ 48\end{array}$	13. $\begin{array}{r}338\\\times\ 19\end{array}$	14. $\begin{array}{r}164\\\times\ 74\end{array}$

15. $\begin{array}{r}503\\\times\ 16\end{array}$	16. $\begin{array}{r}866\\\times\ 29\end{array}$	17. $\begin{array}{r}382\\\times\ 84\end{array}$	18. $\begin{array}{r}167\\\times\ 79\end{array}$	19. $\begin{array}{r}345\\\times\ 36\end{array}$	20. $\begin{array}{r}370\\\times\ 72\end{array}$	21. $\begin{array}{r}257\\\times\ 33\end{array}$

22. $\begin{array}{r}223\\\times\ 35\end{array}$	23. $\begin{array}{r}507\\\times\ 17\end{array}$	24. $\begin{array}{r}750\\\times\ 75\end{array}$	25. $\begin{array}{r}524\\\times\ 63\end{array}$	26. $\begin{array}{r}397\\\times\ 52\end{array}$	27. $\begin{array}{r}155\\\times\ 93\end{array}$	28. $\begin{array}{r}403\\\times\ 68\end{array}$

Set 24 *pages 216–217*

1. $24 \div 6$ 2. $10 \div 2$ 3. $32 \div 4$ 4. $16 \div 8$ 5. $12 \div 3$ 6. $20 \div 5$

7. $4 \div 2$ 8. $27 \div 3$ 9. $45 \div 5$ 10. $15 \div 3$ 11. $24 \div 8$ 12. $18 \div 6$

13. $40 \div 8$ 14. $16 \div 4$ 15. $9 \div 3$ 16. $28 \div 4$ 17. $21 \div 7$ 18. $36 \div 9$

19. $3\overline{)21}$ 20. $5\overline{)25}$ 21. $2\overline{)14}$ 22. $3\overline{)18}$ 23. $9\overline{)27}$ 24. $4\overline{)20}$

25. $6\overline{)30}$ 26. $5\overline{)35}$ 27. $3\overline{)12}$ 28. $5\overline{)10}$ 29. $2\overline{)18}$ 30. $6\overline{)12}$

More Practice

Set 25 *pages 222–223*

1. 6$\overline{)6}$ **2.** 6$\overline{)36}$ **3.** 6$\overline{)18}$ **4.** 6$\overline{)24}$ **5.** 6$\overline{)12}$ **6.** 6$\overline{)42}$ **7.** 6$\overline{)54}$

8. 7$\overline{)21}$ **9.** 7$\overline{)7}$ **10.** 7$\overline{)42}$ **11.** 7$\overline{)56}$ **12.** 7$\overline{)14}$ **13.** 7$\overline{)28}$ **14.** 7$\overline{)63}$

15. 8$\overline{)16}$ **16.** 8$\overline{)56}$ **17.** 8$\overline{)40}$ **18.** 8$\overline{)8}$ **19.** 8$\overline{)48}$ **20.** 8$\overline{)32}$ **21.** 8$\overline{)24}$

22. 9$\overline{)18}$ **23.** 9$\overline{)54}$ **24.** 9$\overline{)9}$ **25.** 9$\overline{)45}$ **26.** 9$\overline{)72}$ **27.** 9$\overline{)27}$ **28.** 9$\overline{)36}$

29. 6$\overline{)48}$ **30.** 8$\overline{)64}$ **31.** 7$\overline{)35}$ **32.** 1$\overline{)7}$ **33.** 3$\overline{)18}$ **34.** 5$\overline{)40}$ **35.** 4$\overline{)36}$

36. 1$\overline{)8}$ **37.** 1$\overline{)6}$ **38.** 3$\overline{)21}$ **39.** 9$\overline{)81}$ **40.** 7$\overline{)49}$ **41.** 4$\overline{)28}$ **42.** 5$\overline{)30}$

43. 8$\overline{)72}$ **44.** 3$\overline{)27}$ **45.** 5$\overline{)35}$ **46.** 6$\overline{)30}$ **47.** 4$\overline{)24}$ **48.** 2$\overline{)14}$ **49.** 5$\overline{)45}$

50. 2$\overline{)12}$ **51.** 2$\overline{)16}$ **52.** 4$\overline{)32}$ **53.** 3$\overline{)24}$ **54.** 9$\overline{)63}$ **55.** 2$\overline{)18}$ **56.** 1$\overline{)9}$

Set 26 *pages 236–237*

1. 5$\overline{)580}$ **2.** 3$\overline{)435}$ **3.** 2$\overline{)288}$ **4.** 7$\overline{)941}$ **5.** 4$\overline{)650}$

6. 8$\overline{)937}$ **7.** 6$\overline{)726}$ **8.** 3$\overline{)982}$ **9.** 2$\overline{)447}$ **10.** 3$\overline{)698}$

11. 6$\overline{)874}$ **12.** 4$\overline{)553}$ **13.** 5$\overline{)648}$ **14.** 7$\overline{)865}$ **15.** 3$\overline{)549}$

16. 940 ÷ 6   **17.** 823 ÷ 5   **18.** 526 ÷ 2   **19.** 984 ÷ 8   **20.** 690 ÷ 4   **21.** 792 ÷ 7

22. 725 ÷ 5   **23.** 943 ÷ 2   **24.** 825 ÷ 3   **25.** 756 ÷ 6   **26.** 785 ÷ 4   **27.** 487 ÷ 2

28. 900 ÷ 8   **29.** 948 ÷ 5   **30.** 872 ÷ 4   **31.** 687 ÷ 6   **32.** 975 ÷ 7   **33.** 629 ÷ 5

34. 999 ÷ 9   **35.** 825 ÷ 6   **36.** 869 ÷ 4   **37.** 629 ÷ 5   **38.** 846 ÷ 7   **39.** 981 ÷ 8

Set 27 *pages 238–239*

1. 325 ÷ 5   **2.** 148 ÷ 2   **3.** 179 ÷ 8   **4.** 251 ÷ 6   **5.** 192 ÷ 9   **6.** 248 ÷ 3

7. 294 ÷ 8   **8.** 223 ÷ 7   **9.** 170 ÷ 4   **10.** 342 ÷ 6   **11.** 480 ÷ 7   **12.** 387 ÷ 9

13. 179 ÷ 2   **14.** 440 ÷ 8   **15.** 182 ÷ 5   **16.** 393 ÷ 7   **17.** 290 ÷ 6   **18.** 614 ÷ 9

19. 285 ÷ 4   **20.** 559 ÷ 7   **21.** 226 ÷ 3   **22.** 437 ÷ 6   **23.** 359 ÷ 4   **24.** 518 ÷ 8

25. 458 ÷ 5   **26.** 155 ÷ 2   **27.** 742 ÷ 9   **28.** 530 ÷ 6   **29.** 852 ÷ 9   **30.** 224 ÷ 4

Set 28 *pages 240–241*

1. 4)428   2. 5)505   3. 2)217   4. 7)719   5. 3)318

6. 8)827   7. 6)613   8. 9)929   9. 5)532   10. 7)734

11. 3)920   12. 6)643   13. 2)203   14. 3)978   15. 7)765

16. 415 ÷ 2   17. 846 ÷ 8   18. 608 ÷ 6   19. 810 ÷ 4   20. 626 ÷ 3   21. 921 ÷ 3
22. 538 ÷ 5   23. 819 ÷ 4   24. 756 ÷ 7   25. 952 ÷ 9   26. 829 ÷ 4   27. 604 ÷ 2
28. 873 ÷ 8   29. 512 ÷ 5   30. 435 ÷ 4   31. 812 ÷ 8   32. 638 ÷ 6   33. 807 ÷ 2
34. 529 ÷ 5   35. 930 ÷ 9   36. 835 ÷ 8   37. 728 ÷ 7   38. 838 ÷ 4   39. 985 ÷ 9

Set 29 *pages 242–243*

1. 3)120   2. 8)245   3. 4)963   4. 7)842   5. 2)141   6. 9)905

7. 5)600   8. 6)304   9. 8)826   10. 3)932   11. 9)994   12. 5)521

13. 2)881   14. 4)403   15. 8)966   16. 7)565   17. 6)604   18. 2)817

19. 6)840   20. 3)602   21. 4)825   22. 3)750   23. 6)484   24. 2)800

25. 5)952   26. 7)706   27. 3)923   28. 8)167   29. 6)659   30. 2)401

31. 3)842   32. 9)638   33. 4)820   34. 7)914   35. 9)920   36. 4)431

37. 3)629   38. 2)480   39. 9)724   40. 6)665   41. 2)815   42. 5)549

Set 30 *pages 246–247*

1. $0.76 ÷ 2   2. $0.85 ÷ 5   3. $2.58 ÷ 6   4. $3.40 ÷ 4   5. $4.50 ÷ 9
6. $2.40 ÷ 3   7. $9.20 ÷ 8   8. $6.35 ÷ 5   9. $8.61 ÷ 7   10. $6.82 ÷ 2
11. $4.38 ÷ 6   12. $7.56 ÷ 9   13. $4.28 ÷ 4   14. $9.60 ÷ 8   15. $6.90 ÷ 5
16. $6.00 ÷ 3   17. $9.44 ÷ 8   18. $6.10 ÷ 2   19. $7.56 ÷ 9   20. $9.15 ÷ 5
21. $7.23 ÷ 3   22. $3.92 ÷ 8   23. $8.30 ÷ 2   24. $7.60 ÷ 4   25. $2.25 ÷ 9
26. $5.25 ÷ 3   27. $9.00 ÷ 6   28. $7.90 ÷ 2   29. $6.12 ÷ 3   30. $8.75 ÷ 5
31. $7.98 ÷ 6   32. $5.00 ÷ 4   33. $7.00 ÷ 2   34. $9.48 ÷ 6   35. $8.80 ÷ 4
36. $7.35 ÷ 3   37. $1.61 ÷ 7   38. $5.48 ÷ 4   39. $8.56 ÷ 8   40. $6.24 ÷ 2

More Practice

Set 31 *pages 304–305*

Compare the fractions. Use > or <.

1. $\frac{3}{5}$ ● $\frac{1}{5}$ 2. $\frac{5}{6}$ ● $\frac{3}{6}$ 3. $\frac{4}{7}$ ● $\frac{5}{7}$ 4. $\frac{5}{8}$ ● $\frac{7}{8}$ 5. $\frac{5}{10}$ ● $\frac{9}{10}$ 6. $\frac{1}{2}$ ● $\frac{0}{2}$

7. $\frac{4}{9}$ ● $\frac{7}{9}$ 8. $\frac{8}{12}$ ● $\frac{12}{12}$ 9. $\frac{4}{6}$ ● $\frac{2}{6}$ 10. $\frac{8}{8}$ ● $\frac{3}{8}$ 11. $\frac{2}{3}$ ● $\frac{3}{3}$ 12. $\frac{6}{7}$ ● $\frac{1}{7}$

13. $\frac{8}{9}$ ● $\frac{11}{9}$ 14. $\frac{0}{6}$ ● $\frac{1}{6}$ 15. $\frac{14}{3}$ ● $\frac{10}{3}$ 16. $\frac{9}{2}$ ● $\frac{5}{2}$ 17. $\frac{4}{3}$ ● $\frac{7}{3}$ 18. $\frac{3}{4}$ ● $\frac{0}{4}$

19. $\frac{9}{7}$ ● $\frac{5}{7}$ 20. $\frac{6}{6}$ ● $\frac{8}{6}$ 21. $\frac{5}{12}$ ● $\frac{7}{12}$ 22. $\frac{5}{3}$ ● $\frac{2}{3}$ 23. $\frac{8}{10}$ ● $\frac{4}{10}$ 24. $\frac{3}{8}$ ● $\frac{7}{8}$

Set 32 *pages 320–321*

1. $\frac{2}{5}$ $+\frac{2}{5}$ 2. $\frac{1}{6}$ $+\frac{3}{6}$ 3. $\frac{3}{8}$ $+\frac{4}{8}$ 4. $\frac{1}{7}$ $+\frac{1}{7}$ 5. $\frac{1}{12}$ $+\frac{4}{12}$ 6. $\frac{2}{8}$ $+\frac{2}{8}$ 7. $\frac{4}{10}$ $+\frac{3}{10}$ 8. $\frac{0}{5}$ $+\frac{2}{5}$

9. $\frac{5}{9}$ $+\frac{1}{9}$ 10. $\frac{2}{4}$ $+\frac{3}{4}$ 11. $\frac{1}{8}$ $+\frac{3}{8}$ 12. $\frac{2}{6}$ $+\frac{5}{6}$ 13. $\frac{2}{7}$ $+\frac{4}{7}$ 14. $\frac{4}{6}$ $+\frac{1}{6}$ 15. $\frac{2}{3}$ $+\frac{1}{3}$ 16. $\frac{2}{3}$ $+\frac{2}{3}$

17. $\frac{2}{4}+\frac{3}{4}$ 18. $\frac{2}{5}+\frac{3}{5}$ 19. $\frac{0}{3}+\frac{1}{3}$ 20. $\frac{5}{6}+\frac{3}{6}$ 21. $\frac{4}{8}+\frac{4}{8}$ 22. $\frac{6}{9}+\frac{8}{9}$ 23. $\frac{5}{7}+\frac{3}{7}$

Set 33 *pages 322–323*

1. $\frac{3}{5}$ $-\frac{2}{5}$ 2. $\frac{7}{8}$ $-\frac{3}{8}$ 3. $\frac{4}{6}$ $-\frac{1}{6}$ 4. $\frac{6}{7}$ $-\frac{4}{7}$ 5. $\frac{4}{9}$ $-\frac{2}{9}$ 6. $\frac{5}{8}$ $-\frac{4}{8}$ 7. $\frac{2}{5}$ $-\frac{1}{5}$ 8. $\frac{3}{3}$ $-\frac{1}{3}$

9. $\frac{8}{10}$ $-\frac{7}{10}$ 10. $\frac{4}{5}$ $-\frac{0}{5}$ 11. $\frac{5}{7}$ $-\frac{1}{7}$ 12. $\frac{7}{8}$ $-\frac{1}{8}$ 13. $\frac{5}{6}$ $-\frac{3}{6}$ 14. $\frac{4}{4}$ $-\frac{4}{4}$ 15. $\frac{7}{9}$ $-\frac{5}{9}$ 16. $\frac{11}{12}$ $-\frac{4}{12}$

17. $\frac{8}{8}-\frac{3}{8}$ 18. $\frac{10}{10}-\frac{3}{10}$ 19. $\frac{4}{5}-\frac{1}{5}$ 20. $\frac{5}{8}-\frac{3}{8}$ 21. $\frac{5}{6}-\frac{1}{6}$ 22. $\frac{7}{10}-\frac{3}{10}$ 23. $\frac{5}{7}-\frac{3}{7}$

Set 34 *pages 336–337*

1. $23\overline{)76}$ 2. $42\overline{)91}$ 3. $51\overline{)74}$ 4. $32\overline{)98}$ 5. $72\overline{)91}$ 6. $33\overline{)72}$

7. $57\overline{)89}$ 8. $36\overline{)82}$ 9. $43\overline{)91}$ 10. $25\overline{)80}$ 11. $32\overline{)64}$ 12. $65\overline{)77}$

13. $87\overline{)94}$ 14. $26\overline{)59}$ 15. $39\overline{)81}$ 16. $52\overline{)67}$ 17. $46\overline{)92}$ 18. $37\overline{)74}$

19. $35\overline{)105}$ 20. $22\overline{)179}$ 21. $49\overline{)152}$ 22. $73\overline{)592}$ 23. $82\overline{)689}$ 24. $64\overline{)384}$

25. $61\overline{)248}$ 26. $75\overline{)692}$ 27. $32\overline{)167}$ 28. $21\overline{)189}$ 29. $44\overline{)278}$ 30. $58\overline{)132}$

31. $73\overline{)542}$ 32. $81\overline{)376}$ 33. $92\overline{)482}$ 34. $34\overline{)238}$ 35. $56\overline{)392}$ 36. $67\overline{)215}$

Set 35 *pages 338–339*

1. $27\overline{)81}$ 2. $34\overline{)62}$ 3. $42\overline{)80}$ 4. $23\overline{)62}$ 5. $37\overline{)92}$ 6. $48\overline{)92}$

7. $24\overline{)91}$ 8. $35\overline{)68}$ 9. $11\overline{)72}$ 10. $13\overline{)65}$ 11. $14\overline{)72}$ 12. $12\overline{)76}$

13. $32\overline{)210}$ 14. $23\overline{)146}$ 15. $43\overline{)170}$ 16. $31\overline{)151}$ 17. $52\overline{)352}$ 18. $45\overline{)202}$

19. $28\overline{)112}$ 20. $47\overline{)331}$ 21. $38\overline{)268}$ 22. $56\overline{)463}$ 23. $49\overline{)294}$ 24. $59\overline{)256}$

25. $62\overline{)484}$ 26. $83\overline{)579}$ 27. $77\overline{)462}$ 28. $65\overline{)572}$ 29. $74\overline{)653}$ 30. $92\overline{)368}$

31. $88\overline{)352}$ 32. $76\overline{)215}$ 33. $68\overline{)363}$ 34. $78\overline{)312}$ 35. $96\overline{)457}$ 36. $87\overline{)255}$

Set 36 *pages 340–341*

1. $32\overline{)713}$ 2. $53\overline{)795}$ 3. $20\overline{)712}$ 4. $36\overline{)757}$ 5. $40\overline{)532}$ 6. $55\overline{)630}$

7. $45\overline{)945}$ 8. $35\overline{)809}$ 9. $41\overline{)935}$ 10. $30\overline{)963}$ 11. $25\overline{)783}$ 12. $46\overline{)526}$

13. $61\overline{)833}$ 14. $50\overline{)726}$ 15. $43\overline{)473}$ 16. $37\overline{)783}$ 17. $26\overline{)547}$ 18. $24\overline{)312}$

19. $34\overline{)725}$ 20. $52\overline{)840}$ 21. $60\overline{)852}$ 22. $41\overline{)913}$ 23. $33\overline{)891}$ 24. $22\overline{)308}$

25. $25\overline{)583}$ 26. $70\overline{)976}$ 27. $13\overline{)275}$ 28. $48\overline{)576}$ 29. $57\overline{)912}$ 30. $12\overline{)497}$

31. $47\overline{)689}$ 32. $14\overline{)188}$ 33. $39\overline{)888}$ 34. $28\overline{)379}$ 35. $15\overline{)173}$ 36. $27\overline{)361}$

Metric System

Length

The basic unit of length is the meter*. The distance from a door knob to the floor is about 1 meter.

Millimeter, centimeter, and kilometer are other commonly used units of length.

The thickness of a dime is about 1 millimeter.

The distance across a fingernail is about 1 centimeter.

The length of ten football fields placed end to end is about 1 kilometer.

Mass (weight)**

The basic unit of mass is the kilogram. The mass of this football is about 1 kilogram.

Gram is another commonly used unit of mass. The mass of a dollar bill is about 1 gram.

The mass of a grain of sand is about 1 milligram.

Capacity

The basic unit of capacity is the liter*. This milk carton holds about 1 liter.

Milliliter is another commonly used unit of capacity. An eyedropper holds about 1 milliliter of liquid.

*The word *meter* may also be spelled *metre,* and the word *liter* may be spelled *litre.* The -er spelling is in common usage in the United States and appears in this program.

**The units of mass are often referred to as units of weight. In common usage and in this program, the term *weight* is generally used to mean *mass* and the term *weigh* to mean *determine the mass of* or *have a mass of*.

Area

Square centimeter and square meter are commonly used units of area in the metric system.

Volume

The cubic centimeter is a commonly used unit of volume. If the cube shown here were filled with water, the amount of water would be 1 milliliter. The mass of the water would be 1 gram.

A cube with a volume of 1 cubic decimeter measures 1 decimeter, or 10 centimeters, on each edge. If a cubic decimeter were filled with water, the amount of water would be 1 liter. The mass of the water would be 1 kilogram.

Temperature

The Celsius scale is commonly used in countries employing the metric system.

Prefixes and Symbols

This table shows the most common prefixes in the metric system, as well as their symbols and meanings.

Prefix	Symbol	Meaning
mega-	M	million
kilo-	k	thousand
hecto-	h	hundred
deka-	da	ten
deci-	d	tenth
centi-	c	hundredth
milli-	m	thousandth
micro-	μ	millionth

This display relates some of the prefixes in the metric system to the base-ten numeration system.

thousands	hundreds	tens	ones	tenths	hundredths	thousandths
kilo-	hecto-	deka-		deci-	centi-	milli-

Here are official symbols for some common metric measures. They do not need periods. You need not add an -s for the plural form.

meter	m
kilometer	km
centimeter	cm
millimeter	mm
liter	L
milliliter	mL
kilogram	kg
gram	g
square meter	m^2
square centimeter	cm^2
cubic meter	m^3
cubic centimeter	cm^3

Tables

Metric System

Length

$$10 \text{ millimeters (mm)} = 1 \text{ centimeter (cm)}$$

$$\left.\begin{array}{l} 10 \text{ centimeters} \\ 100 \text{ millimeters} \end{array}\right\} = 1 \text{ decimeter (dm)}$$

$$\left.\begin{array}{l} 10 \text{ decimeters} \\ 100 \text{ centimeters} \end{array}\right\} = 1 \text{ meter (m)}$$

$$1000 \text{ meters} = 1 \text{ kilometer (km)}$$

Area

100 square millimeters (mm²) = 1 square centimeter (cm²)
10,000 square centimeters = 1 square meter (m²)
100 square meters = 1 are (a)
10,000 square meters = 1 hectare (ha)

Volume

1000 cubic millimeters (mm³) = 1 cubic centimeter (cm³)
1000 cubic centimeters = 1 cubic decimeter (dm³)
1,000,000 cubic centimeters = 1 cubic meter (m³)

Mass (weight)

1000 milligrams (mg) = 1 gram (g)
1000 grams = 1 kilogram (kg)
1000 kilograms = 1 metric ton (t)

Capacity

1000 milliliters (mL) = 1 liter (L)

Customary System

Length

$$12 \text{ inches (in.)} = 1 \text{ foot (ft.)}$$

$$\left.\begin{array}{l} 3 \text{ feet} \\ 36 \text{ inches} \end{array}\right\} = 1 \text{ yard (yd.)}$$

$$\left.\begin{array}{l} 1760 \text{ yards} \\ 5280 \text{ feet} \end{array}\right\} = 1 \text{ mile (mi.)}$$

$$6076 \text{ feet} = 1 \text{ nautical mile}$$

Area

144 square inches (sq. in.) = 1 square foot (sq. ft.)
9 square feet = 1 square yard (sq. yd.)
4840 square yards = 1 acre (A.)

Volume

1728 cubic inches (cu. in.) = 1 cubic foot (cu. ft.)
27 cubic feet = 1 cubic yard (cu. yd.)

Weight

16 ounces (oz.) = 1 pound (lb.)
2000 pounds = 1 ton (T.)

Capacity

8 fluid ounces (fl. oz.) = 1 cup (c.)
2 cups = 1 pint (pt.)
2 pints = 1 quart (qt.)
4 quarts = 1 gallon (gal.)

Time

60 seconds = 1 minute
60 minutes = 1 hour
24 hours = 1 day
7 days = 1 week

$$\left.\begin{array}{l} 365 \text{ days} \\ 52 \text{ weeks} \\ 12 \text{ months} \end{array}\right\} = 1 \text{ year}$$

366 days = 1 leap year

Addition-Subtraction Table

+	0	1	2	3	4	5	6	7	8	9
0	0	1	2	3	4	5	6	7	8	9
1	1	2	3	4	5	6	7	8	9	10
2	2	3	4	5	6	7	8	9	10	11
3	3	4	5	6	7	8	9	10	11	12
4	4	5	6	7	8	9	10	11	12	13
5	5	6	7	8	9	10	11	12	13	14
6	6	7	8	9	10	11	12	13	14	15
7	7	8	9	10	11	12	13	14	15	16
8	8	9	10	11	12	13	14	15	16	17
9	9	10	11	12	13	14	15	16	17	18

Multiplication-Division Table

×	1	2	3	4	5	6	7	8	9
1	1	2	3	4	5	6	7	8	9
2	2	4	6	8	10	12	14	16	18
3	3	6	9	12	15	18	21	24	27
4	4	8	12	16	20	24	28	32	36
5	5	10	15	20	25	30	35	40	45
6	6	12	18	24	30	36	42	48	54
7	7	14	21	28	35	42	49	56	63
8	8	16	24	32	40	48	56	64	72
9	9	18	27	36	45	54	63	72	81

Glossary

Acute angle An angle that has a measure less than 90°.

Addend A number that is added. In 8 + 4 = 12, the addends are 8 and 4.

Angle (∠) Two rays with the same endpoint.

Area A number indicating the size of the inside of a plane figure. The area of this figure is 8 square units.

Associative property of addition The way in which addends are grouped does not affect the sum. Also called the grouping property of addition.
(7 + 2) + 5 = 7 + (2 + 5)

Associative property of multiplication The way in which factors are grouped does not affect the product. Also called the grouping property of multiplication.
(7 × 2) × 5 = 7 × (2 × 5)

Average A number obtained by dividing the sum of two or more addends by the number of addends.

Basic fact A number sentence that has at least two one-digit numbers. The sentences below are examples of basic facts.
7 + 2 = 9   16 − 7 = 9
5 × 3 = 15   8 ÷ 4 = 2

Cardinal number A number used to count or to tell how many, such as *three*.

Central angle An angle with its vertex at the center of a circle.

Circle A plane figure with all of its points the same distance from a given point called the *center*.

Circumference The distance around a circle.

Common denominator A common multiple of two or more denominators. A common denominator for $\frac{1}{6}$ and $\frac{3}{8}$ is 48.

Common factor A number that is a factor of two or more numbers. A common factor of 6 and 12 is 3.

Common multiple A number that is a multiple of two or more numbers. A common multiple of 4 and 6 is 12.

Commutative property of addition The order in which numbers are added does not affect the sum. Also called the order property of addition.
4 + 6 = 6 + 4

Commutative property of multiplication The order in which numbers are multiplied does not affect the product. Also called the order property of multiplication.
4 × 6 = 6 × 4

Composite number A whole number, greater than 0, that has more than two factors. 12 is a composite number because it has more than two factors: 1, 2, 3, 4, 6, and 12.

Cone A space figure shaped like this.

Congruent Having the same size and the same shape.

Cross-products For the ratios $\frac{3}{4}$ and $\frac{9}{12}$, the cross-products are 3 × 12 and 4 × 9.

Cube A prism with all square faces.

Cylinder A space figure shaped like this.

Decimal A number that is written using place value and a decimal point.
3.84   0.076

decimal point

Degree (of an angle) A unit for measuring angles.

90   90 degrees

Denominator *See* Fraction.

Diagonal In a polygon, a segment that connects one vertex to another vertex but is not a side of the polygon.

diagonal

Diameter In a circle, a segment that passes through the center and has its endpoints on the circle.

Difference The answer to a subtraction problem. In $95 - 68 = 27$, the difference is 27.

Digit Any of the single symbols used to write numbers. In the base-ten system, the digits are 0, 1, 2, 3, 4, 5, 6, 7, 8, and 9.

Distributive property A distributive property that relates multiplication and addition is used in this number sentence.
$4 \times (7 + 3) =$
$(4 \times 7) + (4 \times 3)$

Dividend A number that is divided by another number. In $48 \div 6 = 8$, the dividend is 48.

Divisor A number that divides another number. In $48 \div 6 = 8$, the divisor is 6.

Edge In a space figure, a segment where two faces meet.

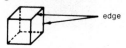

Endpoint The point at the end of a segment or ray.

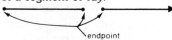

Equal fractions Fractions that name the same number. $\frac{2}{3}$ and $\frac{8}{12}$ are equal fractions.

Equal ratios Ratios indicating the same rate or comparison, such as $\frac{3}{4}$ and $\frac{9}{12}$. Cross-products of equal ratios are equal. $3 \times 12 = 4 \times 9$.

Equation A mathematical sentence that uses the = symbol.
$14 - 7 = 7$

Equilateral triangle A triangle with all three sides congruent.

Even number A whole number with a factor of 2.

Expanded form The expanded form for 5176 is $5000 + 100 + 70 + 6$.

Exponent In 4^3, the exponent is 3. It tells that 4 is to be used as a factor three times.
$4^3 = 4 \times 4 \times 4$

Face A flat surface that is part of a polyhedron.

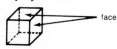

Factor A number to be multiplied. In $3 \times 7 = 21$, the factors are 3 and 7.

Family of facts The related number sentences for addition and subtraction (or multiplication and division) that contain all the same numbers.
$5 + 3 = 8 \qquad 8 - 3 = 5$
$3 + 5 = 8 \qquad 8 - 5 = 3$

Fraction A number such as $\frac{2}{3}$. In $\frac{2}{3}$, the numerator 2 tells how many equal parts or items are being considered. The denominator 3 gives the total number of equal parts or items.

Graph (1)A picture used to show data. The data may be shown by a bar graph, a circle graph, a line graph, or a pictograph. (2)Points on a grid matched with given ordered pairs.

Greater than ($>$) A relation between two numbers with the greater number given first.
$8 > 5 \qquad 9 > 1.4 \qquad \frac{1}{3} > \frac{1}{4}$

Greatest common factor The greatest number that is a factor of two or more numbers. The greatest common factor of 8 and 12 is 4.

Grouping property See Associative property of addition and Associative property of multiplication.

Hexagon A six-sided polygon.

Improper fraction A fraction that names a whole number or a mixed number, such as $\frac{15}{2}$ and $\frac{2}{1}$.

Integers The whole numbers and their opposites. Some integers are $^+2$, $^-2$, $^+75$, and $^-75$.

Intersecting lines Two lines that meet at exactly one point.

Isosceles triangle A triangle with at least two sides congruent.

Least common multiple The smallest number that is a common multiple of two given numbers. The least common multiple for 6 and 8 is 24.

Less than (<) A relation between two numbers with the lesser number given first.
$5 < 8$ $1.4 < 9$ $\frac{1}{4} < \frac{1}{3}$

Line of symmetry A fold line of a figure that makes the two parts of the figure match exactly.

line of symmetry

Lowest terms A fraction is in lowest terms if 1 is the only number that will divide both the numerator and the denominator.

Minuend A number from which another number is subtracted. In $95 - 68 = 27$, the minuend is 95.

Mixed number A number that has a whole number part and a fraction part, such as $3\frac{1}{4}$ and $6\frac{7}{8}$.

Multiple A multiple of a number is the product of that number and a whole number. Some multiples of 3 are 3, 6, and 9.

Multiplicand A number that is multiplied by another number.

$$\begin{array}{r} 7 \\ \times 3 \\ \hline 21 \end{array}$$ The multiplicand is 7.

Multiplier A number that multiplies another number.

$$\begin{array}{r} 7 \\ \times 3 \\ \hline 21 \end{array}$$ The multiplier is 3.

Negative integer An integer less than 0, such as $^-1$, $^-5$, $^-7$, or $^-10$.

Number pair See ordered pair.

Number sentence An equation or an inequality.
$3 + 5 = 8$
$4 < 7$
$9 > 6$

Numerator See Fraction.

Obtuse angle An angle that has a measure greater than 90°.

Octagon An eight-sided polygon.

Odd number A whole number that does not have 2 as a factor.

Opposites Two numbers whose sum is 0. $^+5$ and $^-5$ are opposites because $^+5 + ^-5 = 0$.

Order property See Commutative property of addition and Commutative property of multiplication.

Ordered pair A number pair, such as (3, 5), where 3 is the first number and 5 is the second number.

Ordinal number A number used to tell order or position, such as *third*.

Parallel lines Lines in the same plane that do not meet.

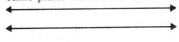

Parallelogram A quadrilateral with opposite sides parallel.

Pentagon A five-sided polygon.

Percent (%) A word indicating "hundredths" or "out of 100." 45 percent (45%) means 0.45 or $\frac{45}{100}$.

Perimeter The distance around a polygon.

Perpendicular lines Two intersecting lines that form right angles.

Pi (π) The number obtained by dividing the circumference of any circle by its diameter. A common approximation for π is 3.14.

Place value In a number, the value given to the place in which a digit appears. In 683, 6 is in the hundreds place, 8 is in the tens place, and 3 is in the ones place.

Polygon A plane figure made up of segments.

Polyhedron A space figure with all flat surfaces. The outline of each surface is a polygon.

Positive integer An integer greater than 0, such as $^+1$, $^+2$, $^+10$, or $^+35$.

Power 3^4 is read "3 to the fourth power."
$3^4 = 3 \times 3 \times 3 \times 3 = 81$
The fourth power of 3 is 81. 4^2 is read "4 to the second power" or "4 squared." See Exponent.

Prime factor A factor that is a prime number. The prime factors of 10 are 2 and 5.

Prime number A whole number, greater than 1, that has exactly two factors: itself and 1. 17 is a prime number.

Prism A polyhedron with two parallel faces, called *bases*, that are congruent.

triangular prism

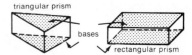

bases

rectangular prism

Probability A number that tells how likely it is that a certain event will happen.

Product The answer to a multiplication problem. In $3 \times 7 = 21$, the product is 21.

Pyramid Space figures shaped like these.

triangular pyramid   rectangular pyramid

Quadrilateral A four-sided polygon.

Quotient The answer to a division problem. In $48 \div 6 = 8$, the quotient is 8.

Radius A segment with endpoints that are the center of a circle and a point on the circle.

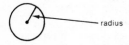

radius

Ratio A pair of numbers that expresses a rate or a comparison.

Ray Part of a line that has one endpoint and goes on and on in one direction.

Reciprocals Two numbers whose product is 1. $\frac{3}{4}$ and $\frac{4}{3}$ are reciprocals because $\frac{3}{4} \times \frac{4}{3} = 1$.

Rectangle A parallelogram with four right angles.

Rectangular prism *See* Prism.

Rectangular pyramid *See* Pyramid.

Regular polygon A polygon with all sides congruent and all angles congruent.

regular hexagon   regular pentagon

Remainder When 20 is divided by 6, the remainder is 2.

Right angle An angle that has a measure of 90°.

Right triangle A triangle with one right angle.

Rounded number A number expressed to the nearest 10, 100, 1000, and so on. 352 rounded to the nearest 10 is 350.

Scale drawing A drawing that shows the shape of a figure but differs in size.

Scalene triangle A triangle with no two sides congruent.

Segment Part of a line, including the two endpoints.

Similar figures Figures with the same shape but not necessarily the same size.

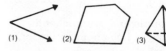

Sphere A space figure with all of its points the same distance from a given point called the *center.*

Square A rectangle with all four sides congruent.

Standard form The standard form for 5 thousands 1 hundred 7 tens 6 ones is 5176.

Subtrahend A number to be subtracted from another number. In $95 - 68 = 27$, the subtrahend is 68.

Sum The answer to an addition problem. In $8 + 4 = 12$, the sum is 12.

Surface area The sum of the areas of all the surfaces of a space figure.

Triangle A three-sided polygon.

Triangular prism *See* Prism.

Triangular pyramid *See* Pyramid.

Vertex (1) The common endpoint of two rays that form an angle. (2) The point of intersection of two sides of a polygon. (3) The point of intersection of the edges of a polyhedron.

(1)   (2)   (3)

Volume A number indicating the size of the inside of a space figure. The volume of this figure is 12 cubic units.

Whole number One of the numbers 0, 1, 2, 3, 4, and so on.

Index